# The Eberly Library
# Waynesburg College

### Waynesburg, Pennsylvania

DISCARD

Class 891.71          Book T882Zf

Marina Tsvetaeva

# Marina Tsvetaeva

THE DOUBLE BEAT OF HEAVEN AND HELL

## Lily Feiler

DUKE UNIVERSITY PRESS    Durham and London 1994

© 1994 Duke University Press
All rights reserved
Printed in the United States of America
on acid-free paper ∞
Typeset in Joanna by Tseng Information Systems
Library of Congress Cataloging-in-Publication Data
appear on the last printed page of this book.

*To my grandchildren*
*Joshua, Zina, Benjamin, and Gabriel,*
*with all my love.*

# Contents

# Acknowledgments

My Tsvetaeva biography began when I first encountered Tsvetaeva scholars at the first Tsvetaeva conference in Lausanne in 1982. I gave a paper on Tsvetaeva's childhood and I was very surprised to find that no one else looked at Tsvetaeva from a psychological perspective.

Without the encouragement of Professor Simon Karlinsky, I would never have finished this biography; he helped me overcome many obstacles on the road to publication. Professors G. S. Smith, Barbara Heldt, and John Malmstad were interested in my approach and have also supported my project.

I am deeply indebted to Lenora DiSio for her inspiration and psychological insights in the early stages of my writing. I am also grateful to Professor Richard Sheldon, the late Rose Raskin, and Professor Svetlana Elnitskaya, who was particularly helpful in discussing her own linguistic approach to Tsvetaeva's work.

Recent revisions, incorporating the new information about Tsvetaeva that has emerged over the last ten years, would not have been possible without my close editorial collaboration with Ruth Mathewson and the helpful suggestions of Judith Vowles.

I am especially grateful to the Tsvetaeva scholar Yelena B. Korkina, and Professors Alexandra Smith and Richard Davis of the Leeds Archive. They helped me immensely by sending me recent materials that in some cases changed my understanding and reshaped the book.

I cannot name all the many friends and acquaintances who were always ready to listen to my interpretations. But I do wish to thank Professors Christopher J. Barnes and Frank Miller; Beatrice Stilman; Anne Stevenson, the poet and biographer of Sylvia Plath; and Lynn Visson of the United

Nations. I checked my psychological interpretations with the psychotherapists Molly Parkes, Gusta Frydman, and Ruth Bachrach. I am also grateful to Eva Vitins, Nina Gove, Jane Taubman, Viktoria Schweitzer, Michael Naydan, Anna A. Tavis, Véronique Lossky, and Laura D. Weeks. I would like to thank Lawrence Malley, formerly of Duke University Press. I especially appreciate the sensitive guidance of Ken Wissoker, my editor at Duke Press.

Last, but not least, I thank my husband, my daughters, and my sons-in-law for their patience and constructive criticism.

# Permissions

Photographs are reprinted from *Tsvetaeva: A Pictorial Biography*, edited by Ellendea Proffer. Copyright © 1980 by Ardis.

Passages from *Marina Tsvetaeva, A Captive Spirit*, translated and edited by J. Marin King (Ann Arbor, Mich.: Ardis, 1980), are reprinted with the permission of Ardis. Copyright © 1980 by Ardis.

Excerpts from *Letters, Summer 1926: Boris Pasternak, Marina Tsvetayeva, Rainer Maria Rilke*, copyright © 1983 by Insel Verlag Frankfurt am Main, unpublished Russian-language manuscript copyright © 1985 Yevgeny Pasternak, Yelena Pasternak, Konstantin Azadovsky, and Mikhail Baltsvinik, English translation copyright © 1985 by Harcourt Brace & Company; reprinted by permission of Harcourt Brace & Company.

Lines from Anna Akhmatova's "Epilogue I" are reprinted from *Poems* by Anna Akhmatova, translated by Lyn Coffin, with the permission of W. W. Norton & Company, Inc. Copyright © 1983 by Lyn Coffin.

Part of Lily Feiler's article "Marina Cvetaeva's Childhood" first appeared in *Marina Tsvetaeva. Trudy I mezhdunarodnogo simpoziuma, Lausanne, 30, VI-3. VII. 1987*, edited by Robin Kemball et al., pp. 37–45. Copyright © 1991 by Peter Lang Publishing Inc.

Parts of Lily Feiler's article "Tsvetaeva's God/Devil" first appeared in *Marina Tsvetaeva simpozium, posvyashchyonny 100-letiyu so dnya rozhdeniya*, vol. 2, edited by Svetlana Elnitsky and Efim Etkind, pp. 34–42 (The Russian School of Norwich University, Northfield, Vermont, 1992).

# A Note on Translations, Transliteration,

# and Punctuation

All translations from Russian and French texts are mine unless otherwise indicated.

Russian names and other words have been transliterated according to a modified Library of Congress system. The generally accepted spelling of familiar names is retained, even if it differs (e.g., Moscow, not Moskva, Pugachev, not Pugachyov). Tsvetaeva is used, instead of Tsvetayeva, throughout.

Note that Russian "e" is transliterated as "e" or "ye" initially and after vowels; "ë" is transliterated as "yo"; "и" as "i" or omitted preceding "y"; "ы" as "y"; combinations "ий" and "ый" as "y"; "ю" as "yu"; "я" as "ya." Soft and hard signs are generally omitted.

Tsvetaeva developed her own idiosyncratic use of punctuation, frequently employing dashes and ellipses in both prose and poetry. Where ellipses are the author's, not Tsvetaeva's, they are marked by brackets [ ]. I have in a few instances changed punctuation for clarity.

# Introduction

*Between the fullness of desire and the fulfillment of desires,*
*between the fullness of suffering and the emptiness of happiness —*
*my choice was made from birth and before birth.*[1]

**M**arina Ivanovna Tsvetaeva (1892–1941) is finally receiving recognition as one of the major Russian poets of this century. In her lifetime she was admired by such renowned poets as Boris Pasternak and Rainer Maria Rilke; Anna Akhmatova saw her as an equal. Yet she had to struggle to have her writings published. Some of her major works appeared only posthumously and remained unknown to the wider Russian audience until recently. In the last twenty years interest in Tsvetaeva — her life and work — has quickened, stirred in this country by Simon Karlinsky's pioneering studies. More and more of her works are published and translated. Joseph Brodsky and Susan Sontag are among her admirers. In Paris, Tsvetaeva books fill the book stores. In New York and Boston, Claire Bloom reads her poems to packed audiences. In Russia, Tsvetaeva scholarship flourishes and biographies of her, her letters, and reminiscences by her contemporaries are widely read. She has also become a cult figure; tours of people old and young visit her Moscow apartment, leaving lines from her poetry on the walls as she used to do. One of her plays has been produced for the first time; new editions of her poetry are sold out. A Tsvetaeva museum is planned.

What brought about this resurrection? Certainly it is the power of her poetry. Tsvetaeva herself stressed that she did not belong to her time, that a poet belonged to no time and to all time, to no country and to any country. She sang about the passion of love and the yearning for a better beyond, about the fate of the poet, about alienation and loneliness. Death was always there.

Tsvetaeva had nothing but contempt for the materialism of the philistines. In her lyrical world what mattered was the intensity of being, heroism, courage, and Rostand's panache. She was never part of a group; she stood alone in poetry as in life. She was oblivious to politics, but her ethical standards inform all her work; she despised the fat, the greedy, and the bigoted. Victory had no meaning for her; hers was the lost cause and her hero was the outsider—the outlaw and the artist. She had no respect for church or state; only the individual mattered to her.

Though she was nurtured by the values of the eighteenth and nineteenth centuries, the rhythm of Tsvetaeva's innovative poetry expressed her own revolutionary time. She became a modern poet, using verbs sparingly, creating her own syntax and mixing the sacred with the vernacular. Language was her companion, her master, and her slave. She would sacrifice everything to find the right word, the right sound. The poet and critic Mark Rudman catches her special quality: "Her meaning resides in her tone of voice, her manner of address, how she says and unsays. She is classical, terse, quick, elliptical: on a tightrope."[2]

Tsvetaeva has often been perceived as a victim of her time. Karlinsky, the eminent Tsvetaeva scholar who introduced her to the American reader in 1966, summed it up in his first book: "Exile, neglect, persecution and suicide may have been the fate of Russian poets after the Revolution, but perhaps only Marina Tsvetaeva experienced *all* of these."[3] She grew up in the cultured milieu of the Russian prerevolutionary intelligentsia only to be thrown— alone with two small daughters—into the turmoil of Moscow under War Communism. Her younger daughter died of starvation there. In 1922 she joined her husband, Sergey Efron—who had fought with the White Army— in Berlin and lived in Prague and Paris until her return to the Soviet Union in 1939. She had to face total condemnation in the Soviet Union and hostility among the émigrés. When she returned to the Soviet Union, the Stalin terror was in full force. Her daughter and sister were sent to the Gulag; her husband was arrested and later executed. Tsvetaeva tried to survive for the sake of her fifteen-year-old son—but in 1941 she hanged herself.

Writing about Andrey Bely, Tsvetaeva commented that "being persecuted and being tortured do not really require persecutors and torturers; for that our most ordinary selves are sufficient."[4] Tsvetaeva knew this only too well, since she had been tortured always by her own demons. I have been looking for those demons. From the very beginning I felt that in Tsvetaeva's early romantic poetry there was a vulnerable, passionate human being who was desperately searching. Searching for what? Did she want to be a mother or an Amazon? Did that troubled and troubling voice call for wild Gypsy love or for death? Did her beloved sad mother ever hear her? Where was her father?

What was the lost paradise of her childhood really like? Whatever carried this voice—ecstasy or despair—it was a compelling, authentic voice. I began my journey into the labyrinth of Tsvetaeva's soul to discover the drama of her life. Not one of the biographies in Russian, German, or French has dealt with these questions, and the English and American studies, though inevitably tracing some emotional patterns, have been interested primarily in other aspects of her life and work. But Tsvetaeva herself was keenly interested in the essence, the "myths" of people and the psychological forces that motivated them. In her portraits of other writers—Voloshin, Bely, Bryusov—and certainly in her autobiographical prose she looked beyond the facts to a deeper understanding of the characters. As Vladislav Khodasevich, her fellow poet, wrote, "in the foreground we have a psychological pattern which is of interest in itself, without regard to the historical and literary personality of the memoirist." [5]

Marina Tsvetaeva's poetry, her autobiographical prose, and her letters leave no doubt that her childhood left her deeply wounded. Pain remained the feeling she knew best, and the memory of the family—whether she idealized or analyzed it—never left her. The need to understand the roots of her early fixation on the mother-child symbiosis—which took different forms, but never changed—made me turn to Freudian concepts and the more recent analytical studies by D. W. Winnicott, Heinz Kohut, Alice Miller, and others. Some studies by Lacan's followers, such as Julia Kristeva, have contributed different insights into the same problems. Svetlana Elnitskaya's linguistic studies have been invaluable for decoding Tsvetaeva's lexicon. [6]

If analytical theories often confirmed my original sense of Tsvetaeva as a "prisoner of childhood" (Alice Miller's term), she never actually fitted any category. She was endowed not only with the genius of her poetic gift, but with a passionate nature and a brilliant mind that made her tragedy unique. What follows, then, is not a case history but an attempt to understand Tsvetaeva's persona through a close reading of her texts, my own interest in psychoanalysis, and the use of psychological theories to lend more substance to my intuitive interpretation. Though I will use psychological terms as sparingly as possible, it is important to define some analytical concepts and to suggest how they apply to the forces that shaped Tsvetaeva's life. These concepts are wounded narcissism and depression.

The narcissistic wound dooms the individual to remain in his or her own world. According to Freud, every child is born with a primary narcissism, with feelings of omnipotence and a need not only for love but also for the acceptance of its individuality, which, in turn, allows it to develop a strong and independent self. Yet when this response is lacking, as it was in Tsvetaeva's case, the child will internalize both the "good" (adored) and the "bad" (rejecting) mother. The result is an internal "splitting," when contradictory drives are invested with equal force and tear the individual apart (Tsvetaeva's duty vs. rebellion, poet vs. woman, control vs. freedom). Barbara Shapiro writes in *The Romantic Mother*, a brilliant study of the English romantic poets, that such a split "prevents both the formation of a mature, cohesive self and the sense of a cohesive, concrete reality outside of the self."[7] If this splitting is not resolved, the child forfeits its chance to leave this primary, pre-oedipal narcissism behind and to enter the world of the Other, the real world. Instead it will remain bonded to the fantasized world of its childhood. The idealized image of the mother will provoke a desire for re-fusion with her, rage for the rejection experienced, and consequent guilt and fear. To gain love and attention, the child may create a "false self" which may find acceptance from the Other, but never security. This loss of the true self leads to the tragedy of the narcissistic persona.

Depression, which Julia Kristeva, in her book *Black Sun: Depression and Melancholia*, calls "the hidden face of Narcissus," that feeling of rejection, futility, and loneliness, can be associated with the feeling of losing one's self.[8] Unless it is resolved it will surface again and again. Often, as in Tsvetaeva's case, depression is temporarily overcome by feelings of "grandiosity"—superiority and contempt. She wrote that "*Ne daigne*" ("Don't condescend") was her motto and she wanted it on her tombstone.

Tsvetaeva had still another defense against depression: intensity and self-annihilation in fusion with nature, with love and pain, with rage and loneliness. That passion fed her poems, but destroyed her life.

Tsvetaeva remained permanently tied to her childhood experience and unresolved primary conflict. She repeatedly stressed the importance of the first seven years of her life. Her mother, Mariya Aleksandrovna—herself deeply depressed and self-centered—was unable to give her the love and response she needed. Mariya Aleksandrovna found in romantic music and romantic literature the excitement she had missed in her life and she transmitted those unreal romantic standards to this daughter. In real life, however, Tsvetaeva's mother treated her with harshness, criticism, and contempt veiled by a pretense of tenderness, security, and "togetherness." She wanted her to compensate for her own emotional frustrations, to be what she wanted her to be, without respecting her individual needs and natural gifts. Tsvetaeva's early poetry conveys her mother's sadness, her powerful, seductive charm, and her own dependence on her. What is missing is any emotional reciprocity, as we shall see in the poem "Mama Reading." The child tries unsuccessfully to get mother's attention while mother is reading and the last lines of the poem shock us with the cruel truth of mother's preoccupation: "Mother wakes up from her flight into fancy: / children are bitter prose."[9]

Tsvetaeva's father, an art historian dedicated to the building of a museum, followed the conventional pattern of his time by committing himself totally to his professional ambition. He was kind but distant. Emotionally he seems to have been almost absent; his absence in the life of Tsvetaeva's mother did not go unnoticed by the child. Tsvetaeva recognized that her Russian heritage came from him; she admired his total commitment to his museum and wrote that his stinginess was "the stinginess of an ascetic, for whom *everything* is superfluous for his body-self and *everything* is too little for his spirit-self, an ascetic who has made a choice between thing and essence."[10]

Tsvetaeva was fourteen when her mother died. She was left without her mother's guidance and without a chance to rebel against that guidance as many more fortunate adolescents do. Mother had again abandoned her and the conflict remained unresolved. Tsvetaeva was left with an insatiable hunger for a total fusion of mother and child as well as with a concealed rage for having been rejected. After years of feeling unseen and unwanted, she could not form an autonomous identity and never knew whether she wanted to be mother or child. She knew only the pain of loss and the yearning for the unreachable.

Thanks to her craft, Tsvetaeva created a world of her own, a world in which she could rise above ordinary people, ordinary life, ordinary love. In real life she saw no place for herself. Her damaged psyche is most obvious and destructive in her many love affairs. She tells us in her autobiographical prose that when she was still a child, her mother asked her which doll she liked best and she chose the one with the passionate eyes. But "it was not the eyes that were passionate: I ascribed my own feeling of passion to those eyes . . . Not I alone. All poets do (and then they shoot themselves because the doll isn't passionate)."[11]

Trying to understand herself, Tsvetaeva believed that she had chosen "the impossible love" subconsciously from childhood on: "That first love scene of mine [Tatyana and Onegin] foreordained all the ones that followed, all the passion for unhappy, non-reciprocal, impossible love. From that very minute I did not want to be happy and thereby pronounced the sentence of *non-love* on myself."[12] Yes, all her love affairs ended in disappointment and pain. But it was not a matter of choice. Tsvetaeva was simply not able to see the Other, to accept the limitations of ordinary, reciprocal love. As a woman and as a poet she needed and demanded love, adoration, communication, but for her love really meant oceanic, magical, transcendent merger in which the Other—beginning with the doll—was endowed with the passion that was her own. Thus she loved men and women. It never mattered to her because she did not see the Other—she was "in love with love," with the fire that burned inside her and needed to be expressed in poetry. Tsvetaeva's desire for passion never died. Yet her basic conflict between the reality of personal relationship and her need for merger with her art remained as well. In her poem "On a Red Steed" the persona sacrifices her childhood, her lover, even her son, in order to be a poet.

What did it mean to Tsvetaeva to be a poet? Tsvetaeva was not conventionally religious, but she subscribed to the concept of poets in the hands of a higher power, the poet's God: "The condition of creation is a condition of being overcome by a spell. [ . . . ] Something, someone inhabits you, your hand is the fulfiller not of you but of him. Who is this? That which through you wants to be." [13]

# 1. Family and Childhood

*Into a red cluster*
*The rowan berries flamed.*
*The leaves were falling*
*I was born.*[1]

n January 1887 Mariya Aleksandrovna Meyn, aged eighteen, reviews in her diary the events that had plunged her into despair two years before.

> I saw him today and he saw me, but we didn't greet one another. How strange! There was a time when we were so close and now we pass each other like strangers. But isn't he in fact a stranger to me? No! Not a stranger. I did love him, so he can't be a stranger to me. How often have I thought that my feeling for him has died in my heart. And I see clearly that to suffer as I suffered then was beyond human endurance—a little more, and I would have gone crazy.[2]

When she and this man—a family friend, identified only as Sergey E.—were alone in the drawing room of her home in Moscow,

> suddenly with a passion I never knew before, I threw my arms around his neck and fell against his breast. [ . . . ] I felt on my cheek that first burning kiss of love and for a moment I forgot myself and the entire world disappeared for me in that instant. [ . . . ] And then with an embarrassed smile I pushed him away and all my blood rushed to my heart. Auntie was surprised at my pallor. But to me it seemed that I had drunk some heavenly nectar and I was in a sweet state of intoxication. [ . . . ] After tea I sat down at the piano and began to play Chopin—I've never played so well. My whole soul poured into the sounds. I spoke through them and he listened and understood.

But he had given her a letter declaring that he had loved her since she was a child, and had never dared to dream that she could love him. He must, however, tell her that he had loved many women, though not as he loved her. He had married one he had compromised, but they had separated the day after the wedding. This young woman was willing to give him his freedom at any time. His love for Mariya was different from his love for the many. "Dared he hope that she would understand?" That night, the diary continues:

> I cannot describe . . . what I felt when I read his letter. It was terrible. I lay on my bed, leaning on my elbows and with wide open eyes looked into the dark. My head was on fire, my blood was throbbing in my temples, my heart was beating so much that I was frightened. I was shaking as in a fever . . . This is nothing, this is nothing, only not to go mad . . . I held my head in both hands and started sobbing. I felt that I was breaking down and an oppressive apathy was taking hold of me as after the funeral of a beloved being when everything is over. In fact, I had buried my happiness the day before.

On the following day she answers his letter.

> If you only knew how sorry I am for you! Have mercy on others; don't behave with them as you have with me, it's too harsh a lesson. You have loved me as you have loved many times before and will love many times after me, but I have never loved and will not love as I have loved you! You should know that I will never remember you with reproaches. [ . . . ] Yet, after everything I have learned from you, we should not see each other. Yes, go away somewhere—as far as possible, where you do not know anyone and nobody knows you . . . I cannot promise you that if things get too bitter, I will not tell my father.

At a concert next day, she gives him her letter and he slips another note into her hand: "Is everything really lost when we love each other and external obstacles could be removed?"

For her everything *was* lost. Her decision was taken. After reading the note she cried through that night too.

> But it was the last flare up of my grief. Since then began that quiet, constant, anxious grief which became part of my character and changed it totally. When I understood that what had happened had to happen, I stopped struggling with my grief and despair . . . I resigned myself. Yes, renunciation of happiness has its own gratification.

Her only consolation lies in sacrifice.

> Isn't it better to live for others than to live for oneself? Happiness . . .
> what is happiness? Just a word . . . By happiness people understand the
> fulfillment of all their desires—isn't that impossible? And where is that
> happiness? And who avails himself of it? But everyone talks about some
> happiness, waits for it, searches for it, rushes toward it . . . Toward what?
> Toward something that does not exist anywhere, has never existed and
> cannot exist . . . [ . . . ] Having lived your life, you will finally look
> back—and what? Where is that happiness for which you have suffered
> and struggled all your life? The ending settles the question—the end is
> the grave. Was it worth living? . . . When you look around with cold
> contempt, life is such an empty and stupid joke . . . a bitter and cruel
> one. If happiness is ever possible, it is so only in childhood and that is
> why childhood appears to us as some kind of lost paradise.

This diary ends in February 1888. In the three years reviewed in its pages
Mariya has tried to fill her life with music—Schumann, Chopin—and books
—Kant, Heine, Turgenev, Goethe. She has looked for the meaning of life:
does it lie in the pleasures of Don Juan? Should one follow the Epicureans or
find a religious faith? She takes none of these paths. Her only happiness is her
memory of that first love.

> In any case, I will never again in my life love as I have loved him; and
> I am still grateful to him because I have something to remember in my
> youth; though I have paid with my suffering for my love, still I have
> loved as I would never have believed that one can love!

On the last page, at nineteen, she writes:

> Everyone is telling me: "You should not read all day, you have finally to
> do something more useful. . . . You are getting ready to be a wife and
> mother and not to give lectures and write dissertations."

Three years later she married Ivan Tsvetaev, a widowed friend of her father
with two small children. He was forty-five, she twenty-one.

Mariya Aleksandrovna, Marina's mother, had a lonely childhood. Her
own mother, a Polish noblewoman, died at twenty-six after giving
birth to her only child. Mariya was reared by her father, Aleksandr Danilo-
vich Meyn, a wealthy Russian-German from the Baltic, and her Swiss gov-

erness, called Auntie ("Tyo"), whom her father would later marry. Mariya knew few other children and turned instead to books, legends, and music to fill her loneliness. In her youth, she remained withdrawn and melancholy. She was a brilliant pianist, whose teachers encouraged her to go on the concert stage. Her father, however, kind but conventional, did not want to see his daughter perform in public, and Mariya sacrificed her career at his bidding.

As we have seen, Mariya sustained another bitter blow in her parting at seventeen from her only love. It is clear from the diary that she makes her decision to break off the relationship immediately, before she tells her father about it. He does forbid her suitor's visits, but that was some time later. Yet, in her writings Tsvetaeva would create the more dramatic myth that her mother "had to choose between her father and her lover," while in fact Marina's mother had no choice in the climate of her time. Why did Tsvetaeva create this myth, one that has been repeated by many scholars? Clearly she sensed her mother's emotional injury, and she read the diary after her mother's death, but she wanted to understand this tragedy in her own terms. "Everything is myth," she would write, "since there is no non-myth, no extra-myth, no supra-myth, since myth anticipated and once and for all cast the shape of everything."[3]

Though Tsvetaeva never knew her grandmother, Countess Mariya Bernadskaya, she cherished her memory. In her myth, at least, that young, beautiful, and passionate woman whose portrait hung in her parents' bedroom had also been in love with another man and had died young. So had her great-grandmother, Mariya Leduchowskaya. Noble, proud, and doomed—that was how Tsvetaeva saw her female ancestors. Obviously she identified with them: "Young grandmother! Who has kissed / Your haughty lips? Grandmother, that cruel / Tempest in my heart / —is it not from you, I wonder?"[4] Unhappy loves and unhappy lives would always fascinate Tsvetaeva; they were, she felt, her mother's legacy.

Marina's father, Ivan Tsvetaev, born in 1846, was the son of a village priest of Vladimir Province. His family was so poor that Ivan and his brothers ordinarily went barefoot, saving their boots for trips to town. The boys learned to work hard and to live according to a strict moral code. Following in his father's footsteps, Ivan almost became a priest. However, while still in divinity school, he took an avid interest in philology and art history, and his request for a traveling grant from Kiev University was approved. This stipend enabled him to tour Italy and Greece, where the sculptures of antiquity so moved him that he dreamed of building a sculpture museum in Russia. His teachers, impressed by his dedication and ability, helped to advance his academic career and in 1888 he was appointed Professor of Art History at the University of Moscow. He also worked as a supervisor and, later, as director at the celebrated Rumyantsev Museum in Moscow. Through these years, however, he never stopped working for his own museum project, which became the central ambition of his life. In 1912 it was inaugurated as the Alexander III Museum of Fine Arts in Moscow, known today as the Pushkin Museum.

Ivan Tsvetaev's first wife, Varvara Ilovayskaya, was the beautiful and talented daughter of a well-known historian, Dimitry Ilovaysky, the author of reactionary history books used in secondary schools throughout Russia. After an unhappy love for "the wrong man," Varvara went to Italy to train her beautiful voice. When she returned to Russia, she agreed to marry her father's friend, Ivan Tsvetaev, without, however, reciprocating his love. They had two children: a daughter, Valeriya, and a son, Andrey. Shortly after giving birth to Andrey, Varvara died. Valeriya was about eight years old.

Only a year after Varvara's death, Professor Tsvetaev married her friend, Mariya. Already a highly regarded scholar, he was looking for a companion and a mother for his children. But Varvara, Tsvetaeva would recall, remained "the first love, the endless love, the endless longing of my father."[5]

In Varvara, Marina's mother—young and passionate—faced a rival she could not defeat. The shadow of Tsvetaev's first wife was forever present; remembrances of her were kept everywhere. A large portrait was on prominent display; trunks filled with her silken dresses, furs, lace, and jewelry appeared every spring in the garden for airing, bringing with them a ghostly aura of Varvara herself—of luxury, magic, and sex. It was during this yearly ritual that Marina saw unmistakably her mother's resentment of her dead rival. When Marina, watching, would remark: "Mama, how ... beautiful,'" her mother would say: "I don't think so. But these things have to be taken care of because they are Valeriya's dowry."[6] Even the Moscow house was Varvara's and would be left to her children.

In this atmosphere of rivalry, it is not surprising that Tsvetaeva learned about her mother's chance encounter with the man she had renounced. When he asked her if she was happy, she answered: " 'My daughter is a year old, she is very big and intelligent, I am completely happy.' " "Oh God," Tsvetaeva would write, "how in that minute she must have hated me, big and intelligent, because I was not his daughter!"[7]

Russia, at the turn of the century, was heading for revolutionary change: it was a time of ferment. Russian liberalism was growing side by side with Russian Marxism, while political terrorism coexisted with mystical idealism. Russian literature, theater, music, and ballet were thriving. Symbolist writers and poets Aleksandr Blok and Andrey Bely succeeded the Russian realists Tolstoy, Dostoevsky, Turgenev, and Gorky. The great Russian composers Mussorgsky and Rimsky-Korsakov, Rachmaninoff and, a little later, Scriabin and Stravinsky were writing their masterworks. Stanislavsky created the new Russian theater and the Russian ballet brought world fame to Diaghilev and Fokine, Balanchine, Bakst, and Benois. In the 1860s decrees had been enacted that emancipated the serfs, reformed the judicial and educational systems, and created local self-administration. Yet the 1870s would bring frustration and disappointment: the peasantry still suffered deprivation, while the intelligentsia was dissatisfied with the slow pace at which constitutional government was introduced. Dissatisfaction would fuel the rise of populist, nihilist, and anarchist groups. Though the assassination of Tsar Alexander II in 1881 signaled a return to a more conservative, repressive government, the country's economic and social changes of the preceding decades could no longer be reversed. A more pragmatic approach to the problems of modernization was sought and new political parties came into being: the Socialist Revolutionary Party (SR) united the populist parties; the Constitutional Democrats (Cadets) represented the more moderate elements; the Social Democrats were a Marxist party that split in 1903 into the Bolshevik and Menshevik factions.

At the same time, the Russian working class emerged and the middle class began to grow in importance. Among the intelligentsia a strong civic protest movement spread, calling for freedom of speech, equality before the law, and constitutional government. The contributions of this movement are eloquently described by Vladimir Nabokov in a letter to Edmund Wilson: "Nothing quite similar to the moral purity and selflessness of Russian *intelligenty* is to be found abroad. Whatever group they belonged to, Bolshevik or Cadet, members of the People's Freedom Party or Anarchists, their daily life during half a century of the civic movement was marked by a sense of duty, self-sacrifice, kindness, heroism; nor were these traits sectarian."[8] Nabokov's perception captures the mood which left its imprint on the Tsvetaev family and on Marina herself. Thus she carried with her into the twentieth century the message of political idealism and the nostalgic mood of nineteenth-century European romanticism.

Marina Tsvetaeva was born on October 9, 1892. Two years later, her sister Anastasiya, usually called Asya, arrived. In early childhood, Marina learned, and never afterward forgot, that both she and her sister were disappointments to their mother, who had wanted sons and had, in fact, already chosen names for them: Aleksandr for Marina and Kyril for Anastasiya.

The children grew up in two houses—the Moscow home on Three Pond Lane and the rented house near Tarusa in Kaluga Province, where the family spent every summer. The town house, surrounded by poplar trees and acacias, shone with affluence, culture, and warmth. The downstairs rooms were spacious and elegant, with high ceilings, polished parquet floors, soft upholstered furniture, potted plants, and gold-framed pictures. In the center of the grand salon stood Mama's grand piano. The parents' books, in separate bookshelves, lined the study walls. Upstairs, on the mezzanine floor, were the simpler, cozier rooms of the children. Marina and Asya shared a room; Valeriya and Andrey had their own rooms. Their summer house was a remodeled old gentry home surrounded by birch trees. It was miles from any habitation, on a high bank of the river Oka. Life there was simple: walks in the fields and forests, reunions with family and friends, the traditional Russian mushroom-picking, swimming, and croquet.

The outer contrasts of these houses mattered little to the children, for what they loved was the atmosphere in both: music and books, holidays and games. The very repetition of the same rhythm, winter and summer, gave their life a sense of security, warmth, and stability—at least on the surface. As an adult, Tsvetaeva would return in her most trying hours to memories of their Moscow and Tarusa houses.

The domestic arrangements in both houses were typical of the Tsvetaevs' class and time: there were maids, cooks, gardeners, nannies, German or French governesses. Although ostentation was frowned upon, comfort was taken for granted. As in many families of their circle, the cultural climate, stressing ethical values and idealism, was predominately secular and liberal. The grownups were concerned not only with Russian political and social issues, but with those of the rest of the world as well: the Dreyfus case and the Boer War were discussed at length. The Tsvetaevs always sided with the underdog. Both parents were highly educated, well-read, and fluent in French, German, and Italian. Parties in the grand salon for the grown-ups and theater outings for the children were festive occasions.

The Tsvetaevs' marriage, based on loyalty and friendship, lacked tenderness and emotional closeness. Tsvetaeva's daughter Ariadna would call it "an alliance of lonelinesses."[9] Professor Tsvetaev was the center of the family, but the center of his world lay in his outside achievements, his professional goals. An able, committed man, he knew how to manipulate his court connections and wealthy patrons to obtain the financial support and court backing he required. Yet, inside the family, both Marina and Asya perceived him not as a father but as a grandfather—"joking, affectionate, distant." [10] And, in this house, filled with music and singing, he knew only one tune, one he remembered from his first wife. As Tsvetaeva wrote: "Poor Papa! That was just the point, that he *didn't* hear; us, or our scales, or our canons and gallops, or mother's streams, or Valeriya's (she sang) roulades. He so utterly *didn't* hear that he didn't even close the door to his study!" [11]

Tsvetaeva came to understand her father's "deafness" as a sign of his absolute, spartan dedication to his work. Both parents, however, were deeply involved in the building of the museum, which the children called their "gigantic brother." The children had only confused ideas about what a museum actually was. They associated the word "ground-breaking" with burials, and Marina resented the fact that while cases of multicolored marble arrived from the Urals, the mountain cat that had been promised by her parents never showed up.

But, whatever her feelings about her father and his museum, it was Mama who claimed the center of Marina's universe. Mama, whose hazel eyes shone with intelligence, but whose lips seemed always to conceal a trace of bitterness. Mama, whose piano playing—Chopin, Beethoven, and Mozart, Haydn and Grieg—filled the house. Mama, who read aloud stories and myths to the girls, who told them tales of heroism and suffering, compassion and separation. Mama, who taught her children the idealism so dear to her, instilling in them contempt for materialistic values and social conventions. With Marina and Asya's help, Mariya Aleksandrovna created a mood of seductive intimacy, an illusion of total union: the three of them, in the quiet winter twilight of their Moscow home, reading under mother's fur coat, or lying in the high grass of the fields around their Tarusa house or sitting under one of Mama's shawls, with Mama telling stories. This closed, unreal world was permeated by their mother's longing and depression. Only the highest standards of morality and courage, duty and renunciation were accepted. But despite the high price of belonging, it was also a world from which no one wanted to be expelled.

Marina sensed from her earliest years her mother's suppressed frustration and rage. Compensating for her empty emotional life, her mother turned to romantic music, romantic poetry, romantic heroes. Perhaps, too, she tried to punish her distant husband by her ill-concealed "suffering," her ongoing *tristesse.* And her constant sense of rejection, of weakness and defeat, was transmitted to her children, as was the underlying anger these feelings concealed.

Two early poems, published in 1912, introduce us to the lack of connection between the parents. In "Advice," a father turns to his daughter and asks: " 'What can I do, dear child, to make the sad trembling tears in your mother's eyes disappear?' " And the child replies: " 'I'll tell you, cover her eyes with kisses.' " [12] In another poem, Tsvetaeva transmits her perception of the parents' hiding behind some conventional props, but never really participating in the family life around them.

> Boring Games
>
> From a chair I picked up a stupid doll
> And I dressed her.
> I threw the doll on the floor.
> Playing the Mama game bores me.
>
> Sitting on that chair
> I looked a long time into a book.
> I threw the book on the floor.
> I am bored playing Papa.[13]

There they are: Mama interested only in "dressing up" the doll; Papa hiding behind his books. No emotional closeness, no connection to life—the boredom Marina saw in her parents' lives is what she dreaded most in her own.

In 1914 Tsvetaeva would begin a correspondence with Vasily V. Rozanov, a popular philosopher and writer, and a family friend. Her letters to him were confessional, a tone she would use later with many of her correspondents, including those she never met: "Mama and Papa were utterly different people. Each carried his own wound in his heart. Mama had her music, her poetry, her longing; Papa had his scholarship. Their lives ran parallel to one another without merging. But they loved each other very much." [14] How difficult it was for Tsvetaeva then to face, to accept—although she knew it very well—the lack of love between her parents. In one sentence she observes the distance between them; in the next, she denies it.

Both Marina and Asya wrote extensively about their childhood. Yet if the facts coincide, the perceptions often clash. Asya's *Memoirs* paint a picture of an almost perfect happiness, concentrating on the family's everyday life and celebrations, her closeness to Marina and her beloved, "wonderful" parents.[15] Marina's early poetry reflects a more complicated feeling of nostalgia: a childhood in "paradise," bathed in the rosy light of romantic illusion, but devoid of warmth and permeated with fear of the world outside — premonitions of separation, dread, and death. Their half-sister Valeriya, however, saw a very different picture: "We were not a warm, undivided, close family. Each one of us carried through life his own injury in his soul."[16] Whatever the facts were, Tsvetaeva would transmit to us the alienation she felt in her childhood, with an ascetic father committed to stone sculptures and a mother who, never having known personal fulfillment, wanted to live vicariously through her daughters.[17]

Although both parents had made their compromise with life, Marina was nevertheless expected by her mother to exceed ordinary reality, to reach all the heights she, Mariya Aleksandrovna, had herself aspired to, to disregard money, fame, and safety, to stand alone against the world. Disappointed by the birth of a girl, Mariya decided as soon as Marina was born that "at least she'll be a musician."[18] Tsvetaeva was acutely aware of the importance of her mother's influence — the inspiration she provided and the prohibitions she imposed: "After a mother like that I had only one alternative: to become a poet. To expurgate her gift to me, a gift that would have suffocated me or turned me into a transgressor of all human laws."[19]

Before Marina was five, her rigorous musical training began. She was made to play the piano for four hours daily — two in the morning and two in the evening. "Mother deluged us with music. [ ... ] Her children, like those poor people's shacks on the banks of all great rivers, were doomed from their inception. Mother deluged us with all the bitterness of her own unrealized vocation, her own unrealized life, she deluged us with music as if with blood, the blood of a second birth."[20]

At the age of four Marina had begun to play with the sound of words, though she knew that her mother wanted her to become a musician. Yet she had "no musical ardor. The fault, or rather the reason, was my mother's excessive zeal, my mother who made demands on me not measured by my strength and abilities, but by all the measurelessness and agelessness of a real inborn vocation. My mother who demanded from me — herself! From me, already a writer, from me, never a musician."[21]

All the same, mother sitting at the piano, the sounds of music, the piano itself — its keys and its pedals — fascinated Tsvetaeva in childhood. Once, while her mother played for hours, she sat with Asya under the piano, Asya cutting out paper dolls and Marina lost in her thoughts. When their mother discovered them there, she was furious. "'A musical ear can't stand thunder like that!'" she shouted, but when she noticed that Asya's lips were trembling, she turned to Marina. "'Asenka can be excused'," she said. "'Asenka is still little, but you, you who turned six on St. John's Day!' . . . Poor mother, how I embittered her and how she failed ever to realize that all my 'unmusicalness' was nothing more than *another* vocation!"[22]

Tsvetaeva sensed at an early age her inner fire, her secret superiority. She was three when she saw in her mother's room a painting, *The Duel*, depicting the dying Pushkin in the snow. It was then that she "divided the world into the poet—and all of *them*."[23] Herself she allied with the poet, and she felt that her mother should have understood her children well enough to seat "me—at the writing desk, Asya—at a bowl of porridge, and Andryusha—at the piano."[24]

Yet, while Asya was allowed paper for drawing, Marina was denied paper for writing. "All my childhood, all my preschool, all my pre-seven-year-old years, my infancy—was one total scream for white paper. A suppressed scream."[25] And not only paper was denied; the Tsvetaev house was a house of prohibitions. "Mother never forbade anything with words; with eyes—everything."[26] What hurt Marina most was Mother's injunction against immoderation: in eating, in drinking, in reading, in feeling.

> They did not give *because I wanted so very much*. Like the sausage which we had only to look at in order surely to be denied. In our house we had no right to ask for favors. Even not to ask by looking. Actually I will never forget the only and unprecedented case—that is why I have not forgotten it—when my four-year-old sister asked for a favor from my mother by printing over an entire page of her drawing pad (drawing was allowed): "Mama, driad [sic] fruits please!" and pushed it wordlessly under the door of the locked study.

To their surprise Mother, for once, yielded and gave "not only to the one who had asked (the favorite, the youngest) but to everyone: to me the unloved, and to my brother the loafer."[27]

These were Tsvetaeva's recollections in the 1930s. But much earlier, at twenty-two, she had caught the intensity of her mother's nature: "Her tortured soul lives in us—only we expose what she was hiding. Her rebellion, her passion, her yearning have become a scream within us."[28] In her *Memoirs*, Asya tells of another attempt at "rebellion." Out with her father on a walk, she asked him for a picture book, knowing that she was not supposed to ask for anything. Returning home happy and smiling with the coveted book, she encountered mother, who with one look turned her happiness into shame. Marina joined forces against this insubordination. As Asya wrote: "Her eyes were slightly narrowed in inexpressible contempt."[29] Contempt—that was one of mother's favorite weapons and Marina learned from her how to use it, against others as well as against herself. When Marina was seven, she dared to ask: "'Mama, what does Napoleon mean?'" "'What, you don't know about Napoleon?'" her mother asked. "'No, no one ever told me,'" Marina responded. "'But . . . it's right in the air!'" her mother exclaimed, refusing to dignify her question with an answer.[30] The child was left wondering what was "right in the air," feeling stupid and disgraced.

Tsvetaeva defended herself against her mother's pervasive contempt by withdrawing into a world of her own, the world of her poetic power. Yet even this refuge was not safe from the ridicule of her family. In an essay written in 1931, recalling her relationship with the poet Osip Mandelshtam, Tsvetaeva describes a scene in which her family, seated around a table set for tea and pastries, listened to her recite one of her early word-plays:

> Fly my spirited steed
> Across seas and meadows
> And shaking your mane
> Take me there!

> There—where? They laugh: Mother (triumphantly, I will never become a poet), Father (kindly), my brother's tutor, a student from the Urals (ha, ha, ha), my brother who is two years older (echoes his tutor), and my two-years-younger sister (echoes my mother); only my older sister, the seventeen-year-old Institute student, Valeriya, does not laugh to spite her stepmother (my mother). And I, red as a poppy, deafened and blinded by my blood rushing up and beating in my temples, by my tears rising but not yet flowing, I am silent, then I scream: "There—far away! There—there!"[31]

Tsvetaeva was hurt and angry by the reception given to her early attempts at writing poetry, but perhaps there was a deeper wound in her sense that her mother lived in a world of her own, where the children were either resented or even not seen. An early poem published in her first collection clearly shows her perception of her mother's preoccupation.

> Mother Reading

> ". . . Stifled whispers . . . daggers glittering."
> "Mama, do build a house of blocks for me."

Mama passionately clasps
A small volume to her heart.

". . . The Count's eyes flare up with anger:
'I am here, Princess, by the grace of fate.' "
"Mama, doesn't the giraffe drown in the sea?"
Far away is mother's mind.

"Mama, look! An ant in my meat balls!"
Reproach and threat in the voice of the child.
Mother wakes up from her flight into fancy:
Children are bitter prose.[32]

Mariya Aleksandrovna, who lived in her books and insisted on her children's listening to her favorite stories, was unavailable to them as a listener. So Marina found for herself two substitutes: Asya's nurse and her friend the seamstress, who would come to visit when mother had gone out to a concert and the "guileless Asya was sleeping." [33] She would tell them about Pushkin's *Gypsies*, her favorite story about love and freedom, about revenge and killing. She had good reason to be curious about Gypsies: she had been told that her wet-nurse had been a Gypsy "who had loved gold so much that when they gave her earrings and she realized that they weren't gold, but gilded, she yanked them out of her ears along with her flesh and, right there, she stamped them down into the parquet floor." [34] That passionate nature impressed Tsvetaeva. Her infatuation with Gypsies would account for her life-long love of silver bracelets, rings, and amber necklaces.

Besides her own family, Tsvetaeva had two extended families: the Meyns, her mother's family, and the Ilovayskys, the family of her father's first wife. While she had never met her father's father, she remembered well her mother's father, Meyn, who visited the Tsvetaev home frequently, along with his second wife, the Swiss governess who had helped him to bring up his daughter and whom the girls called "Tyo" (Auntie). Their visits were associated not only with presents for all the children, with rides, with fun—but with love. Marina was sure that nobody had ever loved her as much as her grandfather, that he loved her more than he loved Asya. It was with that thought that she lulled herself to sleep every night. She was six when Meyn died of cancer abroad. She was grief stricken. Tyo lived near their summer house in Tarusa and in her home there were always flowers under the grandfather's portrait, there were his books and his gold pocket watch. His spirit lived on.

In contrast, Professor Ilovaysky, the father of Tsvetaev's first wife and the grandfather of Valeriya and Andrey, was strict and forbidding. Though the Ilovaysky house was not far from the Tsvetaevs', the girls almost never visited there. Ilovaysky, though, came to see his grandson Andrey, bringing him gold pieces which he put "straight into his hand—even past his hand some-how—without saying a word, without even looking, and only on birthdays or at Christmas." [35] Mama would take the gold pieces away and ask the German governess to wash his hands. "And that is how it stayed with us children and for good: money is dirt." [36]

Marina resented it that Ilovaysky "never saw us at all, not once, that is he did not connect the face with the name, and he did not connect them because he didn't care one way or the other." [37] Ilovaysky was married twice; Varvara had been a child from his first marriage. Soon after the death of his first wife, he married Aleksandra Aleksandrovna Kovrayskaya, a beauty thirty years his junior. His house, his marriage, and his children—Sergey and Nadya—became the center of another biographical essay: "The House at Old Pimen." There was another daughter, Olga, who married a Jew and thus disappeared from the Ilovaysky house and never entered Marina's childhood world. Nadya, about eight years older than Tsvetaeva, personified for Marina beauty and romantic love. "But we were not friends—not because of the age difference, [ . . . ] but because of my shyness in front of her beauty which at that time I was unable to cope with in my poetry. [ . . . ] Simply: we were not friends, because I loved her." [38]

When Tsvetaeva was four she had developed a crush on Sergey; later she believed that he was the first man she had ever loved. When she was older, Sergey encouraged her to read him her poems and did not laugh at them. "Dear Serezha," she wrote years later, "accept my gratitude for that big-headed, short-haired, plain little girl that nobody liked, from whose hands you so carefully took the notebook. With that gesture—you gave her to me." [39] That single rare gesture of acceptance, of approval for her poetic vocation remained precious to Tsvetaeva forever after. Yet perhaps there was more than his appreciation of her poems. It was also a personal gratification for that "plain little girl" to be acknowledged by those she admired. Tsvetaeva, who was always attracted to beauty, was not happy with her looks. As a young girl she was always trying to lose weight; she wanted to look prettier, more romantic. In her photos we see a round face, big eyes, a stern look, rarely a smile.

Tsvetaeva, unlike many memoirists, had a clear understanding of the emotional losses suffered in her childhood, recounting them not only in her mature work but in adolescent letters and — give or take some sentimentalization — her youthful poetry. But her response in the spring of 1926 to a Soviet Academy of the Arts questionnaire sent to her by Pasternak focuses on the cultural legacy, not on pain and loss.

Principal influences: mother (music, nature, poetry, Germany, passion for Judaism, one against all, Eroica). Father's influence no less but not so direct (dedication to work, contempt for careerism, simplicity, self-denial). Combined influence of mother and father — Spartanism. Two leitmotifs in a single home: Music and Museum. Atmosphere of the home neither bourgeois nor dilettantish; chivalrous. Life on a lofty plane.[40]

# 2. Growing Up: Reality and Fantasy

*Between God and Devil there wasn't the tiniest crack*
*to introduce one's will, [ . . . ] to stave*
*off that terrible fusion of roots.*[1]

I n her autobiographical prose of the thirties Tsvetaeva examined her childhood to preserve a lost world and to find a lost self. Writing about other writers or about the role of the poet, she interjected digressions dealing with what was most important to her, her childhood. In analyzing Pushkin's poem "To the Sea" she associates Pushkin's desire to depart for nothingness ("For naught my soul has hastened away") with her own desire "to depart for another family where I will be alone without Asya and I will be the best loved daughter, with a different mother and with a different name maybe Katya or maybe Rogenda, or maybe the son Alexander."[2]

Tsvetaeva needed to be the "one"—superior and chosen. This need for exclusiveness brought about her boundless jealousy, a jealousy that in childhood turned mostly against her siblings, with the exception of Valeriya. Valeriya was exempt since there was no love lost between Valeriya and her stepmother; she resented the woman who had taken her mother's place and she remained almost an outsider in the family. Still, Marina was jealous of the son her mother had wished for, and she had no tender feelings for her stepbrother Andrey, whom Mariya Aleksandrovna favored because he was a boy and very handsome. In childhood the main target of her jealousy, however, was her sister Asya.

In Tsvetaeva's autobiographical essays, Asya appears as a spoiled, silly, whiny little girl. At the piano, missing the right notes, she is a blind puppy who misses its dish, a fly who can't aim, and finally:

One way or another the playing was not only lamentable, but—tearful with streams of small dirty tears and a monotonously mosquito-like:

ee-ee, ee-ee, ee-ee, at which everyone in the house, even the yardman, grabbed their heads with the hopeless outcry: "There, she's at it again!" And just because Asya went on playing, mother, with each passing day, inwardly felt a more hopeless renunciation of her musical career and vented all her hopes on big-headed and tearless me.³

In fact, between Marina and her mother there was a tacit understanding that they shared an intellectual closeness unique in the family. Yet this made her mother's coldness even more painful for Marina. She was placed in a double bind. Once, after reading to the children a poem in German about a hunter, mother asked them who the hunter really was. Andrey gave up and Asya gave the wrong answer. " 'So—you don't know? But then why am I reading to you?' " Mariya Aleksandrovna asked. Then Marina gave the right answer: the hunter was the Devil. At that, mother erupted angrily: " 'And why is it always *you* who know, when I am reading to *all of you?!*' "⁴

Asya was well aware of the arrogant expression in her older sister's green eyes, her moods of jealousy, of rage, of possessiveness. In her *Memoirs* she would recall Marina's "keen perception that everything belonged to her alone, to her, to her, to her—more than to anyone else; her jealousy when someone else (especially I who resembled her) loved trees, meadows, a journey, spring—as much as she did." Her goal, Asya thought, was "to share with no one, to be the only one and the first in everything."⁵

In a short, evocative essay, "A Fairy Tale," Tsvetaeva would later re-create the triangular mother-daughters relationship. Mariya Aleksandrovna tells a story about two sisters and their mother. Before she can get under way, Asya tries to wheedle out of her an admission that she loves her more than Marina. Mother stalls, but Marina needs no confirmation since she knows "very well whom mother loved more."⁶ Naturally, Asya identifies with the younger sister in the story, and Marina with the older one. Mother lets the children contribute to the story because she is frequently lost in her own thoughts. Asya at one point describes how the younger daughter finds a dog on the road and takes it into her carriage: "She noticed by chance that these were not dog's eyes. [ . . . ] This was her older, her old, sister. Immediately, she threw her out of the carriage and she broke into smithereens, into four pieces."⁷ Interestingly enough, in this fantasy within the story, Marina endows her sister with feelings of hatred and aggression. She may well have projected onto meek little Asya her own murderous jealousy and rage.

When mother reveals that the two girls in the story have no father, Asya leaps in to say that he must have died from diabetes or appendicitis. Marina,

WAYNESBURG COLLEGE LIBRARY
93 LOCUST AVENUE
WAYNESBURG, PA 15370

though, believes that a robber is in love with the mother in the tale and must have killed the girls' father. Mother takes up Marina's suggestion, and a robber appears on the scene to demand that the mother choose which of the daughters he should kill. The mother persuades the robber to light two candles, one for each daughter, and to let fate decide: the one whose candle is still burning in the morning will be allowed to live. In the morning, however, the two candles are as tall as they ever were; the robber takes pity and mysteriously disappears.

At this point in the story, Marina's sympathy for the robber, the outcast, is aroused. She declares that she would have married him—that in fact the mother in the story would have married him—because it was she he must have loved. " 'Yes, but you have forgotten completely that he had killed her husband,' " her mother points out. " 'Could anyone really marry the murderer of her children's father?' " [8] Marina concedes that such a thing is not possible. But, all the same, the love need not be lost. " 'Well, then, Mama,' " she replies decisively, " 'I would write poems for him in a notebook.' " [9] Whenever, later in life, one of her passionate love affairs came to an end, Tsvetaeva would write poetry that made the experience immortal.

The bitterness of that rejected love for her mother and her jealousy of Asya remained with Tsvetaeva all her life. In a letter written in the winter before her death she was still hurting: "I was my mother's older daughter, but I was not the favorite. She was proud of me, but she loved my younger sister." [10]

According to "The Khlystovki," an essay written in 1934, Marina's loneliness in her family was relieved by friends among simple people. Near Tarusa, where the Tsvetaevs rented their summerhouse, Marina discovered a group of thirty or forty women and one man who belonged to a flagellant religious sect, the Khlysty. All the women had the same patronymic, Krillovna; the man was called Christ and his companion was called the Virgin Mother. The names alone fascinated Marina; moreover, the Khlystovki lived in the midst of a huge, overgrown, neglected garden in which she could gorge herself on strawberries, raspberries, elderberries, cranberries, and cherries. To gorge oneself, of course, was forbidden by mother.

Marina was enchanted by the strangeness, the freedom, the joy she encountered among these people. But more than that, she was enchanted by their love for her.

The Kirillovnas, I testify to this with delight, loved me more than all the others. Perhaps precisely because of my greediness, my health, my strength. Andryusha was tall and thin. Asya was small and thin; and they [the Kirillovnas], being childless, wanted a daughter like me, one for all of them! "And the Khlystovki love me more!" with that thought I, the insulted one, fell asleep. Mama, [ . . . ] the German governess, and Nannie love Asya more (Papa out of kindness "loved more" everybody), and, to compensate the Khlystovki women and grandfather love me.[11]

One summer day, the account continues, the Tsvetaevs were invited to come for a visit to the Khlystovki—only a carriage ride from their house. Marina, of course, was eager to go, but mother objected. She did not like such outings, especially not with her children. For one thing, Marina always got motion sickness and mother did not hide her disgust from her husband: " 'Papasha [Marina's maternal grandfather] doesn't get sick, I don't, you don't, finally neither Lera [Valeriya] nor Andryusha nor Asya do, but all she has to do is to look at the wheels and *she* is already sick to her stomach.' "[12] Finally, Marina's father offered to sit next to Marina and promised to take care of her if she was sick. Once they arrived at the Khlystovki, Marina was thrown into a frenzy of love, of excitement, of gaiety as they carried her around, passing her from one to the next: "In that paradise, I don't remember my family: not Papa or Mama, not the governess or nanny, not Lera or Andryusha, or Asya. I belonged to *them*."[13] When it was time to leave, one of the women asked Marina whether she wanted to stay with them, to be their daughter, live in the garden, and sing their songs with them. Marina answered: " 'Mama won't allow it.' " She remained silent when they asked her again whether she would like to live with them. A young woman suggested kidnapping her and keeping her hidden behind their wall of bushes and trees. Years later Marina would recall "a wild, burning, unrealistic, desire flared up within me."[14]

Clearly, the unconditional acceptance by the strangers remained a memory Tsvetaeva cherished. So important was it to her that in the essay she expressed the desire to be buried in the cemetery of the Khlystovki,

> under an elderberry bush, in one of those graves with a silver dove, where the reddest and largest wild strawberries in our region grow or, at least, to have a stone set in those hills with the inscription:
>
> Here would have wanted to lie:
>
> MARINA TSVETAEVA[15]

In 1922, in a letter to Pasternak, Tsvetaeva would write: "My favorite mode of communication is beyond this world: the dream. To see in a dream." [16] Sorcerers and vampires, incantations and miracles became important elements of Tsvetaeva's art; flight into a better world, the world of imagination, of dreams, was a leitmotif in her life.

In 1934, Tsvetaeva wrote the essay "The Devil," she wrote in a letter to Vera Bunina: "I am writing 'The Devil', about my childhood with him—and I warm myself with him, that is, I really don't notice that I have been writing for over two hours with the window open." [17]

According to the essay, it was in early childhood that Marina created the Devil fantasy that rescued her from drowning in mother's flood of allurements and prohibitions, hopelessness and demands. The Devil taught her divine pride and rebellion. He made her choose her heroes among outlaws and heretics and he made loneliness and passion her exclusive domain.

She first met the Devil, she writes, when she was five. He came to her in Valeriya's room in Moscow, "a red satiny-silky-damasky room," where she felt surrounded by sensual love. And "not only her [Valeriya's] seventeen-year-old sex reigned in that room, but all the power of love in her race, the race of her beautiful mother, who did not wear out love's force and buried it down among all those satins and moires, eternally sweet-scented and not for nothing so burningly raspberry red." [18] For Marina, Valeriya's room was also the room of "my transgression, of mother's prohibition." [19] There she would read the "forbidden books," not only Gogol and Pushkin, but popular romance magazines and novels. There she discovered Pushkin's gypsies and his outlaws, and—perhaps more significantly—defied her mother's orders and read in secret, hiding the books when she heard mother's steps. She transgressed. The Devil became her ally.

The atmosphere in Valeriya's room, its disorderly dresser drawers filled with things to make a seventeen-year-old girl attractive—makeup, paper flowers, jewelry, and those mysterious pills "*contre les troubles*"—along with the sensuous image of Valeriya's mother (still her father's unending love) brought out in Marina the longing for sex that was personified by the Devil. Later, the Devil would visit Marina in Tarusa, but there, too, always in Valeriya's room.

The Devil sat on Valeriya's bed—naked, in gray skin, like a Great Dane with whitish-blue eyes, like a Great Dane's or a Baltic German Baron's, the arms extended alongside the knees like a peasant woman from Ryazan. [ . . . ] There was no fur; there was the opposite of fur: complete smoothness, even clean-shaveness, fresh-cast steeliness. I see now that my Devil's body was ideally athletic: the physique of a female lion, and the color—of a Great Dane. [ . . . ] I don't remember horns, maybe there were small ones, but they were more like ears. There, unmistakably, *was*—a tail, a lioness's tail, large, bare, strong, and vital, like a serpent twisted gracefully in many coils around statuesquely immobile legs arranged so that from within the last coil a tassel looked out.[20]

This passage clearly demonstrates Tsvetaeva's sexual ambivalence. The Devil's body is *female*, but, nonetheless, he is clearly perceived as a man— a strong, steely, bold man. Yet this fantasy is more complex, because the quoted passage continues: "But the main identifying marks were not the paws, not the tail, not incidentals; the main thing was—the eyes: colorless, passionless and merciless." [21] Those eyes haunted her all of her life: they were critical like her mother's, but the Devil would be her ally. His eyes, unlike mother's eyes, would be critical in their defense of the poet's creativity.

In the Devil fantasy Tsvetaeva tells how the Devil saved her from drowning in the Oka River and she "loved him madly." When he said, " 'And some day you and I will get married, the devil take it!' " she exclaimed: "How that boastful manhood set me on fire down deep to my innermost self!" [22] She could not keep her excitement to herself and told her mother, who swiftly punctured it: " 'Good children are led across the abyss by angels, but children like you . . .' " [23] There are evident connections here with Tsvetaeva's symbolism in "Mother and Music." Whereas there Marina is flooded by her mother's music and her murderous demands, here she is saved from drowning by the Devil. Now, when the Devil has chosen her, she could look down on her mother, "a lonely being like that. He didn't even know that I have a mother. When I was with him, I was *his* little girl, his devil's-own-waif." [24] Yet, while she felt that she had her "own direct inborn tie with the Devil," she could never abandon mother—or the God image associated with her.[25] The Devil serves as an opposing force to mother; he is a force from "down-under," while mother rules far above; he personifies the truth of instinct, while she stands for false emotions.

If the Devil was the personification of Tsvetaeva's self damaged in childhood, the central image of this essay is even more complex. It is the God-Devil. "One of the first secret horrors and horrible secrets of my childhood was: 'God is the Devil,' " Tsvetaeva wrote. "It was me, in me, someone's gift to me in the cradle. 'God-Devil, God-Devil, God-Devil,' on and on that way an infinite number of times." [26] And this merger of the two figures is not the only evidence that Tsvetaeva internalized her mother's image.

Sometimes the attributes of God and the Devil become interchangeable. Who is that God who is inseparable from the Devil? Does he not stand for the authority, control, and power that is associated with mother? It would almost seem that Tsvetaeva wants to share God's power when she describes in this essay, in a brilliant mixture of humor and fantasy, how during services in the icy Holy Savior Cathedral she

> stared at the awesome God in the Cupola, and then felt and saw my-self clearly and in double vision leaving the shiny floor, already flying, pushing the air, paddling like a dog. [ . . . ] And there I was already in a pink flowered ballerina skirt under the very cupola and I fluttered. "A miracle! A miracle!" the people shout. I, however, smile like those young ladies in Sleeping Beauty, fully aware of my superiority and in-accessibility—[ . . . ] Alone, the only one of them all, alone above all of them, next to that awesome God, my little pink skirt in bloom—I am fluttering.[27]

But Tsvetaeva chose the Devil because she felt understood by him and for-given by him. She addresses him directly: "And then came the sudden real-ization—that to confess really, to the bottom of my heart—about all of you in me (to make it clear: about all the sin of your presence in me) in all of me— I could confess only to you."[28] She tried hard to defeat the forces of control, of depression, of guilt and fear by relying on her love affair with the Devil. And, at times, she seems triumphant, but it is always a short-lived victory, and only an intellectual achievement.

If Marina associated the Devil with heat and the color red, with sex and rebellion, she experienced God (and mother) as coldness and whiteness, control and fear. "God was fear for me. [ . . . ] God was a stranger. The Devil was my own. God was coldness. The Devil was heat. And neither one was kind. And neither one was evil. Only I loved one of them and the other one I did not. One of them loved me and knew me and the other one did not."[29]

The essay introduces us to other transformations of the Devil. At the age of seven Marina discovered cards, and her imagination transformed the cards into fantasy figures in which the Ace of Spades was her Devil, the Devil whom she loved. Even more exciting for her was the card game *Schwarze Peter*, in which all the cards were paired off and discarded while he, the Ace of Spades, Peter, remained in the hands of the loser. To keep the Ace that no one wanted, but who was her secret love, was ecstasy: "The game of *Schwarze Peter* was the same as a meeting with someone secretly and burningly beloved—in a crowd: the colder—the hotter, the farther off—the nearer, the more a stranger—the more mine, the more unbearable, the more blissful." [30]

In a routine performed when something was lost in the Tsvetaeva household, a handkerchief would be tied around a table leg, a chair leg, or even a bidet leg and the children would call out: "Devil, play it out, give it up!" Sometimes he did give up the lost object—but not always. As Tsvetaeva wrote: "Something the Devil never gave up to me was—myself." [31] He could not give her the "self" she had lost in early childhood. He did give her, though, a solitary pride, for he "had chosen me to be a poet and not a beloved woman." [32] Like Tsvetaeva herself, he is alone, to be found only "in the lonely prison cells of rebellion or in the attics of lyrical poetry." [33] And from him she took her life's motto: "Don't condescend." [34]

In her essay "My Pushkin" Tsvetaeva would use a fable about the wolf and the lamb to illustrate her point. [35] Mother feels sorry for the lamb: " 'Just think such a white innocent little lamb.' " Tsvetaeva argues: " 'But the wolf—is *also* good!' "

> The whole trouble lay in the fact that by nature I loved the wolf and not the lamb, and in the given instance you must not love the wolf because he *ate* the lamb, but to love the lamb—although it was eaten and white—wasn't possible; love just wouldn't come out here, just the way nothing ever came of lambs and me put together. [36]

The Devil was Tsvetaeva's "secret heat" that consumed her, the transcendent love she would search for all her life. The Devil would appear in her lyrical world as well as in her personal life. Her heroes would be rebels and imposters, murderers and gypsies. They were passionate, proud, loyal, and courageous. Their love was illicit and burning. And she would endow her own lovers with the demonic features and the power she needed.

## 3. Adolescence, Mother's Death

*I am Eve, and my passions are great:*
*My entire life is a passionate trembling!* [1]

In the fall of 1902 Marina's Russian childhood came abruptly to an end. Andrey burst into the room and announced that mother's influenza had turned out to be tuberculosis. She was going to die. Mother, however, quickly reassured the children, telling them that she had to go to Italy, to the sea, for her cure and that, naturally, they would come with her. Marina was ten, Asya eight. (The pictures of the period show two girls with high foreheads and regular features. But Marina's round, broad face carries a serious, inward expression, while Asya, somewhat slimmer and smaller, reaches out with her eyes and her smile.) [2]

On the dreary November day in 1902 when the Tsvetaevs left Moscow, Marina left behind forever the security of an ordered existence; as they were all seated in the carriage, mother said, "I will never return to this house, children." [3] The landscape of Russia would merge with her mother's romantic vision to inspire a lifelong nostalgia for a paradise lost. All the same, this was the first time that Marina and Asya had traveled far from home, and they were filled with anticipation and excitement. Andrey, so as not to interrupt his schooling, stayed behind with his grandfather Ilovaysky; Valeriya, unwillingly, came along.

The next four years opened a new world to Marina. She met new people, new languages and cultures, and a different religion. She came to know the revolutionary mood among Russian émigrés. She also encountered the world of the dying: "How many I have seen of them during my mother's illness, [ . . . ] doctors coughing out the last shred of lung with shining confidence that it's a little bronchitis; fathers of families who didn't think ahead far enough to say farewell to their children." [4]

Nervi, near Genoa in northern Italy, was their first destination. Their father had reserved accommodations for them in the "Pension Russe," so called because it offered a home to so many Russian visitors. At first, mother had to stay in her room, had even to give up her piano playing, leaving Marina and Asya very much on their own. Father was absorbed by his concern for Mariya Aleksandrovna, and Valeriya was too busy to supervise her younger stepsisters. Thus for the first time in their lives they were free. They could behave like children, and they had a marvelous time with the sons of the owner of the pension, climbing the cliffs, lighting campfires on the beach, learning to smoke, getting suntanned and wild.

Italy enchanted them all. Mother's health improved steadily and Professor Tsvetaev left with Valeriya for a tour of Italian museums. A piano appeared on the scene and mother again was the center of attention. The people staying at the pension were a motley group; many of them were political activists who held differing anti-tsarist views.

In 1894, Tsar Nicholas II had succeeded his father Alexander III. His ultra-conservative policy remained basically the same: he opposed all revolutionary and liberal movements, imposed stricter censorship, and strengthened the power of the central government. Nonetheless, Russia's changing economy forced him to bend. Labor legislation was introduced, taxation of the peasants was lowered, and financial policy began to favor new enterprises. Still, discontent among the peasants and the growing urban proletariat spread. Because of closer economic ties with the West, hopes for constitutional reforms penetrated even the Russian nobility and bureaucracy. Yet no progress at all was made in the political sphere, and a revival of terrorist tactics resulted in assassinations and unrest.

Political refugees of all opposition parties found their way to the West, where they prepared for the coming revolution in Russia. Marina and Asya were, of course, attracted to "their" revolutionaries, the ones staying in their pension. In the evening they would gather in mother's room, listen to her piano playing, sing student and revolutionary songs which she accompanied on her guitar, drink tea and discuss politics. If the girls were fascinated by all of these figures, they were smitten by Vladislav Kobylyansky, an intelligent, cynical, handsome stranger whom Marina nicknamed "the Tiger." [5] Asya quickly sensed his immediate attraction to her mother, who seemed responsive in turn. The presence of a young, strong man at their mother's side made the sisters realize what they missed in their father. Shortly before Tsvetaev returned from his trip, Asya found her mother in tears; the girls understood that the relationship with Kobylyansky was over.

Viktoria Schweitzer reports that Kobylyansky, back in Russia after the Revolution, told Tsvetaeva that her mother had wanted to leave the family for him, but at the last moment could not sacrifice her husband's and children's happiness.[6] Yet Valeriya has repeatedly affirmed that her stepmother had not been faithful to her father and had specifically been involved with one of Andrey's tutors about two years before the family left for Nervi.[7] Her testimony, of course, has to be taken with caution because of her hostility toward Mariya Aleksandrovna. Yet it is not surprising that this young woman may have reached out more than once for the love she did not find in her marriage. Asya writes that she came across the last entry in her mother's diary: "'I am 32 years old, I have a husband, children, but. . . .' The rest of the entry had been carefully cut out."[8]

Life slowly returned to its normal rhythm in Nervi, with thoughts of mother's illness and death receding into the background. But the girls were shocked by the arrival of Aleksandra Aleksandrovna Ilovayskaya with her children, Sergey and Nadya, both suffering from consumption. Sergey had always been Marina's "protector"; Nadya was her "great love." Now these beautiful young people were threatened by the dread disease that was all around them. When their condition failed to improve, they returned to Russia.

In Nervi, grown-ups accepted Marina for the first time. They spoke to her about their commitment to "the people." They listened to her poems and encouraged her. Here, too, Marina had her first "metaphysics" lesson from one of the patients in the pension, Roever, an eighteen-year-old German clerk dying from consumption:

> I remember how in the evenings, attracted by his German music and my Russian mother—mother played the piano with a mastery unusual for a woman—to the melody of his holy Bach, in the darkening Italian room with windows like doors, he taught Asya and me the immortality of the soul.
>
> A scrap of paper over the flame of a kerosene lamp: the paper shrinks, turns to ashes, the hand that holds it—lets it go and Die Seele fliegt [the soul is flying]. [ . . . ] The soul is duty. The duty of the soul is flight [ . . . ]. Duty is the soul of the flight.[9]

In the spring of 1903, their pleasant Italian interlude came to an end. Mother's thoughts had turned to the children's schooling. A Swiss boarding school, where they could continue to study their French, was chosen. Since "Tyo,"

Mariya Aleksandrovna's stepmother Suzanne Meyn, had been born and raised in Switzerland, she was chosen to accompany the children to Lausanne.

There, at the boarding school of the sisters Lacaze, Marina and Asya were surrounded by kindness and attention; everyone knew that their father was far away in cold Russia and that their mother was gravely ill in Italy. But an unexpected conflict arose when Marina and Asya were confronted with the strict Roman Catholic upbringing of their new school friends. In Russia, the Tsvetaevs had observed religious holidays, but few of the rituals of the Orthodox Church. Their mother had taught them religious tolerance; she had told them about the persecution of the Jews, had shared with them her respect for the Jewish people, stressing that Jesus had been a Jew. In Nervi, the atheism of their "revolutionary" friends had proven contagious. Now Marina and Asya tried to defend these new convictions with their new friends, telling them that heaven and hell did not exist, that religion had been invented by the rich to subjugate the poor. Nonetheless, the atmosphere of constant religious indoctrination and the regular attendance at Catholic church services, combined with the human warmth surrounding them, brought about a gradual change in the Tsvetaev girls. They began to pray every evening in their rooms. But their mother expressed her concern in a letter and their religious fervor did not last long.

Soon their mother came to visit them. Although her health was improving, she knew that she would have to stay in Italy for another year. Marina and Asya went for walks with her, listened to her stories, and were soon drawn in as before to her ambience of quiet, chronic sadness. Marina's early poems speak of that mood of perennial, aching separation, of resignation to the transience of life, of the flights into lyricism and into the consolation of being together. One of these poems, "In Ouchy," (a suburb of Lausanne) is conventional and sentimental but it does convey mother's manipulation of her daughters. Who could withstand that seductive appeal of avoiding reality, of dissolving in sadness, of fusing with mother for safety?

> Mama held our hands
> Looking deeply into our hearts.
> Oh, that hour on the eve of parting,
> Oh, that twilight hour in Ouchy.
>
> .   .   .   .   .   .   .   .   .   .
>
> We're close together, joined are our hands.
> We are sad. Time, do not hurry!

Oh, that hour on the threshold of torment!
Oh, that rose-hued hour of Ouchy! [10]

In 1904, at the end of the school year, the family was reunited in Germany. Tsvetaev came from Russia, Mariya Aleksandrovna from Italy, and that summer they spent all together in the Black Forest. The future looked safe and predictable: mother would remain in Germany to get used to the colder climate. If all went according to plan, by the following summer she would be well enough to return to Russia, first to the Crimea, and then to Moscow, home.

For the next school year, 1904–5, Marina and Asya were enrolled in a Freiburg boarding school owned and managed by the two sisters Brink. The girls hated the Brink Pension with its strict German discipline, its boredom, its "stewed rhubarb." Mother understood their plight and would take them for three hours every afternoon to the tiny attic room she had rented nearby. And, as always, they read, they reminisced, and they dreamed of the future when they would be together forever. The girls took turns sleeping over from Saturday to Sunday.

That fall, Mariya Aleksandrovna seemed to feel better. She attended lectures on anatomy at Freiburg University; she planned to study Spanish; she was auditioned by a famous choir and was accepted. But a premonition of death still hovered in the air. "Life will fly by and everything will pass and will end," mother would say, "and someone else will sit at the piano. I will not be with you any more." [11] Still, her relapse that winter came as a shock. Returning from a performance with the choir, Mariya Aleksandrovna was taken ill. The fever persisted, doctors were consulted, and her husband was summoned. The prognosis was unclear.

Then a cable reached them: Fire in the museum! Though the fire was soon controlled, Tsvetaev returned to Russia. Mariya Aleksandrovna, too, was upset. She had been in charge of all the foreign correspondence, with a special flair for combining business and personal attention.

But the main secret of her success was, of course, not the apt words, which are only aids, but that ardor of the heart without which the gift for words is nothing. And speaking of her help to father, I am speaking first and foremost about the indefatigability of her spiritual participation, the miracle of a woman's partisanship, the way she entered into everything and emerged from everything—a victor. To help the museum was, first and foremost, to give spiritual help to my father, to believe in him, and when necessary to believe for him too. [12]

After a short hospitalization, mother was taken to a sanatorium, but it was obvious that her sickness had not been arrested. In the meantime, life in school was not getting any easier for Marina and Asya. Marina got into trouble with her teachers, and only the girls' special situation saved them from being expelled.

Marina's unhappiness was compounded when news of Sergey's and Nadya's deaths reached her that spring: "I let myself go completely," Tsvetaeva wrote years later. "For two full years I loved her [Nadya], I saw her in my dreams all the time, and I remember those dreams! And why I did not die then (did not break away to follow her) I don't know. . . . That love I kept secret until—yes, until now! And I carried it within me all through the year 1905." [13] Nadya was the first of Marina's fantasy loves. To feel alive Marina needed to luxuriate in the "secret heat" of her emotions. Nadya was beautiful, romantic, doomed, and unreachable. Separation and death—love in absentia—would become Tsvetaeva's favorite themes.

When summer vacation began, the girls moved with their father into an inn near mother's sanatorium. They felt lonely and lost, sensing their father's need for support. Perhaps for the first time, he talked to them about his museum, took them for long walks, and shared their anxieties. After a few weeks, mother, although not noticeably better, left the sanatorium and moved into the inn. The family began to plan their trip home.

Russia was in turmoil. In February of 1904, Japan had attacked Port Arthur, which had been in Russian hands since 1900. Russia refused to negotiate, expecting an easy victory over the weaker Japanese military. But the war was unpopular and the morale of the Russian troops was low. They surrendered Port Arthur to the Japanese, and the Russian navy was destroyed in the battle of Tsushima.

And then the Tsvetaevs heard the horrible news of "Bloody Sunday." In January 1905, a peaceful demonstration of thousands of workers, led by the priest Gapon, marched toward the Winter Palace in St. Petersburg to petition the tsar for reforms. Gunfire greeted the unarmed crowd, killing hundreds. This tragic event strengthened the opposition to the government, uniting workers, peasants, and political activists.

In the late summer of 1905, the family set off on their return trip. The doctors, however, advised Mariya Aleksandrovna to spend some time in the warm climate of the Crimea before returning to Moscow. After a journey interrupted several times because of Mariya Aleksandrovna's weakness, they arrived in Yalta, where Tsvetaev found them some furnished rooms; a tutor was hired for the girls and, with the practical problems solved, he could return to Moscow to his museum and to his other children.

Russia, forced to accept President Theodore Roosevelt's mediation, signed a peace treaty with Japan at Portsmouth, New Hampshire, in September 1905. Yet the revolutionary spirit of the country was not quelled; when the Tsvetaevs arrived in Yalta it was at the point of exploding into open rebellion. An unstable coalition of peasants, workers, and students demanded a constitutional assembly, an end to censorship, and changes in the condition of the peasantry. Everywhere in Yalta, the humiliating Japanese war and the consequences of that defeat were discussed. Mariya Aleksandrovna only rarely took part in these political debates, but it was clear that she never sided with radical solutions. Tsvetaev was too preoccupied with his wife's illness to take an active interest in public events.

Marina, intrigued by the passionate arguments, defied her mother by visiting Socialist Revolutionaries in the neighborhood, including Gorky's family. She listened to the slogans "Down with Autocracy" and "Power to the Soviets"—and was impressed. The winter of 1905 and the spring of 1906 brought a wave of searches and arrests. Marina was deeply upset by the news of the trials of the revolutionaries and moved by the fate of Lieutenant Schmidt, one of the leaders of a mutiny in the Russian navy.[14] This was the "Revolution" to which Marina responded—one of personal courage and high ideals. In 1926, in answer to the Soviet Academy of Art questionnaire sent to her by Pasternak, Tsvetaeva would write: "First encounter with revolution—in 1902, 1903 (émigrés); second in 1905, 1906 Yalta, Socialist Revolutionaries; no third encounter."[15]

During this difficult winter, tension between Marina and her mother was palpable. Did Marina resent her parents' distance from the dramatic events of the day or was she just rebelling against her mother's strict upbringing? Perhaps her resentment of mother's lack of empathy for her could not be controlled anymore. Then again it may have been simply that Marina was growing up, was becoming aware that other grownups liked her and appreciated her poems, while her mother still regarded her as a child and still insisted on her music lessons.

In the outside world the news was growing more and more dramatic: strikes by the printers, strikes by the railroadmen—finally, a paralyzing general strike. In St. Petersburg the first "Soviet of Workers Deputies" under Trotsky's leadership was formed; for a short time, it took over the city. The government, forced to give in, issued a Manifesto on October 30, 1905, promising a democratically elected legislative assembly, the Duma. Yet the Socialists mistrusted the government, strikes continued, and in December 1905 an armed insurrection broke out in Moscow. Poorly prepared and insufficiently supported by the population, it was soon suppressed. Professor Tsvetaev's reassuring letter came swiftly, but the girls were disturbed by the harsh repression that followed the aborted revolution.

The winter in Yalta had been exceptionally severe and Mariya Aleksandrovna was not getting any better. One night in March the girls woke up to their mother's voice. They found her in her room spitting blood. She was changed, in terror, but still in control: "While her eyes that looked at us said: 'This is the end'. . . her voice said: 'Wake up the landlady, children . . . to Doctor Nozhnikov! and . . . ice!'. . . Illness entered our rooms, settled into them." [16] When their father arrived to take them home to Tarusa, he was shocked by the change in Mariya Aleksandrovna; he dared not travel with her without the assistance of her stepmother, Tyo. So they waited for her arrival. A lawyer came to the house to write Mariya Aleksandrovna's will. For the first time Marina and Asya heard the word "will." It sounded threatening. [17]

The trip home took several days. Approaching the well-known places, looking for the old landmarks, the children's excitement knew no limits and mother shared their joy. Elated by the homecoming, she was transfigured:

> She stood up and, refusing support, took those few steps by herself — past where we stood breathless and immobile, from the porch to the piano — unrecognizable and huge after several horizontal months, in a beige travelling duster which she had ordered made up as a cloak so as not to go through trying on the sleeves. "Well, let's see, what am I still able to do?" She was smiling and, it was clear, talking to herself. She sat down. Everyone stood. And there, from hands already out of practice — but I don't want to name the music yet, that is still the secret I have with her. . . . That was her last playing. [18]

The miracle of that evening never recurred. That summer, mother was dying, lying in her newly redecorated ground-floor room with the jasmine bushes reaching in through the windows. In these summer months, she wanted only Andryusha, her stepson, near her. He had never been given a chance to play the piano or to sing because his grandfather, Ilovaysky, had felt that there was no place for another musician in Professor Tsvetaev's house. But Andrey had taken up, on his own, first the balalaika, then the mandolin, and later, the guitar.

> Mother's last joy was joy at that big, handsome, embarrassedly smiling Neapolitan-stepson (whom she had left behind a short-haired secondary-school boy), with her guitar in his hands on which, sitting lightly on the edge of her deathbed, he shyly, though with confidence, played her all the songs he knew, and he knew all of them. She bequeathed her guitar to him, passed it from her hand to his.[19]

Mariya Aleksandrovna, lying in bed, propped up on pillows, almost smilingly explained to her daughter why she knew so well how to play the German song "Warum" [Why]:

> When you grow up and you look around you, and you ask yourself *Warum* everything came out — the way it did come out, *Warum* nothing at all came out well, not only for you, but for everyone whom you loved, whose music you played, nothing came out for anyone — then you will know how to play *Warum*.[20]

This echoes mother's early diary and it was indeed a terrible message for the fourteen-year-old Marina to hear and to live by. It was not only the final summing up of the futility of her mother's life, but the expression of utterly pessimistic, powerless fatalism.

Mariya Aleksandrovna found it increasingly difficult to breathe. She was quite aware that she would not live to see her children grow up, but "I only regret music and the sun," she told them.[21] On July 4, 1906, she summoned her daughters. Asya has described her final farewell:

> Mama's eyes were fixed on us from the very moment we entered. Someone said: "Go nearer to her." We approached. Mother put her hand first on Marina's head, then on mine. Papa stood at the foot of the bed and sobbed. His face was all wrinkled. Mother turned toward him and tried to reassure him. Then to us: "Live according to truth, children!" she said. "According to truth!"

"My death agony is beginning," she announced on the morning of July 5, 1906.[22] She refused the sacraments and on that afternoon she died.

Marina abandoned the piano immediately after her mother's death and now she began in earnest to write poetry. She believed that she would have become a good pianist had her mother lived longer, but that this would have violated her own musicality, her very essence. She also knew that Mariya Aleksandrovna had never recognized her poetic gift, had not understood the pain she had caused by rejecting her needs. Still, in an essay written years later, Marina could only hope that from the beyond her mother "could see (me, all of me) better . . . that she would grant me, me just me as I am — forgiveness." [23]

Tsvetaeva was fourteen, an adolescent ready to question, to search, to rebel. Her mother's overpowering personality, her pervasive influence, had molded her childhood; now, when she really needed a restraining hand, she was left without one. Although she had found no emotional responsiveness from either parent, her mother had given her a romantic world of illusions, a world Marina now needed to leave, to make room for life. Yet she could not. Her mother's untimely death did not allow her to resolve the conflicts between them. Precisely because there was no one to rebel against, Tsvetaeva was exposed to all the storms of adolescence while chained to her mother's immutable values. Her own emotions, her passions, stayed within herself. She could find no bridge to lead into reality.

The summer of her mother's death proved doubly devastating, for in that same season her father suffered a stroke. After a brief hospitalization, he returned to the Moscow house on Three Pond Lane, but Marina could not bear that motherless home, not yet. Instead, she chose to spend the winter of 1906–7 in a boarding school, coming home only on weekends. At the close of the school year, she was asked not to return because of her rebellious behavior. From the fall of 1907 on, she lived at home once again, attending different gymnasiums. Whatever the school, the time she spent there scarcely touched her life. She would recall this period in a letter to a friend in 1936: "The main thing was — I grew up without a mother, bruising myself against all the sharp edges; *that awkwardness* (shared with all who grow up motherless) stayed with me. But it was rather an inner awkwardness — *being abandoned*." [24]

During this period, Marina grew closer to Asya. She recited her poems to her and they read them aloud together. Many poems in Tsvetaeva's early collections would be dedicated to her, conveying shared moods and experiences. They went to the movies together; Asya brought her school friends home, and Marina enjoyed their company. Their father, as ever, remained unreachable. And when he returned home in the evening, "the house with its half-lit salon and living room changed into some sort of entrance to a temple of science. . . . We would quickly leave and go upstairs into our low-ceilinged, cozy rooms while Papa remained downstairs at his desk with his bookshelves and the replica of the front of his future museum high on the wall, towering above it all." [25]

These years, between her mother's death in 1906 and her first literary success in 1910, were lonely and difficult. One new friend, however, entered the girls' lives: Lidiya Aleksandrovna Tamburer, "the woman in whose friendship we took refuge when our mother died." She was "half Ukrainian, half Italian, of princely blood and romantic soul." [26] A dentist by profession, but close to literary circles, she appreciated Marina's attempts at poetry.

At home, though, everyone lived a separate life, meeting only for meals. Only the knives and forks conversed with one another at those family dinners, as Tsvetaeva would write in an early poem. Furthermore, Tsvetaeva suffered from the typically adolescent pain of hating her looks. Her pink cheeks, her round face, her heavy-boned body didn't at all correspond to the romantic image she yearned to convey. In the manner of self-conscious adolescents, she was shy and arrogant at the same time. Thrown back upon herself, she spent hours and days in her room, reading, writing and dreaming: "At fifteen I escaped from life, from friendships, from acquaintances, from love—into poetry." [27]

But she still had her childhood friends, her books. Undine, the story of a mermaid by the German writer La Motte Fouquet, had been her favorite, as it had been her mother's. Now, in adolescence, she predictably turned to the Romantics, most of them German, but some French: Goethe, Schiller, Heine, Novalis, Bettina Brentano, Victor Hugo, and others. In 1908, she read Rostand's play L'Aiglon, based on the short life of Napoleon's ill-fated son, the Duke of Reichstadt. In the following winter, she devoted all her time to translating the play from French into Russian. Rostand's romanticism, his heroes' bravado and panache in the face of certain death, echoed Tsvetaeva's own impulse to cover up her despair with pride and style. She rejected any criticism of Rostand, who expressed so well her own hopeless defiance. Tsvetaeva needed a new passion to escape her isolation and she turned to a cultlike worship of Napoleon: "At sixteen I fell in love with Napoleon I and Napoleon II. I lived an entire year without people, all alone in my tiny room, in my vast universe." [28]

The red walls of her room were covered with gold stars in imitation of the Napoleonic Bees that were unavailable in Moscow. All over the walls were paintings of the Emperor and his son. An icon on an iron stand was concealed by a painting of Napoleon looking at Moscow burning. Her father, coming into her room unexpectedly, was shocked to find this picture where the icon had hung. When he asked her to restore the icon, Marina flew into a rage, snatched up a heavy candelabrum and stood ready to defend her domain. Her father, seeing that she was beyond the reach of reason, left without saying anything more. Marina desperately needed a world absolutely her own, a need to which her father responded with tolerance, weakness, or perhaps indifference. In any event it seemed too late for words.

Now Tsvetaeva was deaf to the political turmoil around her. Russia had been undergoing a continual crisis since the aborted Revolution of 1905. Rural unrest and pogroms in the cities created a climate of violence and chaos. Finally the prime minister, Count Witte, realizing Nicholas II was too weak to enforce an autocratic regime, prepared an electoral law. But Russia was not yet ready for constitutional government: Witte was dismissed. The first Duma, convened in April 1906, was dissolved in July of the same year. The second Duma, which met in March 1907, also demonstrated the deep gulf between the Duma representatives and the autocracy; both sides were frozen in ideological positions. A third Duma was summoned in November 1907. The Octobrists, a new political party created after the October Manifesto in 1905, played an important role in the third Duma, which was dominated by centrist parties. Uniting merchants, industrialists, and provincial landowners, the Octobrists, with their rightist orientation, supported the policy of the new prime minister Stolypin, a very able administrator who implemented an effective reactionary policy. On the one hand, Stolypin reestablished "order" by the most brutal and repressive means; on the other, he created a new basis of popular support for the autocracy by far-reaching agrarian reform and legislation supporting the new upper-middle class. Thus a new coalition ruled the land, opposing both the extreme right and the extreme left.

If Russian society was in transition in these prewar years, Russian intellectuals, too, were in the throes of change. In reaction to the nineteenth-century literary critics who had insisted on realism and social purpose in literature, a new era of philosophical introspection and individualism was emerging. While a group of writers around Gorky and Andreyev continued to write realistic prose, though with a new emphasis on agnosticism and social justice, the Symbolists were revolutionizing the Russian cultural climate. Since the beginning of the century, a new interest in metaphysical problems, in personal mysticism, and in poetic craftsmanship had appeared in the work of poets like Balmont and Bryusov. The disenchantment of the intellectuals after the defeat of the 1905 Revolution, and the ensuing years of counter-revolution and terror, contributed to the change in the intellectual climate.

The Russian Symbolists had taken their name from the French school, but they were looking for more than a new emphasis on the emotions conveyed by words and sounds, on experimentation and aestheticism; they were in search of a new metaphysical meaning of life. Russian symbolism was at once a literary and philosophical movement and, for many, became almost a faith. The Symbolists' literary salons resounded with passionate debates, and their publishing houses and publications were centers of controversy. Yet their greatest contribution was the creative power of their poets, writers, and philosophers as they brought about a renaissance in Russian letters and philosophy — the Silver Age.

The adolescent Tsvetaeva stood poised before this world — a world of intellectual and artistic experimentation, of spiritual ferment, of political turmoil. Rather than participating in social life or seeking a place among the literary and political groups around her, she chose isolation and her creative work. Having gained some sense of her own power, Marina was ready for her first friendship with a man, with Lyov Lvovich Kobylinsky, a poet, known under his pseudonym, Ellis.

# 4. Dawning Sexuality

*All this did happen. My verse is a diary, my poetry*
*is a poetry of proper names.*[1]

Tsvetaeva had met Ellis—poet, literary critic, and translator of Baudelaire—when she was fifteen, at the home of Lidiya Tamburer. He and Andrey Bely, the Symbolist writer, had been friends since childhood. Both belonged to the "Argonauts," a circle of young Symbolists who met to discuss the "new art" in music, painting, and literature, to search for new guidelines for their turbulent times, and to have fun together. Bely in his reminiscences described Ellis as a unique personality, "utterly uninterested in possessions." His looks were striking, with "keen green eyes, a face white as marble, a short black beard that seems laquered, bright red vampire lips."[2] Twice Marina's age, he was a brilliant conversationalist, bold and entertaining. By the spring of 1909 he was visiting the Tsvetaev house almost daily.

For both Marina and Asya, his visits enlivened their empty house; their father was away on a trip for the museum, and their mother's loss was still a gaping void. Ellis would stay for hours, creating with them and for them a mood reminiscent of their mother's magic. In Tsvetaeva's early poems the sisters travel with Ellis to that dream world, a land of "gigantic orchids, sad eyes and lemon groves," where castles are made of pearls and sapphires, and they visit secret rooms with "fountains spraying mother's tears."[3]

Ellis would talk of Baudelaire and Dante and then all three of them would drink tea and go for walks. In "The Magician," a long poem written in 1914 and dedicated to Asya, Tsvetaeva would convey the special "spell" of these visits, full of music and verses, games and friendship, and solemn oaths never to marry.[4] Obviously the sisters were vying for Ellis's "love" as they had vied for mother's. He is "our angel, our Demon, our ruler—our magician."

When the Ellis of the poem says, "Between Satan and God I am totally torn asunder," we see why Tsvetaeva perceived him as an understanding soul. He liked her verses and he approved of her translation of *L'Aiglon*.

In the summer of 1909, Tsvetaeva obtained her father's permission to travel—all alone—to Paris. She wanted to see Sarah Bernhardt perform in *L'Aiglon* and to visit those places that meant so much to her.[5] There she studied at the Alliance Française and went on dreaming of Napoleon. But Sarah Bernhardt did not perform that summer and she was lonely and disappointed: "I was in Paris for the first time when I was sixteen, alone: grown-up, independent, tough. I stayed on the Rue Bonaparte because of my love for the Emperor and except for the capital N (a triumphant *Non* to everything that was not him) I didn't see anything in Paris."[6]

An undated letter to Ellis, probably from Tarusa, written on Tsvetaeva's return, begins: "Last night I slept with your letters under my pillow and I dreamt about Napoleon and about Mama. I want to tell you the dream about Mama."[7] It is indeed a dream about Mama—about who was she? and who am I? That fall, Tsvetaeva was seventeen, but the problems encountered in the dream would surface throughout her life. The imagery, as well, would recur in her work. While some of the questions asked are those of most adolescents, what is striking here is the pervasive atmosphere of deception and betrayal. Marina's longing for mother turns into an attempt to establish her autonomy, to exorcize mother.

The dream begins when Marina and Asya meet mother on a noisy Paris street:

> I was so happy to meet her in Paris where it is especially sad to be alone all the time. "Oh, Mama," I said, "when I look at the Champs Elysées I feel so sad, so sad." And I raised my hand as though to shield my eyes from the sun, but really because I didn't want Asya to see my tears. Then I urged mother to meet Lidiya Aleksandrovna, "I love you, Lidiya Aleksandrovna, and Ellis more than anyone else." (And what about Asya? it suddenly crossed my mind. No, Asya I don't need!) [ ... ] "How beautiful you are, Mama! [ ... ] What a pity that I don't look like you, but like . . ," I wanted to say Papa, but was afraid that it would hurt Mama's feelings, and I finished for her "like—who knows? I am so proud of your beauty!"

Suddenly Marina realizes that mother is dead, but she is not frightened; she tries to make a pact with her: " 'Mama, make it possible for us to meet again, please do!' " she pleads. "That is prohibited," Mother tells her sadly, "but if some time you see something good, or unusual in the street or at home, remember that it's me or from me." Mother vanishes.

Marina is soon overcome by a feeling of anxiety; something white overtakes her, grabs her and chokes her. Cars and trolleys seem to chase her. Someone must have discovered her pact with mother and wants to set her up against mother. We know of Tsvetaeva's lifelong fears of machinery. Here, however, there is the additional sense of having been set up, a feeling of betrayal and undefined dread.

In the next section of the dream Marina sees a little old woman, an old man, and a child—is this a family? An enigmatic sequence follows:

> I begin to speak about Mama, but the old woman does not understand anything, does not hear. It crosses my mind that I may just think that I am speaking. Perhaps I just stand before her and move my lips. As soon as I think that, it becomes clear to me why she does not hear me, but, still, I keep on thinking my sentence which ends with the words "to annihilate." At that very instant my old woman takes out of her pocket a piece of chalk and writes on the wall "to annihilate," meaning my *unspoken* word.

This painful scene—Marina speaking, but not being heard, seems to repeat her own early experience of being unheeded and the simultaneous awareness of having an inner, unacknowledged link to her mother. Then she starts to question the old woman: " 'Did you know my mother? Did you love her?' " And she receives a surprising answer: " 'A mean little thing she was, a clinging one. Believe me sweetheart.' " Clinging to whom? To her daughters? To Marina? This is a very different image from that of the romantic, beautiful, and powerful mother we see in Tsvetaeva's early poetry. The discovery of mother's hidden dependence brings about Tsvetaeva's ambivalence toward mother. Feelings of guilt for the discovery and rage for the deception surface in her work.

The old woman we meet again in 1921 in the poem "On a Red Steed," where in the unabridged version she appears as "Babka," the simple old woman who also tells a bitter truth to the persona of the poem: " 'Your angel does not love you.' " This allows the persona to leave behind all feminine allure—braids and beads—to strike out on her own and become a poet, owing allegiance only to her own genius.

In the dream Marina then turns to a young girl wearing a pince-nez—near-sighted Marina's double—and asks her a similar question about mother, learning that "everyone envied her because she had so many books." This

may reflect Tsvetaeva's growing conflict between the word and the flesh, between books and life. Not only does she seem to question mother's vicarious
experiences in romantic books but this raises doubts about her own escape
into lonely readings in her room during her adolescence.

The most dramatic development in the dream comes when Tsvetaeva, outraged, screams at these women, " 'Mother was straight as a bow-string! . . .
She was too straight. The bow-string was pulled back too far and, slacken-
ing, it broke her!' " This image brings to mind the Amazons who cut off their
right breasts in order to use their bows in battle. The same image recurs in
the "Poem of the End" when Tsvetaeva describes love as "a bow-string pulled
back to the point of breaking." Tsvetaeva often identifies with her mother to
the point of being unable to distinguish between her mother and herself,
but what is more striking is that the image of the bow-string is used here for
mother and later for love. For Tsvetaeva love must be at the highest point of
tension, and once the tension is released and the string snaps—it destroys
her mother, herself, her love. She seems to sense at seventeen that her own
boundless passion could not be sustained.

Of course, one has to keep in mind that the dream is told in a letter to
a man, to Ellis—a man Tsvetaeva says she loves and who loved her. A brief
reference to her father tells us only that she would rather have resembled
mother. The only active male figure in the dream is a criminal investigator
and he is an "enemy." He first appears in their nursery in Marina's beloved
home, sitting on Asya's bed. To avoid him Marina leaves the room and sees
a small potted orange tree which seems to strain itself beyond its strength,
but does not give up. When Marina realizes that the plant is Mama, her tenderness is moving: "I hug its thin trunk, I kiss the fragile leaves." Later, the
heroine in Tsvetaeva's great poem "The Swain" will also be transformed into
a plant, confirming again her identification with mother.

Then she discovers a note addressed to "Dear Mussya" (mother's name for
her), but immediately suspects that she has been set up again, as she was
by the cars chasing after her. The note is another deception carried out by
the stranger upstairs. The words "criminal investigator" appear on the note.
What is the crime? At times it seems that Marina, too, is conducting an investigation of mother. Perhaps she perceives her own rising doubts about
mother as the crime that will be uncovered by the investigator. She and
the girl with the pince-nez outmaneuver the threatening stranger and he is
picked up by the police. Only feelings of fear and suspicion are engendered
by this male figure in the dream.

Now, together with her double, Marina searches again for a sign from mother. When she sees a young girl on a streetcar platform who resembles Mama, her joy knows no limits. She holds onto that girl when there appears a streetcar, from which protrudes "the red-suited corpse of the detective. He has been hanged." There is no indication that the dreamer is horrified by this violent death. He had to be "annihilated." The dream is saturated with a sense of menace, but the dreamer does not know whether it is mother or the investigator who is threatening. She is torn between her dependence on mother and her fear of men. The absence of her father becomes almost a presence — why did he not protect her?

In the last scene of the dream Marina stands in a square together with her smiling "helper," the girl with the pince-nez, and presses her cold little hand. The girl who resembles mother has been left behind. The threatening stranger is dead. Marina seems to be on her own. Still, however liberating her dream may have been, Tsvetaeva would never be free of mother. Writing in 1931 "The Story of a Dedication," she would observe that, approaching forty, she was approximately the same age as her mother when she died and "if I were a book, all the lines would coincide."[8] This was Tsvetaeva's personal tragedy — she wanted to break out; she knew at seventeen that she had to leave her mother's world and enter her own. She understood as well that she was repeating her mother's pattern. Yet this great poet of passion remained in her own prison, unable to find her place in reality. She did find her place in her creativity and that, too, she understood when she ended her essay on "Mother and Music" with the words: "There are powers which even in a child like that, cannot be vanquished, even by a mother like that."[9]

That fall and winter Ellis came regularly to Three Pond Lane. Yet he absented himself on the night he declared his love for Tsvetaeva and entrusted to his friend Vladimir Nilender a letter proposing marriage. Tsvetaeva was shocked. She had no use for marriage. When Vladislav Kobylyansky, who had courted their mother in Nervi, announced his recent marriage back in Switzerland, Tsvetaeva responded with angry disappointment. How could that "free eagle" marry? Why give in to conventions? Now, Ellis's proposal seemed ridiculous, almost offensive. She refused him on the spot.

That same evening Nilender stayed until the early hours of the next morning. The two sisters and Nilender exchanged confidences and fell in love: Nilender with Marina, Asya with Nilender. It was the sort of evening when love suddenly flares up among young people. It was a complex, erotic atmosphere, involving all four of them. In a short poem, "Two Squared," in her first collection Tsvetaeva admits that the sisters didn't know which of them was the chosen one, nor which of the men they had chosen.[10] We know about Nilender from these early poems, some references to him in her later prose, and Asya's *Memoirs*. Slim and graceful, he was twenty at the time, but seemed older. A Naval Academy graduate, he'd already been married and was separated from his wife. Now he was a poet, studying linguistics and translating Heraclitus's *Fragments*.

Not long after the evening of the Ellis proposal, Nilender proposed to Tsvetaeva and she rejected him, too. Yet, while she did not seem to have suffered from the break with Ellis, the short-lived relationship with Nilender was apparently more complex and emotionally bruising. Tsvetaeva, who had never enjoyed a physical relationship with a man, who had sensed her mother's ambivalent attitude toward sex, was simply frightened. Her poems speak of her undying love, of her tenderness toward Nilender, but they also reveal her fear of leaving her childhood, her "innocence." The decision left her feeling guilty and regretful. In "To the Next One," Tsvetaeva pleads with an imaginary successor to herself in Nilender's affections:

> Be for him what I didn't dare become,
> Don't destroy his dreams with apprehension!
> Be for him what I could not be!
> Love him without measure,
> And love him without end! [11]

In "The Nursery," addressed to Nilender, remorse and despair alternate with declarations of passionate love and confessions of fear to "leave the nursery" and to "exchange the fairytale for passion." In another poem, "Into an Enemy Camp," she tells the men:

> Oh, you're not brothers, no, not brothers!
> You came from darkness and left into the mist . . .
> Wild embraces are for us still
> An unknown trance.
>
> While you're close—we hear laughter and jokes,
> But when you're gone,
> Your words recalled are oddly terrifying,
> And the heart intuits you are enemies.[12]

In Tsvetaeva's adolescent world men had no bodies, only souls, and here she was confronted with a man experienced in love, a man she could not control. She could only say "No." "December and January," addressed to Nilender in Marina's second collection, telescopes this important emotional episode:

> In December, at dawn, there was happiness.
> It lasted — one instant.
> Real, first happiness
> Not out of books!
> In January, at dawn, was sorrow.
> It lasted — an hour.
> Real, bitter sorrow
> For the first time.[13]

In her essay on Andrey Bely, "A Captive Spirit," written in 1934, Tsvetaeva would console herself with the thought that Nilender's love for her could never die:

> I know that if right now, so many years later, or ten more years from now, or even twenty, I were to enter his philological den, the grotto of Orpheus, the cave of Sybil, he would brush aside his young wife with his right hand and with his left he would bring down in an avalanche on my head a ceiling-high heap of old books, and plunge towards me, opening his arms, which would be — wings.[14]

It was certainly not uncommon for a young girl then (or now) to reject her first suitors. Yet for Tsvetaeva this was only the first instance of an emerging pattern: reciprocity in love she could not accept. She would be the mother or the child — and in either role she would be controlling. Actually, Tsvetaeva's rejection of both marriage proposals might not have ended the friendships, if in the spring of 1910 the "Ellis affair" had not occurred, creating a scandal that cut off the sisters' relations with both men. Ellis was accused of tearing out a few pages from some books in the library of the Rumyantsev Museum, where Professor Tsvetaev worked as a director. Whether this vandalism happened deliberately or by mistake, it would have been soon forgotten. But a feud between Tsvetaev and his superior, the minister of education, was already brewing in connection with an earlier theft of valuable engravings from the museum. Tsvetaev feared this new incident could be used against him and, since he had apparently always resented Ellis, he now threatened court action and initiated an official investigation. Eventually the case caused Tsvetaev's dismissal from his post and ruined Ellis's reputation.

Tsvetaeva stood up for Ellis. In one poem, she declares that she is not going to judge a poet who was attacked by everyone; everything could be forgiven for a "weeping sonnet." [15] But she knows her fascination with him had been an illusion and it was over; she knows that "You cannot grab your dream with your hands!"

> You cannot command wavering sadness,
> "Turn into passion! Burn insanely, glow!"
> Such a mistake was your love,
> But without love we perish, oh Magician! [16]

In her Bely essay Tsvetaeva would describe Ellis ungrudgingly as "one of the most passionate of the early Symbolists, a muddled poet, a human being of genius." [17]

In those first months of 1910, after the excitement of two aborted romances had abated, Tsvetaeva was rebellious and unhappy. Asya writes in her Memoirs of her sister's strange behavior, her complete withdrawal, her frustration about her looks. It is in this period that Tsvetaeva may have attempted suicide. Asya mentions a suicide letter addressed to her which she found when she was given access to her sister's papers. This letter has disappeared. There is no corroborating evidence. The text, however, as Asya has memorized it, would indicate that Tsvetaeva shared with her sister the lesson she had learned from the unhappy Nilender affair: Marina advised her sister never to regret, never to rationalize, never to be afraid! (That is, she was telling her: trust your instincts, your emotions, trust the Devil!)

That summer Professor Tsvetaev, traveling to Germany on museum business, brought his daughters to a pastor's family near Dresden in the hope they would learn household skills there. It was not a great success. "I smoke," Tsvetaeva wrote, "my hair is cut short, [I wear] high heels [ . . . ]. I visit the statue of a centaur in the woods, cannot differentiate between a beet and a carrot (in a pastor's family)—my failures are too many to count." [18] Instead of cooking, she prepared her poems for publication.

Tsvetaev took his daughters on a trip to a plaster-casting studio in Berlin where he let each choose a statue. Though Marina really did not like statues, she looked among the many for one "very much *my own*, not selected, but beloved from the first glance, *predestined*." And she found it. The statue was of an Amazon, her "head thrown back toward the shoulders, brows twisted by suffering, not a mouth but a cry." [19] She was precisely Tsvetaeva's self-image.

According to her own testimony, Tsvetaeva had been writing poems since the age of six. Certainly in the years since her mother's death she had turned to poetry for consolation. Now, after her return to Moscow, her poems were circulating, her name was becoming known among poets. Her first published collection, Evening Album, appeared in the fall of 1910. Tsvetaeva's story of that publication is told in her essay "A Hero of Labor": "I published it for reasons alien to literature, but related to poetry. I published it instead of a letter to a man with whom I could not communicate." [20] And the poems are very much like Tsvetaeva's letters: personal, utterly authentic, confessional.

While in her final grade at the gymnasium, telling no one, she simply brought her poems to a printer, selected a cover for the book, and paid with her own money. Once the book was printed, she brought all five hundred copies to a bookshop and then "relaxed." She makes the point in her story that she neither told her father nor sent out review copies. However, Simon Karlinsky informs us that, in fact, she did send out some inscribed copies to important writers—among them Valery Bryusov, the head of the Symbolists, and Maksimilian Voloshin, a poet, writer, and critic.[21]

Evening Album was dedicated to Mariya Bashkirtseva, who was born in Russia in 1860 but spent most of her life in France. After a year in Italy she turned to painting, but her fame rests on her Diary in French. It was translated into many languages and became popular all over Europe. Tsvetaeva evidently identified with Bashkirtseva, whose diary was centered on her passionate inner life. No doubt her death (of consumption) at twenty-four contributed to Tsvetaeva's interest. Karlinsky suggests another affinity, citing Simone de Beauvoir's reference to Bashkirtseva's diary in The Second Sex as "a casebook study" of female narcissism.[22] "I love Mariya Bashkirtseva madly, with a mad, mad pain," Tsvetaeva wrote to the writer Vasily Rozanov in 1914. "For two whole years I lived yearning for her. She is for me just as alive as I am myself." [23] The intensity of this fantasy passion recalls Tsvetaeva's infatuation with Nadya Ilovayskaya. Indeed, the very first poem in this collection is about a dream-meeting with Nadya. In the evening mist, the outlines of a girl's face in the window of a train bring back Tsvetaeva's nostalgia for that long gone, unhappy beauty.

Evening Album was soon reviewed by Bryusov and Voloshin as well as by Nikolay Gumilyov, the maître of the Acmeists. All three critics recognized Tsvetaeva's power. Gumilyov perceived the bold, intimate, confessional qualities of her poetry but emphasized as well that "this is not only a lovely book of a young girl's confessions, but also a book of fine poems." [24] Bryusov, on the other hand, wanted to direct Tsvetaeva's undeniable talent toward loftier subjects, away from the nursery and Mama. Tsvetaeva reacted with anger to his rather patronizing criticism. Voloshin was the most enthusiastic of the three: she belonged, he wrote, to a generation of women poets whose lyrics expressed a new depth of understanding and represented the collective voice of women.

The poems of *Evening Album* (written between 1908 and 1910) are uneven in their quality. Most of them romanticize Tsvetaeva's childhood and lament its loss. Two Russian words, difficult to translate, are at the center of the collection: *uyut*—warmth, coziness, safety—and *zhut*—dread, fright, anxiety. (In her diary shortly before she committed suicide Tsvetaeva would note that there was no more "uyut" in her life.)

While Tsvetaeva's father receives little mention in these poems, her mother emerges in all her seductive power: her sad eyes, her sad lips, her tears, her books, her music, her authority. The poem "To Mama" expresses best the clear message of mother's depression and the daughters' submission to it. Mother's soft voice is heard to the sounds of an old Strauss waltz and lures them away from life into her dream world:

> Tirelessly bending over our childhood dreams
> (You and the moon the only watchers).
> You guided your little ones past
> The bitter reality of thoughts and deeds.
>
> From earliest years, we are close to those who are sad,
> Laughter bores us. We are strangers to hearth and home . . .
> Our ship has cast off in an unpropitious hour
> And sails now at the whim of all the winds!
>
> Ever paler grows the azure island: childhood.
> On the deck we stand alone.
> That, oh Mama, was your legacy to us:
> Sadness.[25]

To counteract the pernicious effect of this deadening influence, to feel alive, Tsvetaeva needed to burn in the fire of her own emotions, as she expressed them in "Prayer."

> I want it all: with a Gypsy soul
> To go toward robbery with a song,
> To suffer for all to the sound of the organ,
> To rush into battle, an Amazon!
> [. . . . . . . . . . . .]

> I love it all: crosses, silks, and helmets,
> My soul is a trace of moments seen . . .
> You gave me a childhood better than a fairytale
> Now, give me death—at seventeen![26]

Evening Album would be followed two years later by Tsvetaeva's second poetry collection, The Magic Lantern, with different backgrounds and experiences but basically similar in mood and style. Some of the poems were written even earlier than those included in Evening Album. Both collections express Tsvetaeva's ambivalent attitude toward the role of women and her unconventional image of women's fate. In the poem "In the Luxembourg Gardens," children are playing, there is laughter, there are quarrels, there is life, and she is overcome by her yearning for children of her own:

> I love women who don't scare in battle,
> Women who can carry a sword and a spear.
> But I know that only enslaved by the cradle
> Will I find my ordinary woman's happiness.[27]

In other poems—"Rouge et Bleue" and "Only a Girl"—Tsvetaeva's bitter resignation to women's fate is painfully evident. However, the beat of her lines in "The Drum" announces Tsvetaeva's allegiance to the special role of the "drummer," the poet. She wants "To be a drummer! Ahead of everyone!"

> Women's lot does not attract me:
> Boredom frightens me, not wounds!
> Everything will be given to me, power and honor,
> By my drum.[28]

Evening Album was published, but Tsvetaeva's life was apparently unchanged. Her father, unaware of her life as a poet, expected her to continue her classes at school, to be Professor Tsvetaev's daughter. Then, one day the doorbell rang and in walked Voloshin. Ilya Ehrenburg has described his mannerisms: "As he walked, he skipped a little; even his way of walking gave him away—he skipped in conversation, poetry and life."[29] Voloshin was a personality, an eccentric, and very much part of the literary milieu. He was thirty-four, a poet, a critic, a painter. He loved to tell stories, to play practical jokes, to mystify. He had spent years in Paris and knew French literature well. Moreover, he was interested in everything—Assyrian art, Cubism, Freemasonry, the myths of antiquity, and much more. Whether or not Voloshin's work survives, his memory will undoubtedly live on in the many memoirs of his contemporaries, including Tsvetaeva's.

That first visit went on for hours. They spoke about her, about her poetry, about poets. He tried to convince Tsvetaeva to read Claudel, Baudelaire, Rimbaud, but she replied that she loved only "Rostand, Rostand, Rostand." So began a friendship that continued until it was interrupted by the Revolution. Voloshin, his house, his mother would offer Tsvetaeva the warm acceptance she craved. He was a friend who regarded her as his equal, a poet who regarded her as his peer. He would introduce Tsvetaeva into the literary society of the day and invite her to Musaget, a publishing house formed by Ellis, Bely, and Nilender, that was also a literary salon, a center for lectures and discussions where new literary theories were formulated and argued.

Tsvetaeva and her sister were invited for that summer of 1911 to Voloshin's country house in Koktebel, near Feodosia in the Crimea. Surrounded by a wild, beautiful landscape, on the eastern shore of the Black Sea, Koktebel was a very special place. Writers, poets, and painters gathered there, paying ludicrously low rents for the cottages on the property to Voloshin's mother, Yelena Ottobaldovna, whom everyone called Pra. Voloshin and his mother loved to bring people together, to create encounters and destinies. Life there was free from conventions and filled with intellectual stimulation, with gaiety and games. Yet, before going there, Tsvetaeva wanted some time for herself. In April 1911, she decided to drop out of school a few months before her graduation and to go to Gurzuf, a mountain village in the Crimea. She was still troubled and restless after her "non-affairs" with Nilender and Ellis. But instead of finding the peace and relaxation she had hoped for, she was depressed. On April 6, she wrote to Voloshin:

> I look at the sea—from afar and from close by, I drop my hands into it—but still I don't own it, it does not own me. To dissolve and to merge is impossible. To become a wave?
>
> But will I love it then?
>
> To remain a person (or half a person, doesn't matter!) to eternally languish, to eternally remain on the threshold. There absolutely must exist a closer merger. Yet I don't know what it is.[30]

All alone, she devoured the books Voloshin had introduced her to: Dumas, Hugo, George Sand. She discovered Heinrich Mann. But reading no longer satisfied her. Now she saw books as a disaster because "a person who reads a lot, cannot be happy. For happiness is always unconscious." On April 18, she wrote again to Voloshin:

> Every book is a theft from one's own life. The more one reads, the less one can or wants to live oneself. [ . . . ] Books and my deep mistrust of real, genuine life are to blame. Books and life, poems and what has inspired them are incommensurate values. I am so infected by this mistrust that I see, I begin to see — only the material, the natural aspect of everything. Isn't this a direct road to hateful skepticism, my enemy! [ . . . ] What remains is a sense of total loneliness for which there is no cure. The body of another person — is a wall, a wall that obstructs his soul. Oh, how I hate that wall!
>
> But I don't want paradise either where everything is blissful and ethereal. Oh, how I love faces, gestures, life! But life where everything is so obvious and so coarse — I don't want either.[31]

These letters demonstrate that Tsvetaeva was searching for a way out of books and into life. In the dream reported to Ellis she had already dealt with her mother's bookishness. Now she was sick of vicarious experience and abstraction. She longed for something more.

# 5. Illusions

*"From a Fairytale — Into a Fairytale"* [1]

Tsvetaeva arrived in Koktebel in early May, still haunted by the memory of Nilender: "I went to Koktebel to get away from him," she would write, "to stop loving him, not to love another man." [2] In Koktebel she entered a new, bohemian world, a world of trust, friendship, and fun.

Voloshin's mother, Pra, was a handsome woman who had built an unconventional, independent life for herself. She had left the father of her son as a young woman and had never remarried, though lovers were not absent from her life. Living in poverty with her son, she had at some point enough money to buy the Koktebel property. She usually dressed in trousers, a silk-bordered caftan, and boots; she smoked hand-rolled cigarettes in a silver holder. "Masculinity meant for two had gone to the mother," Tsvetaeva wrote, "all the femininity — to the son." [3]

As she approached her nineteenth birthday Tsvetaeva was looking for life, for love. She found it in a meeting with Sergey Efron on the pebble beach of the Black Sea. Sergey was a year younger, very handsome — dark-haired, slim, with large sensuous, greenish-gray eyes. Their mutual attraction soon grew into a passionate love affair.

Efron's life had already been filled with drama. His father, Yakov Efron, came from a well-known Jewish family; his mother, Yelizaveta Durnovo, was the daughter of a Russian nobleman, and his father had converted to Lutheranism to marry her. In their youth, his parents were dedicated to the Russian anarchist and populist movements. Both of them joined the underground organization "Land and Freedom" and were entrusted with dangerous missions. In 1880 Yelizaveta Durnovo was arrested and imprisoned; only her father's powerful court connections saved her. She was released and allowed to leave the country. She married Yakov Efron, Sergey's father, who had followed her into exile.

The Efrons had six children before Sergey's birth in 1893, but only three of them—Anna, Pyotr, and Yelizaveta (called Lilya)—survived. After seven years abroad, the Efrons returned to Russia. They were a large and loving family, and after Sergey they had another daughter, Vera, and then a son, Konstantin. At the end of the 1890s, Sergey's mother returned to her revolutionary activities. In the years of repression and reaction after 1905, she was again arrested. When Sergey's father succeeded finally in getting her released, they went abroad with their youngest son. The separation weighed heavily on the adolescent Sergey. Then tragedy struck: Sergey's father died in 1909; a year later his younger brother committed suicide, and his mother, unable to bear her grief, hanged herself on the same day. Sergey came close to a breakdown and contracted the tuberculosis from which he would suffer for the rest of his life.

His family's tragic history only enhanced Sergey's attraction for Tsvetaeva. A sad, handsome young man of noble blood, and with a family of revolutionaries, he seemed to embody all the romantic qualities of her mother's heroes. His Jewish origins added to his image as the exotic "stranger." The son of a "beauty and a heroine," as Tsvetaeva called his mother was apparently made to order to fulfill her fantasies.[4]

Asya, who joined Tsvetaeva in Koktebel, was stunned by the changes, both physical and emotional, she saw in her sister: "The excitement of her happiness fills me with joy for her! For her, never happy since childhood, always lonely, always sad."[5] Tsvetaeva was suntanned and her hair, once cropped, had grown into golden curls. She had adjusted to Koktebel by wearing harem-pants and sandals on bare feet. She looked younger—beautiful.

Later that summer the Tsvetaev sisters separated; Asya had met the man she was to marry, Boris Trukhachyov. He joined them in Koktebel and almost on the same day, the two couples left in different directions—Tsvetaeva and Sergey for a horse farm in the Ufa district where Sergey was to drink mare's milk to gain weight, and Asya and Boris for Feodosia. Because the sisters wanted to keep their new romances a secret from their father, who was abroad, Voloshin agreed to forward his letters to them.

Tsvetaeva and Sergey stayed at the farm for the rest of the summer. To Voloshin Tsvetaeva wrote about "us," about Sergey's diet, about looking forward to their appearance with him at the Musaget. Her happiness spilled over in the letters and her gratitude to Voloshin for having introduced her to his world knew no limits. Her friendship with him was real, and lasting, unusual in its reciprocity.

Back in Moscow, Tsvetaeva and Sergey stayed in the house on Three Pond Lane while Tsvetaeva's father was abroad, but when he returned they moved into the apartment of Sergey's sisters, Vera and Lilya; Pra joined them to help with the housekeeping. But there were tensions. Tsvetaeva was working on her second collection, *The Magic Lantern*, and now Sergey was writing as well. They were too busy and too self-involved to include Pra and Sergey's sisters in their life.

For all her love for Sergey, Tsvetaeva became infatuated with Asya Turgeneva, a grand-niece of Ivan Turgenev, who designed book covers for Musaget, among them *The Magic Lantern*'s. Tsvetaeva's passion followed the same pattern as with Nadya Ilovayskaya: hyperbolic expressions of love, idolization of her beauty, and the sense of a love doomed. Nadya would die; Asya was leaving. In fact, Asya was planning her departure with her lover, Andrey Bely. In her essay on Bely (1934), Tsvetaeva would recall that "from the first instance I perceived Asya as a departing person, as a person lost to me in the long run. The way a dying person is loved, everything all at once, all the final words or no words at all. The encounter began with my unconditional submission on trust, with the complete admission of her superiority." [6] Tsvetaeva's physical attraction to her brings an odd reminder of the Devil's androgyny. On one of Tsvetaeva's visits Asya was

> clothed in a leopard skin that lay on her shoulders, wrapped in the cloud of her curls and the smoke of her cigarette, greeting me scowlingly, shaking my hand the way men do. [ ... ] Her charm was in that particular combination of manly, young man's ways—I would even say her male businesslike air—with the extreme lyricalness, maidenliness, girlishness of her features and outlines. When a huge woman shakes your hand like a man, it is one thing; but a hand like *that*.[7]

As for the leopard-skin shawl: "Suddenly, with the total lack of restraint of a genuine revelation I say: 'Why you're one yourself, Asya, you're a snow leopard! You've taken the skin off yourself and put it on.' "[8] Tsvetaeva's feelings for Turgeneva in 1911 are recalled in lesbian terms:

> There was already the beginning of an undefined jealousy, already a perceptible despondency, already the first stab of *Zahnschmerzen im Herzen* [toothache in the heart] because she is going away, you see, and I will lose her, lose her affection. And there was a nobler, deeper feeling: a

longing for the whole race, the laments of the Amazons for the one who was going away, going over onto *that other shore*, for the sister de-parting — *to them*.[9]

Indeed, Tsvetaeva regarded Asya's departure with Bely as a betrayal. In her poem "From a Fairytale into Life," she laments her leaving: "Do not let any-one — in compassion or in anger — peer into your past. / Happy journey, fallen princess, / Happy journey." [10]

However, another poem written approximately at the same time and dedi-cated to Sergey, "From a Fairytale into a Fairytale," clearly prefers the fairy-tale. She was truly happy and free with Sergey. She wanted to believe that she had left those critical eyes behind. "It is strange, Max," she wrote to Volo-shin, "to feel myself utterly independent. For me this is a surprise, since it had always seemed to me that someone else would shape my life. But now, I will act as I did with the printing of the collection. I will act without hesita-tion. Don't you agree?" [11]

In November 1911, Tsvetaeva was already making plans for a January wed-ding. She wanted Voloshin, who had gone to Paris, to serve as Efron's best man, and was cross when he refused. In a letter to his mother Voloshin ex-plained his attitude: "Marina's and Sergey's wedding seems to me to be only an 'episode' and a very short one. I believe, however, that it is rather good for them since it will immediately make them grow up. And that I believe they need." [12]

When Tsvetaeva told her father that she was going to marry, he understood at once that she would not be deterred by his opposition. He told her at first that he would not attend the wedding, but eventually he relented. Tsvetaev, the son of a priest and the son-in-law of the anti-Semite Ilovaysky, could not easily accept Efron's Jewish origins. The Efron sisters feared that Tsvetaeva would be unable to care adequately for their sickly younger brother. The wedding ceremony took place without much celebration in January 1912, in a church in Moscow. The young couple left on their honeymoon in Sicily, following the route taken by Asya Turgeneva and Andrey Bely. Tsvetaeva was already expecting their child.

When they returned to Moscow, the Efrons settled first in a house they bought with money they had received from Tyo as a wedding present. Their daughter Ariadna was born there. (Two years later they would move into an apartment of six rooms on two floors on Boris and Gleb Lane, the same apartment from which Tsvetaeva would emigrate in 1922.) Sergey, whose poor health had put him two years behind in school, returned to his studies to obtain a high school diploma. Apparently, Tsvetaeva's income from her mother's will spared them financial worries during these years.

From the beginning, their marriage was built on the acceptance of freedom for both partners. Tsvetaeva, heady with her new-found independence from family and school, would hardly have accepted a marriage that set limits. She wrote to Rozanov:

> Our marriage is so different from an ordinary marriage that I don't feel married at all and I haven't changed a bit. I keep loving the same things and keep living in the same way as when I was seventeen.

> We will never separate. Our meeting was a miracle. I am writing you all this so that you shouldn't think of him as a stranger. He is my closest kin for all my life. I could never love anyone else but him. [ . . . ] Only with him can I live as I live — totally free.[13]

The Efrons enjoyed an active social life not only in literary circles but in the world of the theater as well. Efron's sisters Vera and Lilya and his brother Pyotr were all connected with the stage. Lilya was an actress and acting coach; Vera and Pyotr were directors. One of their actor friends recalled Tsvetaeva and Efron as an impressive, elegant couple:

> I see a magnificent head of hair. I stand behind her . . . what a dress she wears! So elegant, made of brown-gold silk, wide, exquisite, down to the floor; her slim waist tightly held by an antique belt. At the slightly exposed neck — a cameo. An enchanting young woman from the last century. . . . She passes by and I notice that she is not alone. Her escort is a young man who does not take his eyes off her. . . . Tall, slim, slightly stooped. The head nobly formed, thick black hair smoothly combed and parted on the slant. In his large grayish-blue eyes a boyish, mischievous and subtle sense of humor flares up quite suddenly.[14]

Here, observed by a stranger, is that boyish mischief Tsvetaeva was attracted to. Yet Efron's friend Nikolay Yelenev had a very different impression. They were guests at a small, formal party given by the famous director Alexander Tairov in honor of Petipa, one of the celebrated actors of the Moscow Art Theater. Tsvetaeva was surrounded by a group of elegant young men. Yelenev was struck by one of them:

That was Efron, Tsvetaeva's husband. With a characteristic gesture, a gesture I observed later on more than one occasion, he shielded his eyes with his hand while talking as though he was defending himself against something. Already that evening I understood that this manly looking hairy hand was betraying an inborn shyness. Thirty years before he faced the firing squad, Efron, subconsciously, was looking for a defense. He felt like an orphan in life. At no time and under no circumstances did Efron overcome the ghetto of his self.[15]

When Tairov asked Tsvetaeva to recite some of her poems, Yelenev observed her self-assured, almost challenging manner: "She recited in a calm slightly mocking voice. . . . Her gray eyes, however, were cold, transparent. Those eyes did not know fear, even less humility, or obedience."[16] The disastrous imbalance between the soft, weak Efron and the steely, arrogant Tsvetaeva was visible even then.

From the very beginning a deep discrepancy in Tsvetaeva's perception of Efron was apparent. She needed to see him as a combination of vulnerability and fearlessness, passion and loyalty, tenderness and firmness, body and soul. She expected him to live up to her own high expectations, just as she would later require of her lovers, her children, and herself. In her early poetry, she implores him to join her in her childhood world and depicts him as "the little grandson," the "little dark-haired boy," and the "little dreamer." But she also endowed him with the qualities of the romantic hero of her eternal quest:

> Through him I am faithful to all chivalry
> To all of you who lived and died fearlessly,
> In fateful times men like you
> Write poetry or mount the scaffold.[17]

By contrast, Efron showed singular understanding of Tsvetaeva's basic drives. The seventeen-year-old Mara in "The Sorceress," a short story in his collection *Childhood*, published in 1912, clearly portrays Tsvetaeva.[18] Mara is visiting at the home of a girlfriend whose two little brothers have been told that Mara is "crazy." She certainly seems strange. At night she walks around her room, she smokes day and night, drinks strong tea or black coffee, eats very little, and scorns a regular routine. When the boys ask her why she is ruining her health, she answers, "'I am in utter need of stimulation, only in excitement am I real.'" She has no use for the simple reality around her. "'Imagination has never betrayed me and never will'," she says. She fears aging and believes that she will die young. Now, at seventeen, she can be everything—" 'a sorceress, a mermaid, a little girl, an old woman, a drummer, and an Amazon—everything! I can be everything, I love everything, I want everything!' "[19]

All this would remain true for the rest of Tsvetaeva's life. Efron would keep a unique place in it, perhaps because he was her first lover and the father of her children. But, even more important, he remained the safe, familiar haven to which she could return over and over. He became first a "son," later a "brother," always coming from the same "cradle." He was her "duty" in life. In her own fashion, she always remained loyal to him. But more than twenty years later, she would write to a friend: "Marriage and love rather destroy a personality, it's an ordeal. [ . . . ] And an early marriage (like mine) is a disaster altogether, a blow for all of life."[20]

Fortunately, Tsvetaeva could not foresee all the blows in store for her. She still lived in a state of optimistic expectation. She was carrying Efron's child. She and Efron had founded a publishing house, which would issue in 1913 *From Two Books*, a volume of her favorite poems from the first two collections. And the opening of her father's museum was approaching. The museum's opening in May 1912 was a formal event, with the tsar and his family attending an official prayer service. The museum was crowded with dignitaries in bemedaled uniforms, their wives in white, high-necked dresses. Marina and Asya, both pregnant, were proud witnesses.


In the fall of 1912, the Efrons' daughter was born. Tsvetaeva recorded in her notebook:

Alya—Ariadna Efron—was born on September 5, 1912, at five thirty in the morning to the sound of church bells.

> A girl! The belle of the ball!
> Or a humble nun, God knows!
>
> .   .   .   .   .   .   .   .   .   .
>
> Let her grow up quiet in sadness,
> Let her grow up tender.

And I called her Ariadna, despite Seryozha who likes Russian names, who loves simple names, [ . . . ] despite friends who call it pretentious. [ . . . ] I called her that because of the romanticism and pride that guide all my life.[21]

Clearly, the name meant a great deal to Tsvetaeva. The legend of Theseus and

Ariadne would become the subject of one of her major plays. Did Tsvetaeva want for her daughter the role of a woman who guides, who controls, who saves her man? Or did she somehow associate the image of the thread with the umbilical cord—that unbreakable link to her own mother and now to her daughter?

Tsvetaeva adored her daughter. Her diary records every minute detail of her looks, her growth, her development. For Tsvetaeva, she was the daughter of a poet and a handsome father, the daughter she wished to possess as exclusively as she had wanted to own a book or love a man or a woman. In September 1913, when Alya was a year old, Tsvetaeva wrote in her diary that when the child called for Efron's sister instead of for her, she felt insulted: "I'm silent, I don't even look at you [Alya] and I feel for the first time—jealous." [22]

For all her devotion, Tsvetaeva did not really see her daughter. In a poem written when Alya was four, she compared her looks to Napoleon's. Later she was to see the same likeness in her son. Tsvetaeva wanted for Alya everything she had wanted for herself:

> You'll be innocent and subtle
> Lovely—and a stranger to all.
> A captivating Amazon,
> An impetuous mistress of life.
>
> .   .   .   .   .   .   .   .   .   .
>
> Everything will submit to you,
> And in your presence everyone will be quiet.
> You'll be—absolutely—like me
> And you'll write better verses . . . [23]

In her own reminiscences, published in 1979, Ariadna Efron would describe her childhood in terms that sound remarkably like Tsvetaeva's early years. At first, there was a succession of nursemaids and her mother spent very little time with her:

Not one of these alternating shadows concealed Marina from me. Marina, so to speak, shone through everyone and all of her was present. I was constantly reaching to her and for her like a sunflower and I sensed her presence all the time inside myself, like the voice of conscience—so strong was the power she radiated, a power that convinced, demanded, dominated. The power of love.[24]

In 1913 Efron was still trying to finish secondary school and Tsvetaeva worried about his health and about his studies. Then in August Tsvetaeva's father died in Moscow from a heart condition. All his children were at his bedside, but a priest was not called to administer the last rites because, Tsvetaeva wrote later, he did not want "to embarrass those near to him, nor [ . . . ] to make an event of his death." [25]

After her father's death, the Efrons spent that winter in Feodosia. Asya joined them with her son, Andrey; she had separated from her husband soon after the infant's birth. They greeted the new year in Koktebel, where they had traveled to surprise Voloshin and to celebrate together. Driving through the blizzard with their old coachman, their exuberance kept them warm.

> It was not cold; there was nothing to feel cold, there was nothing at all, bare, happy souls were riding along unafraid of tumbling out, incapable of any mishap. "Asya!" "Yes Marina, we'll ride along like this *after* death!" . . . And that laughter! When the snowstorm came in sweeps, we were swept with laughter when the Northeaster flew in—the laughter—flew up! [26]

When they arrived, they drank to the new year and, careless and happy, recited poetry. Yet a month later Tsvetaeva wrote:

> I walk along the fortress ramparts,
> In the anguish of the spring evening.
> And the evening lengthens the shadows,
> And hopelessness searches for words. [27]

Her pattern of exuberance and depression surfaced, as it would throughout her life. Death—her own mortality—becomes a motif in *Juvenilia*, her third collection. However, it has changed its face: no longer the great, romantic escape, it was annihilation, dust and ashes, fear and anger:

> Listen! I won't accept it!
> This—is a trap!
> Not me will they lower into the earth,
> Not me! [28]

But she also expressed existential aloneness that suggested growth and acceptance:

> I await the grasshopper, count to a hundred,
> I pluck and chew a stem.

> It is odd to feel so strongly and so simply
> The transience of life and of myself.[29]

When Tsvetaeva returned to Moscow, war was in the air. But actual war held no meaning for her, especially a war against Germany. Her mother, of German descent, had given her a love for German music and literature. And Tsvetaeva herself had come to love Germany, where she and Asya had spent a wonderful summer while her mother was recuperating. Now, surrounded by war hysteria, she did not abandon "Germany—my madness! / Germany—my love!" In any case, she hated war.

> I know the truth! All the former truths—begone!
> Men should not fight men on this earth.
> Look! It is evening, soon it will be night.
> *What for*—poets, lovers, leaders? [30]

By August war had engulfed all of Europe. Efron, now a student at the University of Moscow, was caught up in the patriotic fervor and volunteered for duty at the front. Rejected because of his poor health, he joined the medical corps instead. Since he was stationed near Moscow, the Efrons' life continued its regular routine. But a major personal crisis was in the offing. In October 1914 Tsvetaeva met the poet Sofiya Parnok and responded: "My heart said at once: you are my love." [31]

*Recklessness! — Dear sin,*
*Dear companion and my dear enemy!*
*You have sprayed laughter into my eyes,*
*You have injected mazurkas into my veins.*[1]

svetaeva's love affair with Sofiya Parnok was probably the most passionate, and sexually the most gratifying, of Tsvetaeva's life. For almost two years, the two women lived in a world of their own, alternating between periods of rapture and agonies of jealousy. Close friends of both women knew about the affair; others may have guessed it. Although homosexuality and lesbianism were accepted in Tsvetaeva's circle at that time, for Tsvetaeva this affair had the added attraction of secret, sinful love.

When she was six Marina was taken to see a performance of *Eugene Onegin*, and she would recall in her essay "My Pushkin" that she "had fallen in love not with Onegin, but with Onegin and Tatyana (and perhaps with Tatyana a little more), with both of them together, with love."[2] In her play *Phaedra*, written in 1923, the same idea is introduced in a short epigraph: "I have never written a single one of my works without falling in love simultaneously with both of them (with her a little more), not with the two but with their love. With love."[3]

Her desire to lose herself in the other, to experience total union, was so overpowering that she was ready to make love to men or women, but to women "a little more." Her fantasy lover, the Devil, had the body of a lioness and the male characteristics of a Great Dane. As an adolescent, her hyperbolic expressions of love for Nadya Ilovayskaya showed her response to female beauty. Then, while she was already romantically involved with Efron, she had been infatuated with Asya Turgeneva. Parnok came even closer to fulfilling Tsvetaeva's dream: she was demonic, strong, attractive, a poet; she was the "Devil"; yet Tsvetaeva also saw her as the caring, loving mother. For Parnok, Tsvetaeva became the younger, more feminine, playful child.

The poetic cycle "Woman Friend" contains some of Tsvetaeva's most sensuous and tender love lyrics.[4] When it was published in 1976, in the collection Juvenilia, there was nothing to indicate to whom it was addressed. It was not until 1983 that the work of the Soviet scholar Sofiya Polyakova gave us this information and allowed us to trace the facts of this tempestuous relationship.[5]

Who was Sofiya Parnok and what was the truth of this affair? The daughter of a middle-class Jewish family in the port of Taganrog, Parnok was seven years older than Tsvetaeva. Her father, Yakov Parnokh (Parnok later dropped the h) owned a pharmacy; her mother was a physician. Parnok's childhood was overshadowed by her mother's death in giving birth to twins. Her father soon remarried and there was no closeness between father and daughter. As soon as she had graduated from the gymnasium, Parnok left for Geneva, where she attended courses in a music conservatory and in law school. From adolescence until the end of her life, Parnok had love affairs with women, but, in 1907, at twenty-two, she married Vladimir Volkenshteyn, a poet, who helped her with her verse. The marriage ended in 1909 after only a year and a half because of Parnok's continuing lesbian relationships, but Volkenshteyn remained loyal to her for the rest of her life. Their wedding was performed according to Jewish law, but soon after it Parnok converted to Greek Orthodoxy. She wrote poetry, children's stories, and literary criticism, and translated Baudelaire. She became part of the Moscow literary scene, but her first collection of poetry did not appear until 1916 and she never gained major recognition in her lifetime. Now there is growing interest in her work.[6]

When Tsvetaeva and Parnok first met at one of the many literary salons in Moscow, Parnok was recognized as a talented poet, a sharp, independent literary critic, a powerful personality—and a lesbian. That fateful encounter left its imprint on all of Tsvetaeva's life and work. The poetry cycle "Woman Friend" traces in stark honesty the course of this love affair. Parnok shines through many more of Tsvetaeva's poems and remains in the subtext of her life. In the first poem, dated October 16, 1914, Parnok appears as a romantic femme fatale over whose head hovers sin. She has kissed too many; she is strong, sad, and doomed. Tsvetaeva trembles in happy belief that her new love is a dream and "that you are you, not he." If the poems of that month speak of passion, it is a passion still not entirely understood: "What was it? Whose victory, whose defeat?" Even at this stage the terms are combative; a sense of rivalry is undeniable.

Tsvetaeva threw herself into the affair with Parnok in total disregard of her husband and her small daughter. Utterly intoxicated, she wanted to shower

Parnok with bracelets and rings, earrings and gold chains; she offered her youth and her gaiety. She adored her lover's looks: her dark eyes, her pale complexion, her high forehead, her arrogant lips. Perhaps just because she felt so close to absolute "bliss," she feared abandonment. Soon her anxiety turned into jealousy—a sad and painful jealousy.

In a poem written during the first month of their affair, Tsvetaeva describes Parnok passing by in a sleigh with another woman. Both snow and cold function as metaphors of rejection. The last stanza sounds like the sobbing of a child:

> And I stroked the long hair
> On my little fur coat—without anger.
> Your little Kay froze to death,
> Oh, Queen of Snow!*

In January 1915, Tsvetaeva returns to the very beginning of this infatuation and in two poems conveys the essence of Parnok's attraction.

> My heart said at once: you are my love!
> I forgave you everything, chancing it.
> Knowing nothing—not even your name!
> Oh, love me, love me!
>
> .  .  .  .  .  .  .  .  .  .
>
> Your dress—a black silken armor,
> Your voice slightly hoarse like a gypsy's,
> I love everything about you—to the point of pain.
> Even that you are not a beauty!
>
> Your beauty will not fade through the summer!
> [You are] not a flower—but a small steely stem,
> More wicked than evil, sharper than a cutting edge,
> From which island—were you brought?**
>
> You dazzle with your fan or your fancy cane,
> In every vein and every tiny bone,
> In the shape of every wicked little finger,
> Woman's tenderness, boyish audacity.

*From Hans Christian Andersen's tale "The Snow Queen"
**The reference is to Lesbos, the home of Sappho.

It was this combination of "tenderness and boyish audacity" that would attract Tsvetaeva all her life.

In the second poem Tsvetaeva recalls their first meeting:

> How can I not remember
> That fragrance of White Rose and tea,*
> And those Sevres figurines
> Above the blazing fireplace . . .
>
> I was in a magnificent dress
> Of light golden faille,
> You—in a knitted black jacket
> With a wing collar.
>
> I remember your face as you entered
> Without a trace of color,
> I remember how you stood up,
> Your head slightly tilted, biting your little finger.
>
> And your powerful forehead,
> Beneath the burden of your helmet of red hair.
> Not a woman and not a boy,
> But something stronger than I!
>
> You took out a cigarette,
> And I offered you a match,
> Not knowing what I would do if
> You looked at my face.
>
> I remember how—above a blue vase—
> Our glasses clinked.
> "Oh, be my Orestes!" [7]
> And I gave you a flower.

Parnok broke up with Tsvetaeva's predecessor and moved to an apartment of her own. Not surprisingly, Efron's sisters, as well as some close friends, expressed their concern about Tsvetaeva's increasingly serious commitment to her. Nevertheless, in December, Tsvetaeva and Parnok spent a night together in an ancient Russian town, Rostov the Great, famous for its old monasteries

---

*White Rose was a fashionable perfume.

and churches. Tsvetaeva's poem about that night was inspired by the frenzied happiness they shared:

> How merrily the snowflakes glittered
> On your gray and my sable fur.
> How we looked on that Christmas fair
> For ribbons brighter than all others.
>
> .   .   .   .   .   .   .   .   .   .
>
> How you pressed my head
> Caressing every tiny curl.
> How the flower of your little
> Enamel brooch cooled my lips.

The mood of this poem is unbridled sexual happiness, with Tsvetaeva wishing to satisfy her lover's every desire—to steal an icon for her, to be young and happy for her—forever. The background of churches, monasteries, and religious images combine with the holiday atmosphere of the crowd to create the mood of a wedding. But just beneath this passionate love is a mother-daughter relationship which surfaces throughout the poem. In the last lines, Tsvetaeva seems to see herself as the boy her real mother had desired:

> How I brushed over your slender little fingers
> With my sleepy cheek.
> How you teasingly called me a boy,
> How you liked me that way.

Indeed, in many poems of this cycle Tsvetaeva sees herself as the child and their love as transcending infidelity. If either of them turned out to be unfaithful, she assures Parnok, "everything passes—just whistle under my window."

In her poems addressed to Tsvetaeva, Parnok, the older, stronger, more experienced of the two, offers maternal love. One of them begins with a line from Sappho: "You appeared to me as an awkward little girl."

> Oh, with one line Sappho's arrow has pierced me!
> At night I mused over that curly little head,
> Changing my wild heart's passion into a
> Mother's tenderness.[8]

This high-pitched romance took both women into a private world, a secret world of tenderness and passion removed from the reality of war, of family, of responsibilities. As usual, Tsvetaeva refused to see anything beyond her own preconceptions. Her Parnok was a romantic heroine: pale, red-haired, with a hoarse gypsy voice. Polyakova, however, offers a very different image of Parnok. She writes that in the photographs of that time Parnok's face looks soft, even tender—certainly not domineering. The only feature she had in common with Tsvetaeva's heroine is her high, protruding forehead.[9] To Tsvetaeva it did not matter whether Parnok wore a demonic mask of her, Tsvetaeva's, own making or whether she was really demonic; her infatuation continued unabated, much to the consternation of her friends.

Apparently during this period Efron, too, had an affair. Little is known of his extramarital affairs at this time or later. He was, clearly, discreet. In January 1915, Voloshin's mother wrote: "Seryozha's romance has come to an end without trouble, but Marina's is getting more intense and with such an uncontrollable force that it can no longer be stopped. She will have to suffer it through and who knows how it will end?"[10] That spring Efron was mobilized, but his visits to Moscow and Koktebel continued, sometimes when Tsvetaeva was not present. At the height of her passion, Tsvetaeva was ready—as she would be later—to sacrifice even her poems for love.

> I walk home as quietly as I can.
> The unwritten verses—I don't regret!
> The sound of wheels, the burnt almonds,
> Are dearer to me than all the quatrains.
>
> My head is delightfully empty,
> Because my heart is over-full!
> My days are like small waves,
> That I watch from the bridge.[11]

In May 1915 Tsvetaeva and Parnok went together to Koktebel and in June to Svyatye Gory, a spa in Belorussia. In Koktebel, Tsvetaeva was accompanied by Alya, Alya's nanny, and her sister with her son. Tsvetaeva seems to have played the domestic role, taking care of Parnok's laundry and of her small purchases. She dutifully kept a record which showed that while she liked to dress in colorful, glamorous blouses and dresses, Parnok dressed in a more masculine style.[12] She did not wait for Efron, who arrived in Koktebel a few days after she had left with Parnok. But from Svyatye Gory, Tsvetaeva wrote to her husband's sister Lilya,

In the evenings when dark has fallen, I am terribly worried and anguished: in the light of the tin kerosene lamp, when the fir trees rustle, I can't stop thinking of the news in the papers, and, besides, for eight days already I don't know where Seryozha is. I'm writing to him at random, first to Belostok, then to Moscow, without hoping for a quick reply.

I love Seryozha forever—he is my kin, I will not leave him at any time or for any place. I write to him every day or every second day, he knows all about my life; I try to write to him less often about the saddest part of it. There is always a load on my heart. I fall asleep and I wake up with it.

Sonya loves me very much and I love her—and that is forever and I won't be able to leave her. I feel torn by having to be divided these days; my heart has room for all of this.

Gaiety—simple gaiety—will never be mine, it seems, and, generally, it is not my way. And joy, deep joy, I don't know either. I cannot bear to cause pain but I cannot avoid causing it. . . . [13]

Though the affair with Parnok was still far from over, this letter shows a shift in mood. Tsvetaeva was burdened by the situation between Efron and Parnok. She expected, though, to be the controlling force; she herself would choose either to keep both relationships going or to separate from Parnok on her own terms.

The poems Parnok wrote in Svyatye Gory speak of cold, of tears, of fear of death. She still turned to Tsvetaeva for consolation, but she seemed to know that her lover had passed her by. When they returned to Moscow, Parnok apparently accepted the fact that their love had come to an end. Upon her return to Moscow she wrote:

> It pleases the lips to belong to no one,
> I love my deserted threshold . . .
> Why do you come, you whose name
> Brings to me the winds of all the roads? [14]

But her poem written in October is clearly addressed to Efron and bares her underlying jealousy of him as well as the pain of expecting that other lovers would come into Tsvetaeva's life.

> O youth, you are not the one who broke her spell.
> Marvelling at the fire of those loving lips,
> O, first one, not your name but mine
> Will her lover jealously remember. [15]

Tsvetaeva too anticipated the end. "Gypsy passion of separation! / Barely you met—you tear yourself away!"[16] In another poem, written in November, Tsvetaeva indulges in nostalgic memories of their early love: a sleigh ride in the snow, Parnok kissing the snowflakes off Tsvetaeva's sable coat— yet behind the coachman's back the two heads do not meet.[17] Both women had sensed from the very beginning that their relationship could not last. It was their trip to St. Petersburg in December that brought the tensions between them almost to a breaking point. They went at the invitation of Sofiya Chatskina and Yakov Saker, the editors of *Northern Notes*, the journal that published their poems. Soon after their arrival, Tsvetaeva made plans to attend a literary soirée in a private home where she hoped to meet Anna Akhmatova, the dominant woman-poet of the day, and to hear Mikhail Kuzmin, a famous poet who accompanied his poems on guitar the piano.

Tsvetaeva would describe the scene in a letter to Kuzmin, undated but probably written sometime in 1921:

> This is what happened. I had just arrived [in Petersburg]. I was with someone, that is with a woman.—Oh, God, how I cried!—But that is not important. So, in short, she absolutely did not want me to go to this soirée and because of that she insisted all the more that I go. She could not go because she had a headache—and her head always aches—and when she has a headache—she is unbearable (darkened room, blue-shaded lamp, my tears). But I had no headache, never have one![18]

Tsvetaeva was exasperated by Parnok's objection to her going and annoyed when Parnok tried to convince her to go. She did not believe her. Mistrust had entered their relationship:

> "Sonya, I will not go!"
> "Why not? Anyway, I am—nobody."
> "But I feel sorry for you."
> "There will be many people, you'll relax."
> "No, I feel very sorry for you."
> "I can't stand pity. Go, go. Remember, Marina, Kuzmin will be there and he will sing."
> "Yes, he will sing, and when I return you'll nag me and I will cry. I would not go, for anything."

But she did go. Akhmatova was out of town, but she met Kuzmin and his friends, and Osip Mandelshtam fell in love with her. She wanted very much to stay longer, but she felt she had to leave because of Parnok. Everyone tried to persuade her that Parnok was not a child waiting for her. Inside, she raged ("to hell with Sonya!") but she knew she would never forgive herself if she stayed, and so she left. Parnok was asleep when she returned.

In mid-January, soon after Tsvetaeva and Parnok returned to Moscow, Mandelshtam came to see Tsvetaeva. He had first met her in Koktebel, but her poetry reading in Petrograd had made him feel that he needed to know her better as a poet and as a woman. Tsvetaeva welcomed him to Moscow and showed him around the city she loved. When he left she went to see Parnok. A shocking encounter awaited her: "When I came to her, after having missed two Mandelshtam days—the only times I failed to come to her in years—someone else was sitting on her bed: very big, fat, black-haired." [19] Probably this was Lyudmila Erarskaya, an actress with whom Parnok would live for many years. Little is known about the details of the final breakup. Clearly, there were tensions in the relationship all along. Both women were jealous, both were strong and demanding, neither wanted to give up her independence. Furthermore, Parnok was a committed lesbian and Tsvetaeva was not. Polyakova's belief that Parnok initiated the final rupture seems to be confirmed by the poems and by the letter to Kuzmin. Such a rejection would also explain Tsvetaeva's violent and long-lasting reaction, for it repeated the pain her mother had inflicted throughout her childhood. Tsvetaeva herself did not perceive this wound as self-inflicted, since, in a letter in 1933, she would refer to this period as "the hour of my first catastrophe." [20]

Yet there might be a less obvious, subconscious, element. It is suggested in the dream Tsvetaeva had described to Ellis in 1919—her mother's (and her own) need to keep the bowstring pulled back forever. If she had felt her own passion waning, it would justify the need for forgiveness she expressed in her farewell poem to Parnok, dated April 1916. It celebrates a relationship that would never be repeated and connects it strikingly with her yearning for mother.

> In those days of yore you were like a mother to me.
> I could call you at night,
> Feverish light, sleepless light,
> The light of my eyes in those nights of yore.
>
> Remember, my gracious one,
> Those days without sunsets,

Mother-days, daughter-days,
Days without sunsets, without evenings.

I didn't come to disturb you. Farewell,
Only the hem of your dress I will kiss,
And my eyes will look into your eyes,
Covered with kisses in those nights of yore.

A day will come—I'll die—and a day—you'll die,
A day will come—I'll understand—and a day—you'll understand . . .
And on that day of forgiveness, there will return to us
That irretrievable time of yore.[21]

On the next day Marina addressed her husband in a heartbreaking poem beginning:

I came to you in the dark of midnight,
For the last help.
I—a beggar who had forgotten kinship,
A sinking ship.[22]

The shadow of Parnok falls over other poems, particularly in the cycle "Insomnia," consisting of ten poems written from April to December 1916 and addressed to her (though she is not named) and an eleventh poem written in 1921, dedicated to Tatyana Scriabina, the composer's widow.[23] Svetlana Elnitskaya's brilliant analysis, "The Two Insomnias," establishes the inner connection between Parnok and Scriabina, with whom Tsvetaeva would form a friendship during her years in Red Moscow.[24]

In fact, that "day of forgiveness" with Parnok never came, certainly not one of mutual forgiveness. Instead Tsvetaeva's pain hardened into hostility and denial of the importance of Parnok's role in her life. The wound she had suffered at the hands of a woman she would never forget. When she met another Sonya a few years later, she didn't dare to consummate the relationship. In Tsvetaeva's later relations with women to whom she was sexually attracted, she avoided consummation but her emotional response remained.

The fullest reaction to the affair with Parnok is found in Tsvetaeva's *Letter to an Amazon*, written in 1934, a kind of harangue against lesbianism.[25] Her revenge against Parnok takes here the form of an attack on Natalie Barney, the "Amazon" of lesbian love in Paris. Tsvetaeva's intent in the essay is to wound "the heart of your cause, of your belief, of your body, of your heart." Her main argument against lesbian love is that to love without having children is against nature. She needs to ease the pain of having lost Parnok, of having renounced lesbianism—and she finds her justification in her fantasized "motherhood." She wanted to nurture her children (at the time of writing she had also a son)—physically and spiritually—not in the manner they needed, but so that they would become what *she* wanted them to be. The myth of motherhood, however, became her weapon to destroy the memory of her lesbian experience and the pain of Parnok's rejection.

Tsvetaeva argues that a young woman who sees man as the enemy still will choose him because of her need to have a child; she will leave a woman lover, not because she cannot resist the man, but because she wants a child. A child for her is the ultimate possession, an extension of herself, a protection against the aridity of old age. "This is the only weak and vulnerable point of attack, the only breach in that perfect unity of two women in love." If love between women is doomed, in the end it triumphs because of the power of Tsvetaeva's poetic prose, which leaves no doubt where her heart is:

> Weeping willow! Willow all in tears! Willow, body and soul of women. The willow's neck bathed in tears. The mass of gray hair pulled over the face, seeing no longer anything. Gray hair sweeping the face of the earth.
>
> Water, air, mountains, trees have been given to us to understand the soul of humans, so deeply hidden. When I see a willow in despair, I understand Sappho.[26]

There is a reference to Parnok's death in 1933 in *Letter to an Amazon*, though she is not named. Tsvetaeva wants at first to find out more about her lover's death, but then decides against it: "What for since she is dead? Since I too will die some day, [ . . . ] and, courageously, with the great truth of indifference: Since she had already died for me, twenty years ago."[27]

Parnok, on the other hand, always kept a picture of Tsvetaeva on her night table, she spoke very highly of her talent, and, though there was bitterness in one of her poems dealing with the end of the affair, she finally "forgave." In a poem addressed to another Marina, Marina Baranovich, written in 1929, Parnok evokes her former friend:

> And the same coldness of a serpent's cunning
> and slippery ways . . . But I have forgiven her,
> and I love you and through you, Marina,
> the vision of your namesake.[28]

Yet when Tsvetaeva returned to the Soviet Union in 1939 and was told by Marina Baranovich about the poem and the blessing, she replied indifferently: "That was so long ago."[29] For the subconscious, however, time did not matter. Tsvetaeva jotted down in her notebook in 1940:

> Then I saw in a dream S. Ya. Parnok, of whom I *never* think and whose death I didn't regret for a second—everything burnt out *clean then*—. In short, I saw her with her stupid woman-friend and with her very naive poems. I left them—the friend and the poems—and went to some train compartment of third or even fourth class.[30]

# 7. In the Shadow of the Revolution

*Fate kissed me on the lips,*
*Fate taught me to be superior.*

*I paid full tribute to those lips*
*I threw roses on graves . . .*
*But Fate grabbed me, on the run,*
*By my hair with a heavy hand!* [1]

Tsvetaeva's brief romance with Osip Mandelshtam overlapped her liaison with Parnok. Emotionally, however, it was worlds apart. Tsvetaeva would recall those "wonderful days from February to June 1916." [2] They wrote poems for and to each other; there was a flirtation, but there was no love affair. "Instead of myself, I gave him Moscow as a present," Tsvetaeva would write years later to a friend. [3]

Nadezhda Mandelshtam, the poet's widow, makes it very clear in her memoirs that her husband must have sensed that Tsvetaeva was "the sort of Russian woman who longs to do something heroic and self-sacrificing, to wash the wounds of Don Quixote—though for some reason it always so happens that when Don Quixote is actually bleeding to death such women are always otherwise occupied and fail to notice anything amiss." [4] Indeed, Mandelshtam, in a poem written shortly after he left Tsvetaeva, says that "to stay with such a mist-wreathed nun means to court disaster." [5] And Nadezhda Mandelshtam identifies the "nun" with Tsvetaeva. This rather harsh interpretation of the relationship may well have been due to jealousy, but on the other hand she pays homage to Tsvetaeva's influence on her husband's poetry:

> Bestowing on him the gift of her friendship, and of Moscow, Tsvetaeva somehow broke the spell which Petersburg had cast on him. It was a magic gift because with only Petersburg, without Moscow, it would have been impossible to breathe freely, to acquire the true feeling for Russia and the inner freedom of which Mandelshtam speaks in his article on Chaadayev. [6]

Mandelshtam, for his part, brought another, a broader, vision to Tsvetaeva. Showing him Moscow brought into Tsvetaeva's poetry that city's history and a sense of a larger cultural context.

Mandelshtam wrote three poems to Tsvetaeva; Tsvetaeva wrote nine to him. She called him "divine boy" and "young swan" and spoke of the great tenderness between them. Perhaps the most striking poem is the one in which she predicts his tragic fate:

> They will take you with their bare hands—zealous, stubborn!
> Your screams will fill the night
> They will scatter your wings to all four winds.
> Seraphim! Eaglet![7]

Later Tsvetaeva would write to a friend: "I love Mandelshtam with his confused, weak, chaotic mind, sometimes mindlessness (try to follow logically any one of his poems!) but with the invariable CHARM of each line. The issue is not classicism but magic."[8]

Mandelshtam was less generous in his criticism of her poetry. In his 1922 essay "Literary Moscow," he called women's poetry "a kind of domestic needlework" and specifically attacked Tsvetaeva for the tastelessness and historical inaccuracy of her "pseudo-populist, pseudo-Muscovite" poetry.[9] This angry criticism may well have been inspired more by Tsvetaeva's rejection of him than by his literary judgment.

The summer of 1916 Tsvetaeva spent with her daughter, Asya's son, and their family nanny at her sister's country place near Aleksandrov, their father's native village. Mandelshtam came to see Tsvetaeva, but he felt out of place in such rural surroundings. Tsvetaeva's essay "The Story of a Dedication" describes that visit. As always she interlaces the present with the past, invoking her attachment to Aleksandrov and her father's legacy. She reminisces and she philosophizes, but the center of the essay is Mandelshtam. He emerges as a lost, slightly ridiculous figure accustomed to life in the city, who is at ease in the ancient Greece of his imagination, but terrified when Tsvetaeva takes him on her daily walks to the country cemetery.

Predictably, Mandelshtam fled the countryside—away from Tsvetaeva's sarcasm, from the nanny's hostility, and from the annoying children. In retrospect Tsvetaeva even felt a little sorry for him. She valued him as a great poet, and on her return to Russia in 1939, she would inquire about him. He had disappeared into a prison camp in 1937, never to return.

In Russia, in these war years, innovation and experimentation in all the arts produced an atmosphere of heightened creativity that would continue in the early years of the Revolution. There were public readings and heated debates about the role of art in society. It was a time of intoxication with ideas, with dreams, with freedom—a time that should have allowed Tsvetaeva to find a literary home. She participated in many of these gatherings; she looked for an audience and she enjoyed the company of poets. Yet, she stood apart. She created on her own, needing neither followers nor masters. And she found her new poetic voice.

During this period, she continued to recite in public the poems she had written from 1912 to 1915. Some appeared in *Northern Notes*, but Tsvetaeva was too preoccupied to look for other publishers. When, in 1919, under the Bolsheviks, she submitted her manuscript to the State Literature Department, it was rejected. In emigration—in Berlin, Prague, and even in Paris in 1928—she tried again and again to find a publisher for these poems, but without success. She recited them in public readings, but only in 1976 did they appear in print, entitled *Juvenilia*.

The early poems in *Juvenilia* continue the poet's personal lyrical diary. There are poems to her sister, to her daughter, to her husband; there are self-portraits. And always there is death. The central theme of defeating depression, of overcoming the fear of aging and death by ecstasy erupts in full force. And there is the emerging awareness that she is a poet. Two poetry cycles, "The Magician," addressed to Ellis, and one addressed to Pyotr Efron, Sergey's brother, begin her tendency to group poems in cycles. In her cycle about her affair with Parnok, Tsvetaeva reaches a new emotional level. It marks a watershed in her maturing art as well. Her poems had become more controlled, simpler, less romantic. Her syncopated rhythm and her original syntax—deleting verbs wherever possible, using dashes and ellipses—were emerging as her main formal characteristics.

Tsvetaeva's power reached new heights with her next collections, *Versts I* (1922) and *Versts II* (1921), which cover the years 1916 to 1920.[10] Originally she had planned one volume, but her wealth of poems made her publish them in two. The first volume begins with January and ends with December 1916. In that year, with the war still raging and revolution imminent, Tsvetaeva did not write a single poem dealing with outside events. Instead, we are given the heartbeat of the poet and a new readiness to confront her own limitless desires.

The collections would also include Tsvetaeva's "Verses to Blok," her hom-

age to the great Russian Symbolist poet. Five years before he died, deeply disillusioned by the Revolution, Tsvetaeva already sensed that "his wings were
broken." Using metaphors of stillness, snow, sundown, pallor, and death,
the cycle marks the departure of an angel from this world, leaving Tsvetaeva
behind.

Interestingly enough, the next cycle, dedicated to Anna Akhmatova, is in
full contrast to the angel image of Blok. Akhmatova, the muse of tears, has
a demon asleep in her; storms and black magic are her domain but her eyes
look down from all the icons. Tsvetaeva's worship of Akhmatova seems to
project much of her own myth and her nostalgia for Parnok.

Tsvetaeva dedicated one poem, written in July 1916, to a new man in her
life, noting in the margin that from that point to the end of *Versts* I all the
poems were addressed to Nicodemus Plutser-Sarna, "the only one who succeeded in loving me . . . and it is not simple to love such a complex thing—
me." [11] While the poem dedicated to him speaks of tenderness and giving,
a nightmarish atmosphere of insomnia and dread fills the rest of the book.
Night and storms, frost and darkness create an awareness of death:

On the roads, crackling with frost,
With the royal silvery child
I pass. Everything is snow, everything—is death, everything is dream.

On the bushes are silver arrows.
Once, I had a body,
Had a name—but isn't it all smoke?

A voice I had, burning and deep . . .
They say this blue-eyed
Ermine child is—mine.

And nobody sees on the road,
That for a long time already I am in a coffin,
I am done with my huge dream. [12]

Tsvetaeva always needed the highest intensity of feeling to fuel her poetic
power. Here, instead of love, rage, or contempt, it was her own struggle
with despair that inspired her. It is not clear how much this poem reflects
her second pregnancy.

**S** The next year was a trying one for Tsvetaeva. Her pregnancy was difficult. The pain caused by her break with Parnok was still fresh, and Efron was away most of the time at Officers' Training School. Her inner turmoil was heightened by outside events. At the end of 1916, it was clear that Russia was on the eve of historic upheavals. The news from the front was bad and social unrest in the country was growing. In February, food rioting broke out in Petrograd and soldiers began to join the rebellion. These events culminated in the February Revolution, which brought democratic forces to the fore. Although Moscow was spared the violence and chaos of the capital, it was obvious that a new era had begun.

Tsvetaeva was in Moscow all this time, alone with Alya, expecting the birth of her second child, hoping for a son. She witnessed with rising apprehension the new mood around her, sensing that the impending revolution was not her revolution. On March 2, 1917 she wrote her first "political" poem.

> Azure clouds over the chapel,
> The croak of crows.
> And the revolutionary troops
> Are passing—color of ashes and sand.
> Oh, my aristocratic, my regal longing! [13]

On March 16, Nicholas II was forced to abdicate and the Romanov dynasty ceased to rule Russia. The tsar and his family were exiled to Siberia and later executed. A provisional government, formed by progressive, liberal, and democratic elements, was headed by Prince Lvov; its most prominent members were Aleksandr Kerensky, Pavel Milyukov, and Aleksandr Guchkov. Simultaneously, soviets of workers and soldiers came into existence and competed for power with the provisional government.

While many intellectuals—writers, poets, playwrights—welcomed the new regime and celebrated the defeat of the old one, Tsvetaeva never trusted the emerging social and political order. Instead she felt alienated and antagonized. This uprising of the masses, the violent and vulgar masses, had nothing in common with her romantic vision of the individual rebel. Tsvetaeva, whose sympathy had always been with the persecuted, now defended the tsar and prayed for the safety of the young tsarevich, Aleksey.

Perhaps to overcome her anxieties, Tsvetaeva's joy in life returned and a harvest of romantic poems resulted in the spring and summer of 1917. The birth of her second daughter, Irina, on April 13 of that year did not disrupt the stream of her creativity. The cycles "Don Juan," "Stenka Razin," "Tsar of Darkness," and "Carmen" allowed her to use different disguises to express her consuming, wild passion. In June 1917, she admonished little Alya: "You'd better know one thing: tomorrow you'll be old / Drink the wine, drive the troika, sing at the *Yar* / Be a blue-eyed gypsy." [14]

Tsvetaeva did not indicate to whom her romantic poems were addressed, and it is almost impossible to know when the passion she described was based on facts or when it was invented. Yet whether "Bohème," written in July 1917, was true or imagined, this account of an escapade with a Polish poet shows us a playful Tsvetaeva with no reference to the background of this difficult, exciting period:

> Remember that light-blue cloak,
> Street-lights and puddles?
> How we played you and I
> Husband and wife.
>
> My first bracelet,
> My white corset,
> Your raspberry-colored vest,
> Our checkered blanket?
>
> .  .  .  .  .  .  .  .  .  .  .  .  .  .  .
>
> Do you remember the chest of imitation walnut?
> The cold was cruel!
> My fear, your laughter.
> The landlord's anger.
>
> How the neighbor knocked
> Awakened by the flute . . .
> Kisses—for dinner,
> And verses—for supper. [15]

Meanwhile political events were moving rapidly. In July 1917 Kerensky formed a new government; Lenin and Trotsky returned from abroad, the Russian army was in retreat, the economy was a shambles. The choice that lay before the country was an ineffectual democratic Kerensky government, supported by the army, or Communism. Life in Moscow grew increasingly difficult. Food was scarce, winter cold was threatening. In August, Tsvetaeva wrote to Voloshin, asking him to use his personal connections to have Efron transferred to the south, where she would join him with the children. Somehow that plan went awry, and on the day of Lenin's takeover—November 7, 1917, according to the new calendar—Tsvetaeva was alone in Koktebel. Efron was with his regiment in Moscow and the children were at home.

News of the Revolution traveled fast. In St. Petersburg and Moscow, government buildings, railways, bridges were taken over, telephones and utilities were interrupted. Kerensky's appeal to the army brought no response; the Provisional Government collapsed without much resistance, and Kerensky escaped abroad. In Moscow, street fighting lasted for days as the officers' regiments put up a valiant struggle, but they, too, finally capitulated. The country was in chaos. All over Russia looting and killing were rampant. The news from the capital and Moscow was confused, but there could be no doubt: the Revolution had begun.

On November 14, Tsvetaeva left for Moscow. It was not an easy journey. She spent two and a half days in a crowded train without food or drink. Alarming rumors circulated:

> Soldiers bring newspapers, on pink paper. The Kremlin and all monuments have been blown up. The 56th [Efron's] Regiment. The buildings where the cadets and officers have refused to surrender have been blown up. 16,000 dead. At the next station it is already 25,000 dead. I don't say a word. I smoke.[16]

On the way, Tsvetaeva wrote a letter to Efron, addressing him in the formal "Vy" but screaming her love, her fear of losing him, her utter dependency. Describing him as "a lion who gives his lion-share—life," she wrote: "If God will perform this miracle—and let you live, I will follow you like a dog."[17] Her anxiety about him becomes so overwhelming that she admits: "No thought about the children. If S. is no longer, then neither am I, and neither are they; Alya won't live without me, she won't want to, won't be able to. As I won't without S." Tsvetaeva finally arrived in dark and frightening Moscow. There she found her husband asleep at a friend's house and the children well. That same evening she went back to Koktebel with her husband and his officer friend so that Efron could join the White Army, being formed in the south. It is not clear why Efron, whose parents had actively opposed the tsarist regime, was now ready to fight the Revolution. At that time, however, many saw democracy threatened by the rising terror of the Bolsheviks, who had taken control without consulting the people. The fact that Efron was in an officers' training school and probably felt solidarity with his officer friends may also have played a role in his decision. Perhaps Tsvetaeva's hostility to the Bolsheviks influenced her husband as well.

The situation was still extremely volatile. The children stayed with Efron's family, while their parents left to consult with their friends and Asya about further arrangements. They arrived in Koktebel in a snowstorm and there, after happy greetings and the joy of reunion, Voloshin foretold the coming horrors of the Revolution: "the terror, the civil war, the executions, the barricades, the Vendée, men turned into beasts, the loss of decency, the unleashed spirits of the elements, blood, blood, blood . . ." [18]

On November 25, Tsvetaeva left for Moscow in order to take the children to Koktebel. She intended to stay with Voloshin and Pra near Efron, who had joined the Whites on the Don. It was not to be. By the time Tsvetaeva arrived in Moscow, the Civil War had divided Russia into north and south: Moscow was cut off. Tsvetaeva was alone with five-year-old Alya and six-month-old Irina, unprepared for both the physical hardships she would face and the ordeal of life in this new society whose basic ethos she had rejected from the start.

# 8. Life under Communism

*The new year I met alone.*
*I, the rich one, I was poor,*
*I, the winged one, I was cursed.*[1]

svetaeva returned to Moscow in November 1917. Twenty-five then, with two small daughters, she was ill-equipped to cope with the surrounding turmoil and its attendant hardships. Fortunately, her inborn vitality, her sense of humor, and even her arrogance helped her not merely to survive, but to develop new relationships and to continue to grow as a poet.

Before the Revolution, Tsvetaeva had been critical of the tsarist regime. While she had had her reservations about the February Revolution and Kerensky, she had nonetheless remained essentially in her own private world. Now, she could no longer avoid facing Bolshevik reality: hunger and cold, the supremacy of the state over the individual, vulgarity and violence. Right from the start, she hated it all. She never accepted the Revolution or Communism, as she could not accept any dogma—religious or secular—limiting her freedom as an individual, as a poet. Feeling like a noblewoman among plebians, she turned her aversion into a challenge: "The main thing is to understand from the very first second: Everything is lost! Then—everything is easy."[2]

If the February Revolution had promised democratic reforms and inspired hopes for a more just society, the November Revolution not only abolished the Constituent Assembly, but established the dictatorship of the proletariat. Lenin, Trotsky, and the men around them were building, under fire, a new society in which the end justified the means. For the next few years War Communism became the new governing formula: a philosophy based on the people's sacrifices in order to build and defend a utopian, classless communist society. The government became the sole producer and distributor of goods, introducing a system of ration cards, mobilizing everyone in the defense of the Revolution. Only workers or well-known intellectuals and artists were entitled to ration cards. Intellectuals like Tsvetaeva often went without food or heat, selling their books and bartering their belongings for food and firewood.

Tsvetaeva had nobody to turn to for support. Asya, who had remarried in 1916 and whose second husband died in 1917, remained in the south; her stepbrother, Andrey, was in Moscow, but she seldom saw him. Valeriya was in Moscow, too, but Tsvetaeva had completely lost touch with her. The most trying absence of all was the lack of any news from Efron. All alone, Tsvetaeva had to provide food, firewood, and clothing for the family, a difficult task. She chopped up her furniture to heat their rooms, sold whatever she could, accepted food and handouts from friends and neighbors.

Ilya Ehrenburg has described Tsvetaeva soon after her return to Moscow: "The striking thing about her expression was its combination of arrogance and bewilderment. Her bearing was proud—her head thrown back, with a very high forehead—but the bewilderment was betrayed by her eyes, large and helpless, as though unseeing."[3]

According to the new rules, Tsvetaeva had to share her apartment with strangers; only the dining room and one bedroom were at her disposal. Fortunately, however, there was a small attic room which served as her refuge and became her attic castle. Ehrenburg's vivid description of that apartment is similar to those of many contemporaries: "It would be difficult to imagine greater chaos. Everyone in those days lived in a state of emergency, but the amenities were preserved. Marina, however, seemed to have ravaged her hiding-place on purpose. Everything was flung about, covered with tobacco ash and dust."[4] This was the new "freedom" she had found.

Oddly, the atmosphere of danger, tension, and challenge hovering over Moscow somehow suited Tsvetaeva, removing her from the quotidian existence she abhorred. Money, conventions, comfort had become unimportant; in their place, bedrock issues of life emerged. Common misery united people from every class, people ordinarily holding altogether different social and political views. In this chaotic world survival took precedence over all, emphasizing the timeless themes of love and death, of transcendence and *carpe diem*, which were Tsvetaeva's own. She described her typical day as follows:

> I get up—the upper window is barely gray, it's cold, puddles, sawdust, buckets, pitchers, rags, everywhere children's dresses and shirts. I saw wood, light the fire, wash potatoes in icy water and boil them in the

samovar [ . . . ]. I walk and I sleep in the same brown brushed-cotton dress, ridiculously shrunken for a long time, made for me in my absence in the spring of 1917 in Alexandrov. It is full of holes from falling pieces of coal and cigarettes. The sleeves, which had an elastic band at the wrist, are now twisted and fastened with a safety pin.[5]

After cleaning, cooking, washing clothes and dishes, and feeding the children, she went to bed at eleven or twelve o'clock. "I enjoy the small lamp next to my pillow, the silence, the notebook, the cigarette, sometimes bread."[6] To her long list of chores, Tsvetaeva added: "I have not recorded the main thing: the gaiety, the sharpness of mind, the eruptions of joy over the tiniest achievement, the passionate intensity of all my being—the walls scribbled over with lines of poetry and notes for the diary."[7] When a former tenant, a loyal Communist, unexpectedly visited her one day, he was appalled by her living conditions. " 'How about these dishes?' " he asked Alya. " 'Don't you wash them?' " " 'Yes, we do,' " Alya replied, " 'inside, not outside, and Mama is a poet.' " To his insistence that her mother take a job, Alya's answer remained the same: " 'Mama is a poet.' "[8]

That winter of 1918 Tsvetaeva began to spend time with Pavel Antokolsky, or "Pavlik," a talented seventeen-year-old poet and actor. He also directed at the Third Studio of the Moscow Theater, whose famous director was Yevgeny Vakhtangov. When Tsvetaeva had gone south in October, Efron's friend had recited some poems and she had asked for the poet's name. It was Antokolsky. She found his address and went to visit him, entering his house by the back staircase. The two poets embraced amid all the paraphernalia of Pavlik's kitchen, and immediately, wrote Tsvetaeva, "the meeting was something of an earthquake."[9] Disregarding the misery all around them, they discussed love and motherhood, the role of men and women, Joan of Arc, and such "topical" questions as: "Who was Satan's Judas?"

In her diary Tsvetaeva notes that Efron came to see her for a day or so in January. She does not explain how he had managed to get to Moscow.[10] Many years later, Efron would mention in a letter to Voloshin that even during his stay Tsvetaeva divided her time between him and someone else.[11]

Antokolsky introduced Tsvetaeva to his best friend Yura Zavadsky, an actor and theatrical director of the same avant-garde studio. They were lovers at the time, but that did not prevent Tsvetaeva from falling under the spell of Zavadsky's cold beauty. At first the two friends visited her only together, but soon

Zavadsky began to call on her by himself. Though she came to describe him as a self-centered, indolent, and weak man who was not interested in women, she was attracted to him as she would always be by handsome people.

All through these years, from 1917 until Tsvetaeva emigrated in 1922, Zavadsky's and Antokolsky's friends as well as Tsvetaeva's own friends—writers and poets—gathered in her house for lively talk of love, theater, and poetry. But outside her attic castle, life was grim. In April, peace with Germany was signed, but civil war continued to spread, increasing the power of the Cheka, the newly organized secret police. The summer of 1918 brought several attempts to overthrow the Bolsheviks: Uritsky was assassinated, Lenin wounded; trials, executions, and terror followed. Viktor Shklovsky, the formalist writer, described St. Petersburg in the aftershock of the Revolution as a city "grown quiet, as after an explosion, when it's all over, when everything's blown up. Like a man whose insides have been torn out by an explosion, but who keeps talking. Imagine a group of such men. They sit and talk. What else are they to do—howl?" [12]

Shklovksy's dire image, however, gives only part of the picture. Though many writers, poets, and artists had lost their moorings, others believed that a new era had begun and that art would assume a more important role than ever before. In these early revolutionary years, the Party was too busy to control all cultural activities and anarchy prevailed. Traditions and conventions were thrown overboard while avant-garde art movements like Futurism and Constructivism thrived; theater, ballet, and films celebrated the new era. Yet these artistic movements could not survive for long in a society where the major function of literature and art would be to follow the Party line. Tsvetaeva still refused to become part of any group, but her spirits were high. Her work, increasingly bold and original, reflected her personal perception of a new reality. The transition she was forced to make from her privileged existence to life in Bolshevik Moscow turned up again and again in her diaries and essays.

One of her diary entries describes an evening in the company of near strangers where she was asked to recite her poems. "Since there is a Communist in the room, I recite the 'White Guard'. 'White guard, your way is set high . . .' " [13] Tsvetaeva, who was afraid of cars, of elevators, of wide-open spaces, who lost her way in unfamiliar surroundings, showed remarkable courage when it came to moral issues. She was convinced of her truth and stood up for it whatever the circumstances. It is this absolute commitment to her values that endows her poetry with a passion difficult to resist. The powerful poems she addressed to the White Armies speak of the suffering of war on both sides, and glorify the courage and loyalty of the Whites, the Swans. Tsvetaeva had never seen the Whites in action, and so she mythologized them into the "last dream of the old world: / Youth—Daring— Vendée—Don."[14] While some of these poems seem to deal with events of the day, the source of their fervor was Tsvetaeva's romanticism and the Russian past. Into these poems she poured all her identification with the "persecuted," her longing for the past, her love for the mythologized Sergey. As political statements they were superficial, but on a deeper level they were metaphors for stability and valor, honor and duty.

In these poems, published for the first time only in 1957 in Munich and now in a bilingual edition entitled The Demesne of the Swans, Tsvetaeva's simple language and her compelling rhythms invoke heroism and sacrifice, courage and lament:

> Who survived—will die, who died—will rise up.
> And then the descendants remembering the past:
> "Where were you?" The question will peal like thunder.
> The answer will peal like thunder: "On the Don!"
>
> "What did you do?"—We suffered,
> Then got tired and lay down to sleep.
> And in the dictionary the pensive grandsons
> Will write after the word "Duty," the word "Don."[15]

Tsvetaeva had always been very close to her daughter. Now, in Communist Moscow, separated from her old world, she shared with the six-year-old Alya her thoughts, her loneliness, her romanticism. She took her along on her walks, to visit friends, to the theater, and to poetry readings. Alya was very pretty; she had Efron's beautiful eyes and Tsvetaeva's high forehead; she was quiet but bright and in those years wrote a diary and poems which her mother considered good enough for publication.[16]

But, like her own mother, Tsvetaeva needed to be the center of her daughter's life; like her own mother, she "stuffed" Alya with her favorite writers and stories. By imposing her own standards on her daughter, Tsvetaeva forced her out of childhood and into the dangerous intimacy she herself needed. Many contemporaries observed how brainwashed, how rehearsed Alya appeared. Not daring to rebel openly, she often played tricks behind her mother's back. Once, when Tsvetaeva and Alya slept in a friend's communal apartment, they were instructed to leave the room in perfect order. Alya, taking advantage of Tsvetaeva's short-sightedness, wrote all over the walls: "Here on such and such a date slept Marina with Alya." She would also hide things Tsvetaeva liked, or throw out "treasures," like food that Tsvetaeva had hunted down. She always addressed her mother with the formal "Vy," for it was clear to her that Tsvetaeva's special role as a poet rendered her superior in every respect.

In her reminiscences Alya includes a description of her mother written in 1918:

> My mother is very strange. My mother doesn't look like a mother. Mothers always adore their children, and children in general, but Marina doesn't like children . . . She is sad, fast, loves verses and music, she writes poems. She perseveres, always perseveres. She can be angry and she can love. She is always in a hurry. She has a great soul, . . . a fast gait. Marina's hands are covered with rings. Marina reads through the nights. Her eyes are almost always mocking. She does not like to be bothered by stupid questions, she gets very angry then.[17]

Once, when returning home from one of their "expeditions" in search of food, they heard the newspaper boys screaming that Nikolay Romanov had been executed. Tsvetaeva turned to Alya and said in a loud, choked voice: "Alya, they've killed the Tsar of Russia, Nicholas II. Pray for the peace of his soul!" Alya crossed herself three times, and bowed down deeply. At that moment Tsvetaeva thought, "Too bad she is not a boy. He would have taken off his cap."[18]

Poems to Alya, written in 1918–19, are imbued with tenderness for her daughter, whom she loved "like a son." Yet she reveals an unmistakable truth: she can define neither herself nor her daughter. Is Tsvetaeva mother or child? Is she playmate or sister? This ambivalence was bound to burden the child.

> I don't know where you are and where I am.
> The same songs and the same worries,
> We are — you and I — such friends,
> We are — you and I — such orphans.[19]

Tsvetaeva also shared with Alya her longing for Sergey:

> And where is Papa? Sleep, sleep, soon the sandman
> Will come on his steppe-steed.
> Where will he take us? To the Don of the Swans.
> There — don't you know? — a white swan is there for me.[20]

Tsvetaeva's younger daughter, Irina, played a much different role. It is not known whether she was born with a genetic defect or whether bad care and nutrition had delayed her development, but at two she was hardly able to walk or talk properly and could only sing a melodious tune. It seems clear that Irina's imperfection was both a reproach and a burden for Tsvetaeva. She never called her anything but "Irina"—never "Irinochka" or "Irochka," as would be usual in Russian families. There was never a hint of that jealous, possessive love that Alya knew from birth. Only two small poems were dedicated to her in her lifetime. Both speak more about the ominous circumstances of Irina's birth—civil war, revolution—than about the child or Tsvetaeva's feelings for her.

In one of her diary entries, Tsvetaeva describes untying Irina from her chair when she came home with Alya from their many forays for food, for wood, for company and fun.[21] Irina had to be tied up, Tsvetaeva explains, because she had once crawled over to a cupboard and eaten half an uncooked cabbage head. Tsvetaeva's contemporaries also described the half-dark room where the little girl spent hours alone, tied to the bed or the chair, her head bumping from one side to the other. Many wondered how Tsvetaeva could leave the child like that and go about her business discussing poetry and metaphysics. But Tsvetaeva herself had no doubts about her priorities: she and poetry came first.

Since the poems had to be written, Tsvetaeva refused to look for work. Yet in Moscow, at that time, she had no prospects of a literary income. Finally, in November 1918, she gave in and accepted the job with the People's Commissariat for Nationalities which her former tenant, an influential Communist, kept offering her. In her essay "My Jobs," Tsvetaeva recalled her five and a half months in this office. Her keen observation and her sense of humor re-create a scene of bureaucratic boredom that sounds quite contemporary: people pretending to work, drinking tea, gossiping. She arrived "clumsy and shy. In a man's mousy undershirt, like a mouse. I am dressed poorer than all the others, and that doesn't cheer me up. My shoes are tied with string. I may have some shoelaces somewhere, but . . . who cares?"[22] Her assignment was to write summaries of newspaper accounts or to paste and file for the archives clippings dealing with the defeats of the White Army. Tsvetaeva was bored and escaped into her daydreams: the Commissariat was located in an old mansion and the elegant surroundings inspired her romantic fantasies.

On her way to the kitchen she imagined seeing Natasha Rostova, the heroine of Tolstoy's *War and Peace*, on the palatial steps of the stairway, and when she passed the tall statue of a knight in the hall, she would "tenderly stroke his iron foot." Her co-workers were "two unkempt, gloomy Jewesses somehow like herrings, ageless; a red-faced, blond Latvian also terrible, like a person who has turned into a sausage." There was "one with a nose, but no chin, another with a chin but without a nose," and behind her "a seventeen-year-old child—pink-cheeked, healthy, curly-haired"—whom Tsvetaeva dubbed a "white Negro."[23] Her supervisor, an enthusiastic propagandist for the introduction of Esperanto, did not care about politics and played along with Tsvetaeva to their mutual advantage. He asked her to cover for him when he wanted to take days off and in turn did not mind her late arrivals.

Tsvetaeva made friends with her "white Negro," and with another young woman, whose fiancé had been executed for sheltering a wounded White Army officer. She was obviously attracted to the white Negro, who shared her bread ration with her and to whom she gave a ring. One day they went together to the chapel that had been preserved in the building. Tsvetaeva never liked church services but she watched the young woman and wondered: "Love—and God. How does that coexist in people? [ . . . ] She prays, her eyes are innocent. With those same innocent eyes, with those same lips that have been praying. . . . If I were a believer and if I loved men, love and God would fight within me like wild dogs."[24]

The job was not without its benefits. On one occasion, Tsvetaeva raced home to get Alya's broken sleigh when she learned that frozen potatoes were going to be distributed. She braved a crowded line and slippery steps to the cellar to reach the precious potatoes, and then dragged the heavy load home. Her face covered with sweat and tears, she felt that she was "one with her sack of potatoes." But some soldiers, recognizing her despite her tattered clothing as a bourgeois lady, jeered at her: " 'They call themselves the upper class! The intelligentsia! Without a servant they cannot wash their faces!' "[25] Finally, she made it home, her potatoes and her sense of humor intact.

One day, on her way to work, she helped an elderly woman carry some things to her husband at Moscow's central prison. When the woman said that she no longer knew whether to envy the dead or the living, Tsvetaeva replied: "One should live and do the best one can, for others to live."[26] Life was hard, but still Tsvetaeva found it easier to deal with external fear than with internal anxiety.

She brought her notebooks to her job and used her free time to write; she took days off and fabricated clippings she had missed. But, when she was assigned to classify some documents, she found it impossible to handle the task. On April 25, 1919, she left her job. She tried another, but soon ran away in tears, swearing never to take a job again, "Never, even if I die." [27]

# 9. Passion and Despair

*He who's abandoned — he should sing!*
*Heart — sing!* [1]

For Tsvetaeva, the end of 1917 belonged to Antokolsky, the winter of 1918 to Zavadsky, and the spring of 1919 to Sonya Holliday, an actress of the Third Studio. These Moscow years under Communism tested Tsvetaeva's physical and moral strength in many ways, yet it was a productive period. Through her new theater friends, she became involved with the stage and in 1918–19 wrote five plays, primarily to provide roles for Zavadsky and Holliday: "The Snowstorm," "Stone-Angel," and "Fortuna" for Zavadsky; "The Adventure" and "Phoenix" for Holliday. The plots of these plays, which were never produced, are thin and inconsequential, the atmosphere is romantic, the time is the past — the sixteenth to the eighteenth century. Tsvetaeva took refuge from the chaos of the time in the romanticism she loved.

Tsvetaeva met Sonya — or Sonechka — during a reading of "The Snowstorm." "Before me a living fire," she wrote years later. "Everything is ablaze, all of her is burning. Her cheeks, her lips, her eyes on fire, the white teeth fire-proof in the flame of her mouth [ . . . ]. And the look, out of that fire — such bliss, such despair, as if to say: 'I am frightened! I am in love!' " [2]

In April 1919, a couple of months after that first meeting, Holliday came to see Tsvetaeva. She, too, had been in love with Zavadsky, and feared that Tsvetaeva would take him from her. But it soon became clear that their love, the love between the two women, far surpassed their unrequited infatuation with Zavadsky. Holliday's fine chiseled features, her pale complexion, her dainty appearance, were the kind of beauty that Tsvetaeva had always desired for herself. In Sonechka, she saw her own idealized image at fourteen, the age when she had lost her mother. In reality Tsvetaeva was only two or three years older than Holliday, but now she became Sonechka's "adored mother."

She described Holliday as both masculine and feminine—the same terms she had used for Asya Turgeneva and Sofiya Parnok. To Tsvetaeva, Sonechka displayed "the saucy challenge of a young boy (with the looks of extreme femininity, maidenliness, girlishness), mischievousness—an imp."[3] This time, though, Tsvetaeva was the older, experienced partner, and she yearned to protect this lovely child. She wished for an older, protective male lover for her and now felt superior, strong, adored, needed. Years later she remembered her as "a beloved object, a gift, with that feeling of joyous possession which I never before or since have had for a person, but for beloved objects—always."[4] Her vulgarity held additional "devilish" charms for Tsvetaeva: people distrusted her, she had kissed many men, she enjoyed banal poetry and cheap songs.

Sonechka often stayed overnight at Tsvetaeva's untidy place, or Tsvetaeva visited Sonya early in the morning in her clean and orderly surroundings. Their relationship changed in character when a man entered the scene: Vladimir Alekseyev, an actor, called Volodya. He had been visiting Tsvetaeva for some time, arriving after his performances in the theater to stay until dawn. Yet their relationship was purely cerebral; they watched the stars together and spoke of Napoleon, of Joan of Arc, and of things of the past they both loved. In Tsvetaeva's words: "I had no one with whom to share what in me was manly, straight, and steely. . . With Volodya I exposed my manly soul."[5] Nonetheless, when Volodya and Sonechka met one day at Tsvetaeva's, his presence seemed to charge her erotic fantasy. He was the "man" who—however absent or distant—was always a presence: her father, the son her mother had desired, the stepson her mother had loved, the young men with whom her mother had flirted, the men Sonechka was constantly talking about, and, of course, Efron, who had been gone so long that Tsvetaeva had turned him into a myth. Possibly, too, Tsvetaeva needed a third person in her relationship with Sonya to avoid being flooded by her own feelings as she had been with her mother.

Tsvetaeva soon endowed Volodya, the perfect vision of a statue, with her father's characteristics:

Straightness, firmness and even inflexibility. While completely open— he was impenetrable, not in the sense of being inwardly enigmatic, mysterious, but in the plainest sense: the stuff he was made of. Such a person you don't touch with a hand, and if you do, you will reach nothing with the hand, you will not change anything by that hand. That is why it is senseless to touch. It is exactly the same with a statue: palpable, reachable, but impenetrable. In some sense, a thing without a resonance.[6]

Volodya and Sonya began to visit Tsvetaeva every night to listen to music on the record player, to talk about love and death, to fall in love with one another. Tsvetaeva would describe the relationship in 1937, after learning that Sonya had died. The style of this book, called *The Tale of Sonechka*, differs from that of her multilayered autobiographical prose. Its exaggerated use of diminutives and hyperboles, echoing Sonechka's speech patterns, its romantic intoxication and nostalgia create an atmosphere both dreamlike and hollow. It suggests that, with her encouragement, Sonechka and Volodya became lovers. When they left late at night, she would think: "Do love one another well, you who have both loved me, and say my name in a kiss." Volodya never revealed anything about his relationship with Sonechka, but "he knew that I knew that this was the last step granted him *toward me*." It was not a separation: "Kissing her, he kissed me, too; when he kissed her, her little face—he kissed all of us: himself, her, me, all three of us and all of the spring of the year 1919."[7]

Here was Tsvetaeva's love fantasy, an erotic cloud enveloping the three of them, flowing from one to the other, without delineation. It was the perfect family, the perfect love:

> We the adults with the child in the middle; we the loving ones with love between us. Embracing, of course, we, our arms linked over her shoulders, she between us in our distanced embrace, separating us and bringing us closer, giving each of us a hand and each of us all of herself, all of love.[8]

Tsvetaeva carried this image of herself, between Sonechka and Volodya—loved, loving, and controlling—forever after. She could return to it without guilt, perhaps because through that implicit control she felt for the first time that she had taken hold of "life," a decisive stance that she may have hoped would liberate her from Parnok.

How long could this game continue? Fortunately for all three, life's demands supplied the answer. In late June, Sonechka's theater group left for the provinces and so "there was the last evening, the last record-player music, the last threesome, the last farewell—and the last dawn."[9] Soon afterward Volodya, on his way to join the White Army in the south, came to say goodbye. When Tsvetaeva saw him in bright daylight, she was astounded to see that his hair was reddish-blond, not black. Volodya commented rather bitterly: " 'Marina Ivanovna, I'm afraid [ . . . ] that you have also seen all the rest of me your way!' " And, he added, " 'Here I have turned out to be blond, and tomorrow you might find out that I am boring.' " [10] Tsvetaeva took him to the train. He embraced her and for the first time kissed her on the lips. They, too, never met again. He was declared missing in action that same summer of 1919.

Though Sonya wrote Tsvetaeva letters from the provinces declaring her undying love, she came to see her only once, between two trains. After that brief meeting, Tsvetaeva remained in Russia for about three more years, but never attempted to get in touch with Sonya. "I knew that we had to part," she wrote. "If I had been a man—this would have been the happiest love, but this way, inevitably, we had to part [ . . . ] Sonechka left me for her woman's fate." [11]

What made the relationship with Sonya so different from most in Tsvetaeva's life was the way it ended, without disenchantment or anger. With a fantasy that had served its purpose, Tsvetaeva had only to invent a rationalization for Sonechka's leaving her and she was ready to let her go. "My whole miracle with her was that she was outside me and not inside, not a projection of my dream and my yearning, but an independent thing outside my imagination, of my conjecture; that I had not dreamed her up, had not conjured her up, that she was not in my heart, but in my room—that she was." [12]

This is a striking instance of Tsvetaeva's paradoxical combination of insight into herself and self-deception. She knows that she projects, that she conjures people up, but at the same time she denies this knowledge. One has only to reverse this passage to get at the true picture. The "whole miracle" was that Sonechka was inside Tsvetaeva, not outside her, a projection of her dreams and her yearnings, not independent, outside of her imagination, of her conjecture. She had dreamed her up. Sonechka was not in her room, but in her heart. In a way, she did not exist.

In July 1919 Tsvetaeva gave a public reading of her verse play "Fortuna"; its hero was the Duc de Lauzun, a French nobleman who fought with the forces of the Revolution and was guillotined during the Reign of Terror. In his final speech, reaffirming his loyalty to the cause of equality and to his own noble roots, he emerges in the play as the victim of his executioners' ignorance and cruelty. Lunacharsky, the commissar of education, was present at the reading. The irony of the situation was not lost on Tsvetaeva. "The monologue of a nobleman in the face of a Commissar—that's life!" She only wished she could have read it in front of Lenin or the entire Lubyanka, the prison of the Cheka.[13]

After the reading, her feelings of loneliness and alienation surfaced again: "I am as much a stranger here as I have been among the tenants in the house where I have lived for five years, as I was in my job, as I was in all seven Russian and foreign pensions and gymnasiums, as I have been everywhere, always."[14] Yet at that time Tsvetaeva had many friends; she was respected and admired among theater people and her reputation as a poet was growing. But it was never enough.

Now that she had left her job, the struggle for survival became desperate. She tried to earn some money by sewing pages of her poems together (notebooks were scarce) and leaving them in bookstores for sale. Her friends and neighbors were tired of helping, but she insisted on using her time for writing. As always, she found some solace not only in her work but also in new relationships, in the intensity of being. Among her new friends were Vera Zvyagintseva and her husband Aleksandr Yerofeyev. Both were poets involved with the theater; they knew her sister and were delighted to meet Marina. Soon they became close friends; Tsvetaeva always felt welcome in their home. Zvyagintseva has described Tsvetaeva's house.

> I came to Boris and Gleb Lane from the kitchen door and saw an immense kitchen chock-full of pots, flat irons, and the Devil knows what. . . . Marina stood there in a Moravian costume and—I swear—played an accordion. Word of honor! . . . Soon a little girl [Alya] came in and said: "Marina, the sunset today is like a sea."[15]

By then, Tsvetaeva had simply given up any attempt to maintain an orderly household: her house was monstrously dirty, the dishes unwashed, but she did wash her hair every day, and every night she visited friends, often Vera and Aleksandr, to sing White Army songs, recite poetry, flirt, and talk until dawn. Still, she was ill-fed, ill-clothed, and cold. Finally, in November, her impoverished circumstances forced her to take her children to a state children's home in Kuznetsevo. She saw herself then as "a poet and a woman alone, alone, alone, like an oak tree, like a wolf, like God, surrounded by all the plagues that beset the Moscow of 1919."[16]

On February 17, 1920, Irina died. Although Tsvetaeva had neglected her, she felt crushed by her death. A few weeks earlier, while visiting the children, she had discovered that Alya was running a high fever. She immediately took her home and nursed her through attacks of malaria, but she did not visit Irina. Later, when she went to a central administration for children's welfare to inquire about a place for Alya to recuperate, she ran into some people from the Kuznetsovo home who told her that Irina had died, but that the funeral had not yet taken place.

Efron's sister Lilya had offered to take Irina to live with her in the country, but she wanted to keep her for good and Tsvetaeva refused. Now, after the tragedy, the Efron sisters and their friends blamed her. Tsvetaeva was devastated. She probably had never loved or even accepted this little girl, but she could not admit to herself that she had failed Irina all along. When she was working at the Commissariat she had written in her journal of hurrying back "to my place, to Casanova [she was working on a play about him], home!" Irina was still alive then, but she didn't mention her. No doubt her death was the ultimate horror. But Tsvetaeva showed no natural maternal response. Her letters to Vera and Aleksandr tell it all: her guilt, her self-pity, her panic, her demands on others, but little real mourning for the loss of Irina.

Moscow, February 20, 1920

Dear friends!

I have a great sorrow. Irina died in the children's home on the 17th of February, four days ago. And it is my fault. I was so busy with Alya's illness and so afraid to go to the children's home, that I left it all to fate. [ . . . ] Irina died without an illness, of weakness. And I didn't even go to her funeral. Alya had a fever of about 103 degrees that day, and to tell you the truth, I simply *could not*. Oh, friends! So much could be said. I'll only say that it is a *bad dream* and I keep thinking that I'll wake up. At times, I forget completely. I'm happy that Alya's fever is falling or that the weather is nice and then, suddenly—Oh, my God! I simply don't believe it yet. I live with a choking sensation in my throat, at the edge of an abyss. I understand so much now: it is all the fault of my adventurousness, of my easy-going attitude toward difficulties, and finally of my health, my own monstrous physical resistance. When one feels good, one doesn't believe that the other feels bad. And, finally, I was so deserted. Everyone else has someone: a husband, a father, a brother— I had only Alya, and Alya was ill. I immersed myself totally in her illness—and then God punished me. [ . . . ]

Friends, tell me something, explain to me. Other women forget their children because of balls, love, dresses, or celebrations of life. My celebration of life is poetry, but I didn't forget Irina because of poetry; I hadn't written anything for two months! My greatest horror is that I didn't forget her, that I had not forgotten her; all the time I tortured myself and kept asking Alya: Alya what do you think? And all the time I intended to pick up Irina and all the time kept thinking: So Alya will get well and I will take care of Irina! And now it is too late. [ . . . ] Friends, if I have to take Alya to a sanatorium, I'll come to live with you. I could even sleep in the corridor or in the kitchen—for God's sake—I can't stay in the Boris and Gleb apartment, I'll hang myself there. Or take both me and Alya. It's warm in your apartment. I'm afraid that if Alya is left in a sanatorium, she will die too. I'm afraid of everything. I'm in a panic. Help me! [ . . . ] I implore you: perhaps you can scratch out the dining room from your tenants? You know that Alya's disease is not contagious and not chronic. You'd have no trouble. I know that the help I'm asking is beyond belief, but, friends, you love me, don't you! [ . . . ]

I kiss both of you. If possible, don't mention this to any of our mutual friends for the time being. I'm like a wolf in his lair, hiding my sorrow. People make it hard on me.[17]

This letter was written on a Friday; on the following Wednesday, Tsvetaeva, who was staying with Alya at another friend's house, addressed a second letter to Vera:

Verochka!

You're the only one I can talk to now. Perhaps because you love me. I'm writing on a piano top, the sun is flooding my notebook, my hair is hot. Alya is asleep. Dear Vera, I'm utterly lost. The way I live is frightening. I'm completely like an automaton: build the fire, go to Boris and Gleb Lane for wood, wash Alya's shirt, buy carrots, shut off the heating pipe—by then it's already evening. Alya falls asleep early. I'm left alone with my thoughts; at night I dream of Irina. I dream that she is still alive. I still haven't grasped the fact that she is no more. I don't believe it. I understand the words, but I don't feel it. I can't accept the irreparable, and so I keep thinking that it will pass, that it has been a lesson in a dream and that I will wake up at any moment. [ . . . ] What I need now is someone to believe in me, someone who would say: "You're a good person, don't cry. Sergey is alive, you'll meet again, you'll have a son— everything will still come out all right."

Dear Vera, I have no future, no will power, I'm scared of everything. It seems to me that it is better to die. If Sergey is dead, I won't be able to live, anyway. Just think what a long life lies ahead—immense and strange—strange cities, strange people. Alya and I are so abandoned— she and I. Why prolong the agony, if one can avoid the suffering? What ties me to life? I'm twenty-seven years old, but I'm like an old woman. Anyway, I'll never have a real life. [ . . . ]

Vera, dear, I'm writing in full sunshine and I'm crying because I have loved everything on this earth with such intensity.

If only a circle of people would surround me now. Nobody thinks about the fact that I, too, am human. People come and bring food for Alya. I thank them, but I feel like crying because not one of them, not one, not one in all that time has patted me on the back, has stroked my hair.[18]

After Irina's death, Tsvetaeva addressed one poem to her in which she again developed the notion that she had saved Alya at the price of Irina. This was her defense:

> Two hands lightly lowered
> On a child's head!
> I was given two little heads
> One for each.
>
> But with both of them,
> Clenched, in frenzy, with all my might,
> Grabbing the older one from darkness—
> I could not save the younger one.
>
> Two hands to caress, to smooth
> The tender curly heads.
> Two hands—and now one of them
> Overnight became empty.
>
> The fair one—on a thin little neck
> Like a dandelion on its stalk,
> I have still not grasped
> That my child is in the earth.[19]

Tsvetaeva could not allow people to judge her, so Irina became a sacrifice to her "love" for Alya. She soon found somewhere else to place the blame: on Efron's sisters. "Lilya and Vera are in Moscow," she wrote to Voloshin. "They work and are well, but I broke off with them long ago because of their in-human attitude toward the children. They let Irina starve to death in the children's home under the pretext of hating me. That is the absolute truth." [20]

When Tsvetaeva left Russia in 1922 she listed in her notebook the things she took with her; there was not a single memento of Irina.

# 10. Years of Frenzy and Growth

*Oh, my steed is all fire—insatiable devourer!*
*Oh, fire rides it—insatiable rider,*
*My hair mingles with the red mane . . .*
*A fiery streak—into the heavens!* [1]

After Irina's death Tsvetaeva obtained a ration card for herself and Alya, enabling her to devote more time to her writing. In a frenzy she wrote more poems though few were published. Later she grouped them in the two collections *Versts* I and *Versts* II. Inspired by the premonition of the defeat of the Whites, they mourn the dead of both the White and Red armies. The last stanzas of one poem, written in December 1920, convey a humanism applicable to any war:

> White he was—red he turned:
> Blood painted him crimson.
> Red he was—white he turned:
> Death blanched him.

> Who are you?—A White?—Cannot tell! Do stand up!
> Or did you end up with the Reds?—Ryazan.

> And from the right and from the left
> And from the back and from the front
> The Red one and the White one:
> —Mama!

> No will—no anger—
> Long-lasting—unyielding
> Up to the heavens:
> —Mama! [2]

Her prose of this period was brilliant in its various forms: descriptions of life around her, reflections, aphorisms, disjointed thoughts. Even when she wrote about trivia, she was invariably concerned with the essence of people, of events, of nature, of things. Her sole interest was the deeper meaning as she perceived it.

In the spring of 1920 she spent a lot of time with the painter V. D. Miliotti, with whom she began what she called "a series of misbehaviors." He was "the first 'thing' I smiled at after all the horror," she wrote.[3] We know little about this relationship, but her friend Vera Zvyagintseva has recalled other men in Tsvetaeva's life at that time. Zvyagintseva was not entirely unbiased about Tsvetaeva, who apparently flirted unsuccessfully with her husband. Still, her portrayal of Tsvetaeva is striking:

> Marina used to wear a winged coat — a coat with a cape, a ridiculous dress: some simple dress with pink buttons fit for a street fair which did not belong here. Since she was always tightly belted I called her "horseman". . . . Marina washed her wheat-colored hair in our bathroom whenever she came. And she went to sleep without taking off her shoes, though I had given her our last clean sheet that I had washed myself. Her hair was very beautiful and fluffy. Her pale face was puffy from a diet consisting mainly of frozen potatoes; her eyes were green — "salty peasant eyes," as she wrote.[4]

Zvyagintseva speculated that Tsvetaeva had some kind of romance with Volkenshteyn, Parnok's ex-husband, with whom she often came to their house; she also suspected "that there was something between Marina and Tatyana Fyodorovna, the [second] wife of Scriabin."[5] But she was quite explicit about Tsvetaeva's behavior with Valery Bebutov, a theater director in whom Zvyagintseva was also interested. Tsvetaeva met him at a party at Zvyagintseva's. Bebutov and Tsvetaeva were put up afterward in the dining room, and as Zvyagintseva recalled:

> She grabbed Bebutov from me immediately, while he was still warm. When, in the dark, I went to the dining room for matches (Marina had taught me to smoke, she and hunger) they were already lying "in position." She lay on top of him and was casting her spell with words. She often said that her main passion was to communicate with people; that sexual relationships were necessary because that was the only way to penetrate a person's soul.[6]

Sex and poetry played a similar role for Tsvetaeva: both were subordinated to the urge to reach another person, to break out of her isolation.

Tsvetaeva also met Prince Sergey Mikhaylovich Volkonsky at Zvyagintseva's house. Volkonsky, a writer, former director of the Imperial theaters, and the grandson of a Decembrist hero, was much older than Tsvetaeva, but she was attracted to him at once. She saw in him a teacher, a teacher she wanted to serve, and she copied hundreds of pages of his works-in-progress.

In that same spring of 1920, Tsvetaeva met Nikolay Vysheslavtsev, a painter who lived in the Palace of Art on the same floor as Miliotti. The Palace of Art was a meeting place and an auditorium, and also housed artists and writers. There Tsvetaeva heard a poetry reading by Blok and attended a celebration of the twenty-fifth anniversary of Balmont's creative career. In that spring and summer Tsvetaeva addressed about thirty poems to Vysheslavtsev, poems which disclose the fervor of her feelings. Never before had she dedicated so many poems to one individual. The throbbing pain conveyed throughout this cycle demonstrates the persona's gratification through suffering. The cycle's climax is the long poem "Nailed Down," whose central theme is guilt, punishment, and pain.[7] The persona, a woman, stands in the street, begging for happiness, but holds in her palm only "a handful of ashes." If she cannot have love, she wants pain—just to feel something. Yet these poems are contradictory; however masochistic the persona is, her resentment of her lover's lukewarm response to her fire is apparent in such lines as "To love a little bit—is a great sin" and "You are made of stone, but I sing / You are a monument, but I fly."[8] Whatever this short-lived but passionate liaison meant to Tsvetaeva, Vysheslavtsev's portrait of her, painted in 1921, exposes a frightening vision: large unseeing eyes, lips tightly clenched—not a human face but a frozen mask of hopelessness.

In the summer of 1920 Tsvetaeva wrote her first long folkloric poem, *The Tsar-Maiden*. The basic plot was adapted from two Russian folk tales collected by Aleksandr Afanasiyev: the story of the star-crossed love of the weak, passive, feminine Tsarevich-musician and the strong, aggressive, masculine Tsar-Maiden who longs to conquer him. Tsvetaeva's masterful handling of this material, however, was her very own. This form permitted her imagination to soar beyond the bounds of reality. She used dreams, magic, and surrealistic techniques to create her own fantasized world. In a perceptive essay G. S. Smith finds that "the focus of interest in the poem as elsewhere in Tsvetaeva's work is spiritual rather than physical reality. . . . The characters exist not as studies of credible human beings but as channels for the exploration and expression of emotional and spiritual states."[9]

The Tsar-Maiden faces a powerful rival—the Tsarevich's young step-mother, who turns to the tutor-sorcerer and induces him to teach her the use of a blood injection which puts the Tsarevich to sleep whenever a meeting with the Maiden is planned. The injection works and the lovers never really meet. The scenes of the Tsarevich's seduction by the stepmother allow Tsve-taeva to show the earthy, erotic strain that counters her spiritual concerns.

As for the Maiden, she sees the Tsarevich only when he is sleeping, while the Tsarevich sees their encounters only in his dreams. Happiness is defeated by the "third element" to come between them. The tragedy of failed meet-ings, of love bypassed, is a growing presence in Tsvetaeva's work. The poem's most interesting aspect, however, lies in the choice of the androgynous nature of the lovers as her subject. Tsvetaeva had loved men and women. She had learned the limitations of sexual passion. Now she was searching for a love beyond that gratification. So the Tsar-Maiden's love for the Tsarevich traces her own pattern: elemental, possessive, maternal:

> The child [the Tsarevich] sleeping here is
> Mine—in grief and in happiness,
> Mine—in power and in sickness,
> Mine—in dance and in strife,
> In a Tsar's palace
> And in a Tsar's dungeon.
> In silks—or straw,
> Mine—in the grave and in thunder.[10]

The special love for which the Tsar-Maiden strives can exist between a man and a woman, between two young women, between two young men, or between two angels, and it culminates in total fusion, the wondrous self-contained union of two complementary lovers or of mother and child.

When, after the last encounter with the sleeping Tsarevich, the Tsar-Maiden realizes the futility of her efforts, she breaks her sword and tears out her heart, leaving her message:

> I am nowhere.
> I disappeared into the void.
> Nobody will overtake me.
> Nothing will make me return.[11]

The Tsar-Maiden leaves reality—the earth and life—for the void. Just as Tsve-taeva escaped from reality into her dreams.

**[SY]** Yevgeny Lann, a poet, arrived in Moscow from the south in November 1920 with greetings from Asya. Tsvetaeva was ready for another "great love"; Lann, unfortunately, was not. He stayed in Moscow only about three weeks, but Tsvetaeva's letters to him show the impact that he made upon her, both as a man and as a poet. "If I knew that you—that you needed me, oh, every hour of mine would be a winged one and would fly to you," she wrote.[12] And she thanked him for "the huge creative upsurge I experienced from meeting you."[13]

Crushed by Lann's rejection, Tsvetaeva could no longer deny her emotional crisis. Bitter experience had taught her something about the futility of expecting inner peace through yet another romantic love—though, to be sure, she never stopped trying. Moreover, she was plagued by uncertainty about her husband's fate. As the defeat of the White Army forced her to consider the possibility of exile from her beloved Russia, her chronic depression resurfaced. As ever, when under pressure, she turned to her work. In five days, she wrote the pivotal poem "On a Red Steed," which brought her not merely personal solace but a leap forward in her creative growth.[14] On January 19, 1921, she wrote Lann about this new poem: "So here it is. For two weeks I wrote nothing, not a word which is very rare for me. [ . . . ] Then I began writing poetry—utterly in a frenzy!—from morning to night! Then 'On a Red Steed' [was born]."[15]

The interior journey on which Tsvetaeva embarked in this long poem was indeed a long and arduous search for answers to her most urgent questions: Who am I? What am I? Why do I continue to love and hope, to lose and suffer? What is my purpose on this earth? Why am I different from others? "On a Red Steed" leads us through the labyrinth of her tumultuous struggle for answers, for comprehension: it is her self-analysis. It is crucial for understanding Tsvetaeva the woman, as well as Tsvetaeva the poet. Yet it has received less critical attention than her other long poems.[16]

Although the structure generally follows folkloric patterns in which the hero in his quest faces temptations and dangers, and although the poem itself was part of the sequence of what Tsvetaeva called her "Russian pieces"—The Tsar-Maiden (1920), "Sidestreets" (1921), and "The Swain" (1922)—it is nonetheless unique. In the other poems Tsvetaeva used Russian folklore plots, but "On a Red Steed"—permeated by a dark, different mood—is hers alone. It is a stark poem of loss: lost childhood, lost love, lost motherhood, lost faith, leading at last to the discovery of a world beyond all earthly concerns.

The dramatic cadence of the poem is enhanced by the metrical shifts reflecting alternating moods. Through occasional use of Church Slavonic, the language used only in the church, Tsvetaeva signals her return to the deepest roots of her existence: eternal Russia—perhaps even her father's priestly origins. Yet the repetitive images of fire and destruction, of confusion and turmoil, reflect the atmosphere of her own time: revolutionary Russia.

The poem begins with a denial, with a negative, the apophasis characteristic of the folk song or *bylina*; it defines something as what it is not rather than what it is.

> Not the Muse, not the Muse,
> Over my poor cradle
> Sang to me, led me by the hand.
> Not the Muse warmed my cold hands,
> Cooled my hot eyelids,
> Not the Muse—brushed my forelock from my forehead,
> Not the Muse—led me away into wide fields.
>
> Not the Muse, no black braids, no beads,
> No stories, only two blond wings—
> Short wings—above the arched brow.
> A figure in armor.
> A plume.

Whatever, whoever, it is that controls the heroine, it is certainly not the Muse, no loving maternal figure. The figure on the red steed is male—cold, unyielding, demanding. His face is concealed—we see only a plume—his body is concealed—we see only armor. He conveys only nobility and harshness. The epigraph reads:

> And wide open, wide open
> Arms—two.
> Flat on my back! Stamp on me, Rider!
> Until my spirit soars from my ribs—to you,
> Not born of mortal woman!

After the introductory stanzas, the poem leads us through the stages of the heroine's development. The first three dreamlike sequences unfold to reveal an identical pattern, in which we recognize the sad repetition of the poet's emotional life: Tsvetaeva moving instinctively, impulsively, almost unconsciously, impelled by her feelings but sensing the inevitable destruction of all that she holds most dear. The first image is fire, Tsvetaeva's favorite symbol for the intensity she craves. The heroine here is a little girl whose house is in flames, and whose "soul is on fire." Fire, tocsin, destruction: all of them evoke the Revolution, and evoke, too, the heroine's inner turmoil. In the following stanzas, the little girl falls deeper and deeper under the spell of the fire: "Prancing along with the terrible beauty / I applaud the burning hearts of torches / I scream, I whistle / I roar—I cast sparks!" The girl's feelings pull her headlong into the conflagration until the boundaries between them melt away, until she and it are one and the same. Still, she disregards the danger. She is beyond fear. At last she is wholly outside reason and wholly inside feeling.

Then, at the last moment, although she doesn't quite know how, she is rescued. Yet the experience remains dreamlike: "I cannot wake up!" All she understands is that she is suddenly safe, though still mesmerized by the roaring destructive power. In fact, the mounting chaos, the smashing of traditional wealth and of the traditionally wealthy seems increasingly to delight her: "Let the pillars collapse!" Since her own world is gone, she has nothing left to lose and "nothing to desire." Then, in a flash, she remembers her doll, left behind in the burning house. She screams in anguish. At once the mysterious Rider appears, giving her a "commanding glance," rescues the doll, then frowns and orders: "'I saved her for you, now break her! Liberate Love!'" Thus the beloved doll is returned, but in the next breath its sacrifice is demanded, this time by her own hands. Automatically, the heroine obeys. Yet the actual moment of this compliance does not appear in the poem. We witness only the moment before and the moment after; we see the hands stretching out after the Rider: "the little girl without a doll."

In the second section the persona behaves just as willfully and impulsively, but she is older now, a young woman in love. The image of the fire has changed to a raging, foaming current; above this torrent, she stands and embraces her lover: "I—all his harems, he—all my emblems." The emblems evoke Tsvetaeva's fascination with nobility, chivalry, heroics. Further aroused by her passion, the young girl dares her beloved to jump into the current to prove his love for her. And then, as before, she realizes too late that something dreadful has happened. "Numbly—I watch / as my life is drowning." Again, at the last moment, the Rider appears and saves the beloved. Again, he frowns and orders the heroine to kill her loved one, to "Liberate Love!" And again we witness not the act but its aftermath: "the young girl without her beloved!"

Predictably, the third sequence repeats the near loss, the rescue, the bitter command obeyed, and the final irrevocable loss. This sequence, even more than those preceding, swiftly creates a mood of "murky darkness," of eerie premonition, while the reader is carried along by the persona's obsessional drive to overcome every obstacle. Now a young mother, she urges her small son onward, impelling him to scale with her the mountain before them: "Climb upward, my first-born! Inch by inch, the heights will be ours!" They are surrounded by eagles, whose "fierce fluttering of wings and drilling claws" make a pitiful contrast to the small boy's hands. The mother, possessed as she is by her wish to have her first-born reach the mountain's peak, has no idea how to protect him against the dangers along the way. In this section, the poem's repetitive process of threat, rescue, and arbitrarily demanded sacrifice takes on a ritualistic air, while the crescendo of pain keeps mounting. Again, the act of killing is omitted in the poem, but the sequence's final stanza is unbearably cruel:

> What is it that suddenly crunches—No!
> That's not dry wood.
> Two hands—after a rider stretching—
> A woman without a womb!

The central unifying theme of these three episodes is the narrator's recognition of the excesses of her own nature and the recognition, as well, of the implacably cruel nature of the powerful Rider, to whom she apparently belongs. Headstrong, heedless, the narrator has challenged the forces of nature—fire, water, and wind—until reality with its immutable laws robs her over and over again of her dearest possessions. These are then returned, only to be destroyed forever, this time by her own hands. Submitting to the Rider's cruel demands, she remains abandoned, "emptied out," stretching her hands after him. Obviously the heroine is ready to sacrifice the lives of others in order to obey the Rider.

How to explain the Rider's terse command at the end of each of these three events? Is he teaching the woman an obedience to a force far stronger and more relentless than any she has hitherto known? Perhaps, but this fails to explain why she obeys the Rider automatically, without any real sense of what she is doing. Only later will she come to understand. But at this point, she believes that she herself has brought about these appalling losses.

In her despair and loneliness, the woman yearns to hold on to something, to the Rider. The Rider, however, knows better. Each time he exhorts her to "Liberate Love!" he is ordering her to liberate herself from the attachments of personal love, to free herself for that loftier "Love," her inspiration. The pleasures that usually belong to women are not for her. Neither doll nor lover nor child will ease her years on earth, enrich them, give them meaning.

The next sequence opens with an "evil dawn." The heroine is in despair; she has given up everything to please the mysterious Rider. But he keeps disappearing into the whirlwind of snow, with the Russian storm evoking political as well as personal and natural turmoil. In her pursuit, the woman braves the perils of that storm, but all the while the Rider remains elusive. As she runs after him, reaching for him, confusion overwhelms her: What is real, what is she imagining? Is it his plume she sees or is it a branch waving? She turns for help to the elements, the winds. The winds respond, and they blow stronger. But with their growing power, her confusion mounts. The shape of a church appearing in the distance seems like the longed-for refuge, and the narrator appeals for protection to God, "the Tsar of all armies." But again the Rider interferes; overtaking her, he "storms into the altar" before she can reach it. And now the howling storm winds break into the sanctuary. The cupola shakes, church lanterns sway, and the icons themselves grow dim.

The destructive power of the storm, which brings down the church and leaves a sense of devastation and chaos, seems to intoxicate the persona as the fire had done before. The temple is destroyed, but the spirit is liberated. Again, the persona seems to merge with the fury of the elements. Falling to the ground, she appeals to Christ. The Rider, however, is now above her. Once more he comes "galloping from on high" and "flat on my chest he plants his horse's heel." There is no question that she belongs to him. No other faith can claim her.

In the following short section, deleted from all later publications, a startling shift in imagery occurs, revealing an altered state of mind: no more powerful elements, lofty metaphors of God and tsars, no more heroes from classical mythology, but a simple peasant woman—a *babka*—bent over a steaming cauldron, drinking some cheap vodka from a bottle. And to this earthy, even coarse woman, the heroine brings her question: " 'What kind of dream am I having?' " And she receives for the first time an answer, a flat, pragmatic statement: " 'Your Angel does not love you.' "

It is a terrible statement, but the heroine recognizes its truth. No doubt, under the various disguises, the goal of her quest was "love." Every answer she had hoped to find, had hoped to get from the Rider, has brought only further bewilderment, further tragic losses, further questions. At last, now, she has turned to her own instinctual voice, to her own intuition in the form of the *babka*. And that response, painful though it is, is liberating. Now, she can dispense with the constraints of womanhood and love. She is free. If her Angel does not love her, she need not please that Angel, need not act like a woman, using a woman's traditional devices. Instead, she can become the proud Amazon who leads her troops on a white horse and challenges the Rider as an equal: "We'll see, oh, now we'll see—how well will he fight, the proud one on a red steed!" Appealing to the spirit of her forefathers and to her own vitality, she defies and accepts death and rides into battle and glory. On she goes, exhorting her troops to advance. But her forward drive hesitates: "Have you failed? Again / Another line—across the ditch!" And again comes the sudden realization of her recurrent confusion: "What's that / on the snowy armor? Dawn? Blood?" Panic seizes her: "Soldiers! Who's the enemy? Who are we fighting?" and then the climax: "In the breast, a chill—a flame, / and enters, and enters with a steel lance / under the left breast—a ray."

Finally, the chilling flame brings about her illumination, her new consciousness. The quest for the self, for her voice, for serenity, is coming to an end. Humbled and suffering, she hears from the Rider himself that this is how he has desired her, that this is why he has chosen her. Now, she is his bride, at last. The sexual imagery of the union with the Rider is glaring, but they are not united in the fire she craves. Instead, she is a "bride in the armor's ice." Still the Rider claims her exclusively for himself, forever, thus fulfilling her own deepest desire: never again to fear abandonment. She vows to belong to him while "clutching the wound," the wound she now accepts as the price for being chosen.

Thus "On a Red Steed" ends with comprehension and compliance. In retrospect, it seems clear that the heroine's greatest error was believing herself to be a woman among other women, like other women; she is not, was not, ever. She has been chosen from the start. Her difference—her high passions, her intensity, her creativity—condemns her to destroy any chance for lasting personal happiness and empowers her to sacrifice the lives of her dear ones. The poem's diction and cadence reflect that transformation, and the final stanzas in their calm simplicity are its triumph. The clarity of the message in these last four stanzas mirrors the poet's final acceptance of her fate and her newfound serenity.

> Not the Muse, not the Muse, not the earthly ties
> Of kinship, not your shackles,
> O friendship! Not by a female hand,
> The fierce knot has been tied around me.
>
> So awesome a union. In the dark ditch
> I lie, but the sunrise is shining.

> Oh, who has hung these weightless wings
> On my shoulders?
>
> A silent witness
> Of living storms
> I lie and observe
> Shadows.

In writing "On a Red Steed," Tsvetaeva worked through another of her depressive moods. In fact, she more than compensated for her suffering as a woman by acknowledging her eternal bond with the "male" in herself: the Genius who inspired her, who reminded her of her superiority, who shielded her against the pain of life. The poem's ultimate purpose, then, is to justify her life.

Several aspects of this poem recall her childhood "Devil" fantasy. Of whom does the Genius-Rider remind us, if not the Devil? The Devil, too, had cold and merciless eyes; he, too, had chosen her because she was an outsider; he, too, was steely and authoritarian. Like the Genius, the Devil, too, had chosen her to be a poet, "not a beloved woman." Yet the Devil took Marina to his heart, and he had a warm female lioness's body, while the Genius remains covered in armor. The Devil always waited for Marina, while in "On a Red Steed" she was forced to run after her Genius. These differences reveal a shift in the direction of Tsvetaeva's maturation as a poet. In coming to terms with her creative destiny she loses hope of personal happiness.

In Tsvetaeva's Genius we see both her own fierce, masculine nature and the cold, denying, pain-inflicting nature of her mother. Didn't she learn from her mother that one had to give up all instinctual gratification for the higher cause of "duty and soul"? Didn't her mother's romantic heroes teach the child to reach for the unobtainable? To replace reality with imagination? Didn't her mother's lack of response wound her so early and so deeply that her most frequent feeling was pain? With "On a Red Steed," the contradictory sides of Tsvetaeva's personality achieved some sort of integration. The God/Devil was fused, however temporarily, and for a while was at her service, leaving her free to find ever greater faith in her own voice. "On a Red Steed" is finished," she wrote to Lann:

> The last dash has been placed. Should I sent it to you? What for? The steed exists, so Lann, too, exists—forever—upward! And I didn't want to come to you as a beggar—only with poetry. I didn't want to come to

you (feminine pride and Tsvetaeva pride — always post factum) as I had been before, yours, while now I am feeling so *free*.

Life had to change its base. And so, Comrade Lann (the address is ironic and tender) I stand before you again as on the day when you entered my house for the first time (excuse the definition): gay, free, happy — myself.[17]

## 11. New Poetic Voice and Departure

*My youth — I do not call you back.*
*You were a load and a burden to me.*[1]

Early in 1921, soon after Lann had left, Tsvetaeva met Boris Bessarabov, "an eighteen-year-old Communist. Without boots. Hates Jews."[2] Reporting to Lann in minute detail the progress of her new romance, she wrote that Bessarabov was a Red Army man, exceedingly handsome, like a hero out of a Russian epic tale, a *bogatyr*. Predictably she was quick to call his facial blush "raspberry red," always her color for connoting sexuality. Tsvetaeva saw in him many of the qualities she admired: his seriousness, his disregard for material things, his guilty feelings about all the sins of the Soviet regime, and his willingness to help those in need. Primarily, however, she was attracted by his "childlike, helpless, sad, frenzied love for his recently deceased mother."[3] As Tsvetaeva put it in another letter to Lann: "It is obvious, Lann, only boys who love their mothers passionately and who are lost in this world can love me — this is what I need."[4]

After their first meeting, Boris accompanied Tsvetaeva home: "At the doorway, Lann, do praise me, we separated."[5] On the next day, though, they separated at the same doorway at 8 A.M. after spending the night together. It was a night of confessions, of intimacy, but not of love making. Again, Tsvetaeva gave a full report to Lann: they kissed, they laughed, they had a wonderful time, just like children. Then Tsvetaeva turned to Boris and the following dialogue ensued:

Marina: Boris, this does not oblige me to anything, does it?
Boris: What?
Marina: That you're kissing me?
Boris: Marina Ivanovna, not at all!!! And what about me?!

Marina: What do you mean?
Boris: Marina Ivanovna! You are not like other women!
Marina, innocently: Really?
Boris: Marina Ivanovna! Don't you know that I don't like all of that.
Marina, emphatically: Boris! And I *hate* it! [6]

Tsvetaeva's physical enjoyment of the caressing, tender love-play with the boy seemed real enough:

Lann, if you still remember me a little, be happy for me! I don't know how many evenings we have spent together, but the boy is strong. My bones crack, his lips touch mine lightly; we have a good time chatting about nonsense, talking about Russia and everything as it should be: for him and for me.

Sometimes, tired from all that tenderness, I say: "Boris! Maybe?" "No, Marina Ivanovna! Marinochka! We shouldn't! I respect women so much and particularly you, you are a first-rate woman; I have come to love you very, very much, you remind me of my dearest mother, and then the main thing is you are leaving soon, you have such a difficult life and I want you to have good memories of me!" [7]

Tsvetaeva's lack of interest in the sex act as such was striking. What she needed, then and always, was to be held, to be caressed, to be loved like a child or by a child.

Boris used his Party connections to help Asya, who had stayed in the south with the Whites, to join Tsvetaeva in Moscow in May 1921. According to Zvyagintseva:

Marina was terribly worried about Asya, who had stayed with the Whites. She spoke of her every day: "Asya, how is Asya, what is happening to Asya?" Then Asya arrived—totally toothless, with naked gums from scurvy. A few days later Tsvetaeva came alone, asked me to come outside, and said: "I cannot live with Asya, she irritates me." I just stared in bewilderment. That was typical of Marina. [8]

Asya, too, felt the estrangement between them. Both, however, kept up an illusion of harmony, as they would their whole lives long—Marina because Asya was her sister, with whom she shared memories, and Asya because she had always looked up to Marina.

**S** Though Tsvetaeva made no secret of her beliefs and was never seduced by the attraction of participating in the building of a new art, still she knew and was known by those on the Soviet literary scene. She remained outside of literary factions, but she participated in readings and literary discussions. She met the young poets Yesenin, Khlebnikov, Kruchyonykh, Pasternak, Mayakovsky, and many more. It was Mayakovsky whom she admired most. Though they were worlds apart in their views—Mayakovsky looked for his salvation to the future and to a new society; Tsvetaeva looked back to the values of the past and into her own private world—as poets they had much in common. They believed in their genius and poetry was their life. Perhaps more than any similarity in their work, it was a similarity in temperament that made them understand each other. In their poems about love and loneliness, each echoed the other; and it was probably this empathy that would inspire Tsvetaeva in emigration to stand up in defense of Mayakovsky, the bard of Soviet Communism

If poetry was the main focus of Tsvetaeva's relationship with the young poets, she had friends to whom she was devoted in purely human terms. Konstantin Balmont, one of the first Symbolist poets, was much older than Tsvetaeva, but their friendship sustained them both during these difficult years in Communist Moscow. Tsvetaeva brought him precious potatoes and he shared his cigarettes with her, but mostly they both knew how to disregard the misery around them and to keep their spirits high. "How Marina's friendship with Balmont came about, I don't remember," Alya wrote. "It seemed to have been always there."[9] And it would survive in emigration.

Aleksey Chabrov, an actor, understood Tsvetaeva's poems as she wanted them understood. She dedicated one of her most obscure poems, "Sidestreets," to him, and Alya remembered that Tsvetaeva was attracted to him because of his troubled moods and "because in those times without gifts, he gave her the gift of a rose."[10] In the last years before her departure, Tsvetaeva was also very close to the Kogans. Pyotr Kogan was a prominent Marxist literary critic and his wife Nadezhda was Blok's last love. This romantic circumstance probably attracted Tsvetaeva. The Kogans helped her to obtain the ration card without which it would have been difficult to survive. Ilya Ehrenburg, who managed to travel in southern Russia and to go abroad, was another friend. He had always been an admirer of Tsvetaeva's poetry and he was to become a messenger between Tsvetaeva and her husband.

One of the high points of this period was an "evening of poetesses" in February 1921. Tsvetaeva attended at the invitation of Valery Bryusov, the major Symbolist poet who had recognized Evening Album, albeit rather patronizingly. Now he had joined the Bolsheviks and become very influential in the new literary "establishment." Though Tsvetaeva needed the money badly and she knew she would be paid a fee, it took a lot of convincing to get her to agree to attend. She believed that gender was irrelevant when it came to the writing of poetry.

> Since I was born I have had an aversion to everything that is marked by some kind of female (mass) separateness as for instance: women's courses, suffragettism, feminism, salvation—the entire notorious woman's question except for its military resolution: the legendary kingdoms of Penthesilia, Brünhilde, Maria Morevna, and the no less legendary Petrograd Women's Battalion. [ . . . ] There is no woman's question in creativity, only women's answers to human questions such as those of Sappho, Joan of Arc, Saint Theresa, Bettina Brentano.[11]

Nine women poets participated, all dressed up for an audience of young Red Army men and students. Tsvetaeva herself demonstrated in her costume her loyalty to the officers of the White Army. She wore "a kind of green cassock, which one could not call a dress (translated into the language of better times it was a coat), tightly belted with a military strap, not an officer's belt even, but a Junker's belt, or even rather the belt of a tsarist ensign. Across the shoulder an officer's pouch (of brown leather for field glasses or cigarettes) which I would consider treason to take off." [12]

Bryusov reminded the audience that since time immemorial women had written about love and passion, for their only passion was love. Then he introduced Tsvetaeva. She read her most passionate poems, not those about love, but about courage and loyalty: hailing the White Army and the battle at the Don, demanding that the poet join the battle. A moment of silence followed every poem, and then a storm of applause. Tsvetaeva was stunned and happy. The last poem she read was most dear to her but does not appear in any of her collections. It begins:

> My hand on my heart:
> I am not a lady!
> I am a rebel with my head and my womb.[13]

Here she was, the wife of a White Army officer, confronting Red Army men and Communists, standing alone against the world exactly as her mother had taught her. Later, having suffered from the lack of response to her poetry by the émigré community, Tsvetaeva would explain that in poetry it is not the content that matters but the sound and the rhythm. That night in 1921, she transmitted to the Red Army audience the courage and commitment that she felt inspired the White Army. They understood her, as her fellow Russian émigrés would not.

In the spring of 1921 Lenin introduced a New Economic Policy (NEP) to save the Soviet Union from economic collapse and popular unrest. Some fundamental changes (though temporary) were introduced; concessions were made to private ownership and management in agriculture, industry, and trade. This led to a changed social atmosphere: the new "entrepreneurs" brought with them greed and vulgarity. In November 1921 Tsvetaeva wrote to Voloshin about these changes: new food stores with fancy names were filled with merchandise but "people are just like the stores: they give only for money. The general law is mercilessness. Nobody cares about anyone else. Believe me, dear Max, I am not envious. Even if I had a million I would not buy whole hams. All this smells too much of blood." [14]

During her last two years in Moscow, Tsvetaeva wrote poems that were to be published in Berlin in 1923 under the title *Craft*. The collection was addressed to Prince Sergey Mikhaylovich Volkonsky, whom Tsvetaeva had met at Zvyagintseva's house and to whom she had been attracted at once. She called their relationship an *amitié littéraire*, a friendship that lasted until Volkonsky's death in 1939. With him she shared her deepening wish to transcend everyday life, her concept of the contradiction between "existence" and "being." Volkonsky later dedicated his book *Existence and Being* (Byt i bytiye) to her, addressing her in the introduction:

> This was during those terrible, loathsome Moscow years. Do you remember how we lived? The filth, the disorder, the homelessness? But that is nothing! Do you remember those impertinences in military fur caps breaking into the apartment? Do you remember the insolent demands, the insulting questions? . . . Was there ever a dawn without victims, without tears, without horrors? . . . Well, that was Soviet existence.

> But do you remember our evenings, our rotten but lovely "coffee" on the kerosene heater, our readings, our writing, our talks? You read to me your poems for your future collections. You copied my *Wanderings* and *Laurels*. . . . How much strength there was in our inflexibility, how much reward in our steadfastness! That was our *being*! [15]

Volkonsky was indifferent to women, so when Tsvetaeva wrote a poem about her worship for him, she changed herself into "a fair-haired boy."

In *Craft* Tsvetaeva's poetic power exploded beyond the limits of conventional form and language. As Efim Etkind writes in his introduction to this collection, "the cycle 'The Pupil' opens the collection to announce from the first lines a new beginning, a new chronology in the life of the author. . . . And simultaneously, the meaning of 'The Pupil' is the author's declaration of irrefutable autonomy, of her independence from anyone, even from the beloved teacher." [16] Tsvetaeva's voice had hardened, leaving behind romanticism and traditional forms. She discarded the often "unnecessary" verb and employed neologisms, enjambments, a new syntax. Fascinated by the language of the people, by folkloric elements, she turned to pure sound and rhythm to express the intensity of her vision, using her craft to experiment with words and expecting to be understood even when she spoke in a different, sometimes enigmatic idiom.

The mood of the collection is dark; essentially, it is a summing up, a good-bye to her beloved Moscow. As she wrote to Lann:

> Sometime [ . . . ] I will get my courage together and send you the poems of these last months, poems that are difficult to write and inconceivable to recite (I to others). I write them because I am jealous of my own pain. I don't speak of Sergey to anyone—and there is no one to speak to. . . . These poems—are an attempt to work myself up to the surface: it succeeds for half an hour.[17]

Five poems are addressed to Efron: "Separation" tells of the poet's disorientation, her despair, her fears. It is also interesting from a purely biographical point of view because Tsvetaeva speaks here more than once of suicide as the only way out, associating death with going "home," that safe, lovely home of Tsvetaeva's idealized childhood memories which always beckoned her. Perhaps she turned to that home in her last desperate hour. In the poem, though, she is saved by a young winged warrior, the genius of her poetry.

At that time, Tsvetaeva had no knowledge of Efron's whereabouts, but in fact the long awaited reunion with him was not far off. In one three-stanza poem she prepares Efron for her transformation: she has not grown prettier, her hands have coarsened, they have grabbed bread and salt. Her language, too, has become less refined to express the harsh reality of those years. She appeals to him to understand, to appreciate the change she has undergone. She has reached a new level of consciousness.

The theme of renunciation, heard in "On a Red Steed," sounds louder and louder now, and joins with a new tolerance and maturity. Tsvetaeva has not forgotten the volunteers of the White Army, she knows that "the ball is over," but in one poem she pays her respects to the dead Red rebels who fought valiantly for the wrong cause.

The last poem in this collection, "Sidestreets," differs in its content and tone from the others. It vibrates with incantations and rhythmic chants; magic—good or evil—fills the air. Despite its linguistic virtuosity or perhaps because of it, "Sidestreets" remains enigmatic. All the same, it was one of Tsvetaeva's favorite poems. Again she was inspired by an old Russian folk epic about the struggle of the hero with an evil sorceress. Many years later, Tsvetaeva called it "a story of ultimate seduction." The sorceress seduces with words, with the "power of her soul." [18]

In July 1921 Tsvetaeva heard from Ilya Ehrenburg that her husband was alive and had escaped to Czechoslovakia. The White Army had been defeated. At the same time, the New Economic Policy had changed Soviet society but had not made Tsvetaeva feel more at home. She was anxious to join Sergey. When his first letter arrived, she "turned to stone." She who never had trouble expressing herself could only write: "I don't know where to begin: there where I will end: my love for you." [19] Distance had enhanced his image. She went toward him as toward a safe harbor.

The formalities required to obtain an exit visa took some time, but by the spring of 1922 Tsvetaeva and Alya were ready to leave for Berlin, where Sergey was expected to meet them. They said good-bye to their friends and packed their things. From Tsvetaeva's notebook Alya later copied a list of "valuables" they took with them:

A pencil stand with a portrait of Tuchkov-IV
An ink stand with the figure of a drummer, a present from Chabrov
A plate with the picture of a lion
Seryozha's tea-glass holder
Alya's portrait
A sewing box
An amber necklace (she had bartered for it in the countryside with
     bread and kept it until her death)
Alya's felt boots
Her own boots

A red coffeepot
A blue mug, the new one
A kerosene heater
A velvet lion [20]

They also took along the plush blanket given to Tsvetaeva by her father shortly before his death, some Russian toys, several new Soviet children's books, and very few clothes or shoes. They set out, crossing themselves whenever they passed one of Moscow's many churches. They were leaving behind them Russia, home, and were going toward the unknown, toward exile. As Tsvetaeva would write later: "From a world where my poems were as necessary as bread, I came into a world where no one needs poems, neither my poems nor any poems; where poems are needed like—dessert; as if anyone needs dessert." [21]

# 12. Russian Berlin

*One's motherland is not the conventionally accepted*
*territory, but the immutability of memory and blood.*[1]

On May 15, 1922, Tsvetaeva and Alya arrived in a Berlin that was already the center of a thriving, heterogeneous Russian émigré population with a climate of political freedom and intellectual stimulation. Monarchists and nationalists, Constitutional Democrats, Socialist Revolutionaries, and Mensheviks had different hopes for the future, but they were united in their opposition to the Soviet regime and shared a sense of dislocation and readjustment. They lived in the same German pensions and met in the same cafés to debate political and literary issues. Fear of arrest had been replaced by heated discussions about political loyalty, and the memory of executions by plans for new literary and cultural activities.

Visitors from the Soviet Union contributed to the vitality of the Russian colony: Soviet writers like Vladimir Mayakovsky and Andrey Bely, Ilya Ehrenburg and Viktor Shklovsky mixed with such prominent émigré writers as Aleksey Remizov and Georgy Ivanov. Some of the Soviet writers returned to Russia, but many remained abroad, fearing the regimentation of Soviet literature. All of them needed publishing houses, and new enterprises sprang up overnight; Ogonyok, Helikon, Grezhebin, and other houses printed Russian books in great numbers. Russian dailies and literary periodicals also flourished, and Russian ballet and theater companies played to capacity audiences.

Even before Tsvetaeva's arrival, Ehrenburg and Balmont had spread the word that a major new poet was emerging to take her place beside Akhmatova. And in fact her output at the time was considerable: *Versts I*, covering the year 1916; *Versts II*, covering 1917 to 1921; and *Craft*, covering the year 1921 to 1922. *Versts I* and II had been accepted for publication in Russia, along with *The*

*Tsar-Maiden.* Now she wanted to find publishers in Berlin to reach the larger émigré readership. Ehrenburg had been able to have two small volumes of her poetry published there: *Separation*, which included "On a Red Steed" and "Verses to Blok." Tsvetaeva herself arranged for the publication of *Craft, The Tsar-Maiden,* and *Psyche.* With her poetry beginning to appear in major Russian literary journals in Berlin and Paris, she was received with great enthusiasm.

At first, Tsvetaeva and Alya stayed in Ehrenburg's apartment, moving soon to a room in a German pension. In general, Ehrenburg and his wife tried to be helpful to them in finding their way in a strange city. He introduced Tsvetaeva to the literati, and his wife went shopping with her and Alya. Tsvetaeva had almost forgotten what it meant to shop; now, she bought presents for Sergey, a dress for Alya, and one for herself. She wore that dress, a dirndl, every summer for the rest of her life.

Life seemed, at last, to offer hope for a new beginning, with new friends and new opportunities. Soon after she arrived, Tsvetaeva asked Ehrenburg to introduce her to Roman Gul, a man of letters familiar with Russian publishers and journals in Berlin. Gul later became the editor of *Novy zhurnal* (The New Journal), a major Russian-language literary journal. The first time he entered Tsvetaeva's room, he wrote in his reminiscences, he was surprised to see her lying on something like a trunk covered with a rug. He was struck by her appearance. "Tsvetaeva was fairly tall for a woman, slim, dark complexioned, with an aquiline nose and straight hair cut in bangs," he recalled. "Her eyes were nothing special. Her glance was quick and intelligent, her hands without any feminine tenderness; hers was rather a mascline hand, one that made it immediately clear she was not a 'fine lady'. . . . As a woman Tsvetaeva was not attractive. She walked with big steps, her feet shod in what looked like men's shoes." [2] From the very beginning their relationship was extremely friendly; Gul found it interesting to talk to Tsvetaeva about "everything: about life, about literature, about trivia," and he enjoyed the way she spoke "in something approaching poetic prose or 'free verse'." [3]

Tsvetaeva also became very close to the two daughters of the writer Yevgeny Chirikov, Lyudmila and Valentina. Lyudmila, an artist, designed the cover of Tsvetaeva's *Tsar-Maiden,* published in Berlin in 1922. Both sisters were fond of Tsvetaeva and shared her scorn for the material world. They would remain friends with the Efrons for the many years of emigration.

Tsvetaeva also met Mark Lvovich Slonim, a young, handsome critic who was the literary editor of *Freedom of Russia* (Volya Rossii), a weekly publication in Prague that was in the process of becoming a monthly journal. During a visit to Berln, Slonim suggested to Tsvetaeva that she bring her poetry to his office in the center of Prague. Familiar with her poems glorifying the White Army, he warned her that the journal was an organ of the Socialist Revolutionaries. But when Tsvetaeva heard that Slonim's editorial office was located in an eighteenth-century building where Mozart was supposed to have written his *Don Giovanni*, she replied, "I am not interested in politics, I don't understand it, and of course Mozart is more important."[4] Slonim was convinced that she became a contributor because the strongly nostalgic surroundings were more important to her than the politics of her time.

One day shortly after her arrival, Tsvetaeva joined Ehrenburg at his table in the Prager Diele, one of the Berlin cafés frequented by Russian writers, poets, and publishers. To her astonishment, in walked Andrey Bely, whom she revered as a great poet, the idol of Ellis and Nilender, and the husband of her adored Asya Turgeneva. Now he stretched out his hands to her in a foreign land. Thereafter the two writers spent days and nights together exchanging memories and impressions. They discovered their common bonds: their past, their love of poetry, their helplessness in the real world. They were as happy as children, or—in Tsvetaeva's words—as "orphans and poets."[5]

Bely was under great personal stress at the time. Asya, his wife, had left him for another man, and he shared with Tsvetaeva not only his present agony but the memories of his complicated relationship with Blok and his wife. He also spoke to her about his involvement with Rudolf Steiner's anthroposophy and his quest for metaphysical answers to his many questions about life. Tsvetaeva responded with total acceptance.

Tsvetaeva's publisher gave Bely a copy of *Separation*, which had been published that spring by Helikon. Bely read it through the night. "You know, it's not a book but a song: a voice, the purest of any that I've ever heard," he wrote Tsvetaeva in a letter the next morning. "The voice of longing itself: *Sehnsucht*."[6] He immediately wrote an article about Tsvetaeva's distinctive melodic rhythms.

Like many of his fellow writers, Bely was still undecided about returning to the Soviet Union. When Tsvetaeva arrived in Prague on August 1, 1922, she tried to arrange some financial support for him from the newly formed Czech government, which under Masaryk offered not only asylum to Russian refugees but financial support to Russian émigré scientists and writers. Bely, however, had already left for Russia.

Tsvetaeva's original purpose in going to Berlin had been to join her husband, but even before Efron arrived from Prague, she had fallen in love with Abram Vishnyak, whom she called Helikon, the name of his publishing house. In her poetry of the previous two years she had proclaimed that her destiny was to be a poet and to renounce ordinary human happiness. Now she faced in real life the dilemma of being a poet and a woman. Little was known about this liaison until 1982 when Serena Vitale, an Italian Tsvetaeva scholar and translator, brought from Moscow Tsvetaeva's letters to Vishnyak and published them in French and Italian under the title *Le notti fiorentine*.[7] They were obviously meant for publication. Tsvetaeva wrote in 1933 to a friend that she had translated into French nine of her own letters to a man and a single one in response from him, with an afterword and a description of their last meeting five years later. She was submitting the manuscript to publishers, she added, but no one wanted to publish it.

Tsvetaeva translated these letters between 1932 and 1934, at approximately the same time she wrote *Letter to an Amazon*, about lesbian love, also in French. Vitale has combined these writings in a single volume, believing Tsvetaeva's themes in them to be the same: the "non-meeting," the emptiness of sexual love between women and between men and women. Of course, neither the letters nor the poems of the period offer a realistic account of Tsvetaeva's infatuation with Vishnyak. But how much of it was dreamed up or mythologized is irrelevant. Tsvetaeva's pain, and her passion, were real. She met Vishnyak soon after her arrival in Berlin, though her first letter to him is dated June 17, 1922. He was a close friend of Ehrenburg's and had already published a volume of Tsvetaeva's poetry. A young, good-looking man, he was happily married and had a four-year-old son; he loved her poetry and was attracted to her. She was captivated by his sensual, dark Jewish warmth and stunned by the onslaught of tenderness, his and her own: "All these last years," she wrote to him, "my life has been so different, so hard, so icy that now I can only raise my shoulders and my eyebrows: is this me? You soften me (make me more human, more woman, more animal) as fur does."[8]

Her surrender to the heat of an unexpected passion was so complete that she was ready to give in to her most vulnerable feminine self, a self that was hidden successfully most of the time. But she was not ready to surrender her maternal role. She addressed Vishnyak in her letters as "my child" and "my little boy." "My little one!" she wrote. "It is four o'clock in the morning. I am with you, my forehead against your shoulder, I would offer you all my poems—the ones that have come, that are coming."[9] At the height of her passion Tsvetaeva was ready to exchange her poetic gift in return for being loved as a woman. She had offered it to Parnok and would offer it to others.

She was aware that it was Vishnyak's sensuality that attracted her, not his soul: "I know everything, Man, I know you are superficial, easygoing, hollow, but your profoundly animal nature touches me more deeply than other souls. You know so well how to feel cold, to feel warm, to be hungry, thirsty, sleepy." [10] Soon enough, she perceived his irritation, his boredom with her patronizing "lectures." Sensing her own inability to follow him in simple enjoyment, she began to build her defenses: "I can be without you. I am neither a young girl nor a woman; I can do without dolls and without men. I can be without all of them. But perhaps for the first time, I wish I were not able to." [11]

Now her compulsive pressure to uncover—or to invent—Vishnyak's soul began in earnest: "Don't think that I have contempt for your simple earthy personality. I love all of you, your look, your smile, your mannerisms, your laziness—inborn, natural, native—your obscure (for you, not for me) soul: full of goodness, of compassion, and of renunciation." [12] Tsvetaeva wanted to change the easygoing, pleasure-loving Vishnyak into a spiritual human being, one who would search for a loftier, more intense union than sex alone could offer. She wanted him, essentially an Epicurean, to accept her own favorite words by Beethoven: "Joy through pain." But she soon realized that her hope was in vain. In the margin of one letter she wrote: "Hope has wings. My hopes are stones on my heart: desires which have not had time to become hopes, but which have turned immediately, in advance, into despair, into weights, into heaviness! Grant me, Oh God, never again to have hopes for myself!" [13]

Alya, now ten, seems to have understood better than her mother that, in fact, there was no conflict in Vishnyak because "he does not have much soul, since he needs quiet, rest, sleep, comfort—all that is exactly what the soul does not need." [14] She also saw clearly the gap between Vishnyak and Tsvetaeva. "Marina speaks with Helikon like a giant and he can understand her as little as an inhabitant of the Orient can understand the North Pole, and it is just as enticing." [15]

When Vishnyak left for the seashore with his wife and son, Tsvetaeva understood that he was choking on her love. She believed that he had loved her through her poetry, while others had loved her poetry because they loved her. With keen insight she added: "In both cases they have endured rather than loved. To clarify: there has always been something excessive in me for those close to me; for 'something' read 'a large half,' a whole self too much; either my living self or the living self of my poetry." [16] What a bitter truth for a woman who yearned all her life for total acceptance.

On July 9, Tsvetaeva described in one of her letters how, lying on the hard floor of her balcony, she waited for Vishnyak. Listening to the steps outside, she knew that he would not come. Still, she hoped. Her response, as always, was control and defiance in the face of despair. Comparing life to a garment poorly cut and patched together, she refused to kneel down to pick up the leftover pieces from the floor: "No, no, and no. Both hands behind my back. And the back very straight." [17]

One can safely assume that Vishnyak's reaction to Tsvetaeva's flood of emotions, demands, and scoldings was to return as quickly as he could to his family, friends, and normalcy. His only letter to Tsvetaeva—which she included in her translation—is stilted and cold, listing in businesslike fashion the things he was returning to her: letters, notebooks, books. The only personal sentence reads: "I remember you, on the balcony, your face toward the black sky, implacable toward all of us." [18]

Tsvetaeva wrote a poem about that balcony on June 30, a poem that conveys better than all her letters what Vishnyak had meant to her:

> The Balcony
>
> Ah, from an open precipice—
> Down—into dust and tar!
> The failure of earthly love,
> One salts it with tears—for how long?
>
> A balcony. Through the salty downpour
> The tar of angry kisses
> The sigh of unending hatred:
> Will breathe into verse!
>
> .   .   .   .   .   .   .   .
>
> Yes, this battle with love
> Is wild and heartless.
> Soaring up from the granite overhang,
> To breathe out into death! [19]

In an afterword to the letters, Tsvetaeva dismissed Vishnyak: "As much as you existed—to that extent you are no more. [ . . . ] The absolute can be nothing else but the absolute. Such a presence can only turn into such an absence. Everything — yesterday, nothing — today." Just as she had with Parnok, Tsvetaeva needed to forget the moments of bliss, of hope, of exposure she had shared with him. Both Parnok and Vishnyak had pierced her defenses. Her revenge was to reshape the past by establishing her superiority: lesbian love made no sense without a child, she claimed. Nor could heterosexual love last without a total union of souls. In a letter to Pasternak, less than a year after her departure from Berlin, Tsvetaeva wrote: "I was then friends with Helikon who was in love (I shrug my shoulders) with my poetry. He was a black, velvety mediocrity, a charming one."[20]

In mid-June Efron arrived in Berlin to find Tsvetaeva being lionized by the Russian literary set. She was in love with Vishnyak and seeing a lot of Bely. Efron knew full well that the role he played in this reunion after an absence of more than four years was a minor one. During that long separation, Tsvetaeva had not only survived on her own under the most grueling circumstances but had acquired a strengthened sense of direction and identity. She knew now that she was, first and foremost, a great poet. Efron, on the other hand, had experienced the defeat of the White Army and was not even sure that he had fought on the right side. Since November 1921, he had been living in dreary student quarters in Prague, where he had been granted a scholarship along with many other Russian refugees.

Alya detected the dissonance between her parents. Though she described in her reminiscences the hugs and kisses that accompanied her father's arrival, she also noticed Efron's youth and his weakness in the presence of her powerful mother: "Seryozha, who would be twenty-nine in the fall, still looked like a boy who had just gone through a serious illness: so slim and large-eyed, he was still as lonely though Marina sat beside him. She, indeed, looked an adult — once and for all! Up to the strands of early gray that already glimmered in her hair."[21]

Efron, who had inspired some of Tsvetaeva's most passionate poems, who had personified for her the courage of the doomed volunteers of the White Army, and for whom she had longed and prayed, now left center stage. After their reunion she addressed just a few poems to him. He would always remain her "duty," her son, her brother, but he was no longer her inspiration, although she continued to need him as the living witness of her past, a past that remained her spiritual and emotional "home." Now, in Berlin, he stepped aside as he had with Parnok, as he would many times more. Probably to avoid more pain, he returned to Prague, cutting short a reunion he had dreamed about for years. Tsvetaeva and Alya were to follow him to take advantage of the financial support offered by the Czech government. But for now, Tsvetaeva was busy negotiating with publishers. She was also plunging into a new worship of Pasternak.

On June 27 Ehrenburg transmitted a letter to Tsvetaeva from Boris Pasternak, who was in Moscow. Tsvetaeva and Pasternak had met casually there, had listened to each other's readings, but at that time had been preoccupied with their own work. Now Pasternak had read Tsvetaeva's *Versts II*, published in Moscow in 1921. He called her his "dear, golden, incomparable poet" and told her he could not keep from sobbing when he read some of her poems aloud. He reproached himself for having missed her in Moscow and asked her forgiveness. Later he would write in his autobiography: "I was instantly won over by the great lyrical power of the form of her poetry, which stemmed from personal experience, which was not weak-chested but wonderfully compact and condensed." [22] Thus began a correspondence that lasted until the mid-thirties, though its high point was reached in 1926 when Rilke joined Tsvetaeva and Pasternak to form an unusual epistolary triangle.

In her answer to Pasternak's first letter, Tsvetaeva reminisced about their encounters in revolutionary Russia and admitted that she had never read his poems. His book *My Sister Life* was soon in her hands, and once she opened it, she did not close it until she finished it. She carried it around the city, to the zoo, and took it along to dinner and to bed. She wrote later to Pasternak: "It was summer then and I had my own balcony in Berlin. Stone, heat. Your green book on my knees (I sat on the floor). For ten days I lived by it — as on the high crest of a wave: letting myself go, I yielded (obeyed) and did not choke." [23]

In July, Tsvetaeva wrote her essay "A Cloudburst of Light" about Pasternak's poetry. She recalled their meetings in Moscow and described his looks better than anyone else ever has:

> In his face there is something both of the Arab and of his horse: an alertness, an attentiveness, a full readiness to gallop away at any moment, [ . . . ] a pronounced, also horselike, wild and shy slant of the eyes — thus he gives the impression that he is always listening to something intently, only to burst suddenly and prematurely into words, as if a rock or an oak tree had spoken. [24]

Tsvetaeva examined in the essay the essential qualities of Pasternak's poetry, not the specifics of rhythms and rhymes. "That is to be done by specialists in poetry," she wrote. "My special field, though, is Life." [25] Comparing Pasternak's poetry to a cloudburst, she said that she was "drenched" by the power of his verse. Clearly, she identified with his spirituality and found in him what she had missed in Vishnyak. His power as a poet resembled Mayakovsky's, or perhaps her own—they were all three, she felt, poets of a new time.

Pasternak came from a background similar to Tsvetaeva's: his father was a professor, his mother a musician, and his family belonged to the liberal intelligentsia of prerevolutionary Russia. Like Tsvetaeva he was committed to his art. He tried to keep out of politics, claiming that nature provided the focus for his poetic world. This was enough for Tsvetaeva's imagination to fantasize a total communion and to build a new idol. Nevertheless, she left Berlin for Prague on August 1. Pasternak arrived two weeks later. Was she afraid that reality would disappoint her? Or was she simply too tired and bruised from her weeks in Berlin? By the end of her stay there, her friendship with Ehrenburg was floundering. He had asked her not to publish her White Army poems and he did not like her "Russian poems," such as "The Tsar-Maiden" and "Sidestreets." And the Ehrenburgs were close friends with the Vishnyaks. Tsvetaeva would later write to a friend that the breakup with Ehrenburg came "because of the immeasurable gap between our feelings." Much later, Tsvetaeva summed up her opinion: "Ehrenburg is submission to everyone, *spinelessness*." [26]

Tsvetaeva had arrived in Berlin glad to leave behind the hardships of the Moscow years and full of hope for the future. She left only ten weeks later, hurting from her "non-meeting" with Vishnyak and disappointed in her reunion with Efron. She may also have sensed a slight cooling in the émigré community's response to her work. The vast majority of émigrés, whether liberal or reactionary, were united in their hatred of the Bolshevik regime and their contempt for Soviet culture. By now, few believed that they would return to a Russia liberated from the Bolsheviks. While Tsvetaeva was admired for her early lyrical poetry and her poems inspired by the heroism of the White Army, she was criticized for her daring poetic technique, which struck the émigrés as "revolutionary," and for her refusal to join in the chorus of anti-Soviet fanaticism. Tsvetaeva wrote a year later from Prague, "I ran away from Berlin as from a nightmare." [27]

Tsvetaeva's mother and maternal grandfather. Photo from *Tsvetaeva: A Pictorial Biography*, ed. Ellendea Proffer (Ann Arbor, Mich.: Ardis, 1980, p. #62. By permission of Ardis. Unless otherwise stated, all photos are from this source.

Tsvetaeva's father, founder of the
Alexander III Museum (1912).

Tsvetaeva with sister Anastasia (1905).

Portrait of Tsvetaeva by N. Vysheslavtsez
(Moscow, 1920s), from author's collection.

Tsvetaeva in Prague (1924).

Tsvetaeva in Paris (late 1920s).

Tsvetaeva after her return to Moscow (1940).

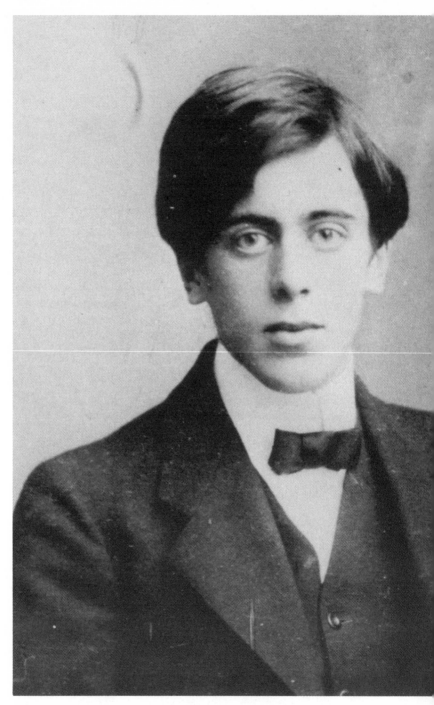

Tsvetaeva and Efron before their marriage (December 1911).

Efron in Paris (1937).

Tsvetaeva's daughter Ariadna (1925).

Tsvetaeva with son Mur at the
Mediterranean (1935).

Sofia Parnok (ca. 1915), from
author's collection.

Sonya Holliday (ca. 1919).

Konstantin Rodzevich (1923).

Boris Pasternak (1920s).

# 13. Prague, Creative Peak

*One does not wait for happiness like that,*
*One waits like that — for the end.*[1]

In Prague, the long-awaited family reunion became a reality, if not quite the reality that Tsvetaeva and Efron had imagined. Not only had they been separated for four years by the revolution, but Tsvetaeva's affair with Parnok and Efron's military service had interrupted the normal course of their lives for another three years. After the stormy weeks in Berlin, the rift in their relationship needed time to heal. Yet they had little time together. Efron spent four days a week in his dormitory in Prague, where he studied law and edited a students' periodical, *Our Own Ways* (Svoimi putyami). When he joined his family, he was burdened with work and was too tired even to take walks with them. All the same, Tsvetaeva was loyal and supportive. She was concerned for his health and encouraged him to return to his writing. In a poem written in September 1922, addressed to him, she described a new relationship built not on romantic love but on an acceptance of their long history together: "The gold of my hair / turns quietly to gray, / Do not regret! Everything has happened, / Everything has merged in my bosom and has harmonized." She ends the poem: "You, too, have turned silvery / My companion!"[2] She tells him in another poem, "Even the joy of mornings / is too crowded for two / [ .... ] / (Since the spirit is a wanderer / and walks alone)."[3]

When Tsvetaeva and Alya arrived in Prague, they faced the problem of finding a place to live. Because the city was expensive, they lived for a while with some of Efron's student friends, finally settling in Mokropsy, a village nearby, while Sergey kept his room in the students' dormitory. Tsvetaeva described her life to Pasternak:

I live in [ . . . ] the last house of the village. At the foot of the hill is a brook. I go there for water. A third of the day is spent on heating the huge tile stove. The daily routine is not that different from life in Moscow, it may even be more difficult, but there is something more than my poetry: the family and nature. For months I don't see anyone. All morning I write and I walk; the hills are beautiful here.[4]

Tsvetaeva's first year in Czechoslovakia was a period of reflection and emotional relief. The Czech subsidy—a scholarship for Efron and an added annuity for Tsvetaeva—helped them make ends meet. She hoped that with additional literary fees she would be able to create the right conditions for her work. Meanwhile, she, Efron, and Alya were a family again. Alya remembered life that winter as "happy, busy, and friendly though difficult."[5] When Efron was home, the family would linger at the table after dinner. He would read aloud to them while Tsvetaeva and Alya mended or sewed. At bedtime Tsvetaeva and Efron would tell Alya a story; at Christmastime, Alya recalled, they festooned their tree with homemade decorations. When the time came each week for Efron to return to Prague, Tsvetaeva would take him to the station with Alya. She was no longer just her mother's daughter but now Efron's daughter as well.

Like the Efrons, many Russian émigrés could not afford to live in Prague, so they settled in outlying villages. Most of them were struggling to survive on their meager subsidies. A certain esprit united them; as Tsvetaeva wrote to a friend, "Life is not communal (everybody is very busy), but friendly; people help one another in need. No scandals or gossip, a great feeling of purity."[6] The Efrons were fortunate to have friends nearby: Lyudmila Chirikova and her family were neighbors, and Nikolay Yelenev, who had fought at Efron's side, was now studying with him. He and his wife Katya were fond of the Efrons. So was Anna Teskova, the head of the Czech-Russian cultural society, Jedinota, who invited Tsvetaeva to give a reading. Tsvetaeva also deepened her relationship with Mark Slonim and became friends with Vladimir Lebedev, another editor of Freedom of Russia.

That journal became Tsvetaeva's literary home, the place where all the work she offered was published without deletions. At the same time, Craft and Psyche appeared in Berlin, and four of her plays were published in émigré journals. Even though she enjoyed the rank of a major Russian poet, she was unable to place her Moscow prose or her White Army poems. Yet she did not give up. She was recopying her prose, proofreading and correcting the galleys of her publications, and drowning in poems that had to be written.

Then in April, the Efrons' landlady initiated court proceedings against them, claiming that they had not taken care of their lodgings properly. Tsvetaeva was upset and angry. "Seryozha is tormented and unnerved by the forthcoming trial," she wrote to Lyudmila Chirikova, who had moved to Paris. "I am altogether exhausted by life on this earth. I dread to think of all the scrubbed and all the unscrubbed floors that the future holds in store for me—all the boiled and unboiled milk, the landladies, the pots and pans, etc."[7] Fortunately, the Efrons were acquitted of any wrongdoing. But now, even Berlin seemed better to her than Czechoslovakia.

For Tsvetaeva, time and distance would always enhance places, people, feelings. By the time the Efrons moved to Paris, Tsvetaeva would remember Prague, too, as a paradise.

In Prague, Tsvetaeva was at the peak of her creativity. In the next three years, 1922–25, she wote her most mature lyrical poetry, published only in 1928 under the title *After Russia*. The volume of her work and the level of her poetic achievement were astounding, considering the hardships of her existence. It was at this point that her commitment to poetry hardened. To have time to write, she insisted that ten-year-old Alya take care of many of the household chores. When a friend objected, she responded:

> It is either she who has not yet manifested herself, who is still in the future, or I—my life, my creativity. I *exist* already and I cannot sacrifice my poetry. [ . . . ] If you have not learned to remove everything, to step over all obstacles, even if it harms others, if you have not learned absolute egotism in your fight for the right to write, you will not create a great work.[8]

Tsvetaeva wanted to create "not for the millions, not for one special person, not for myself. I write for the poem. The poem writes itself through me."[9]

During these first months in Czechoslovakia she was still recuperating from Vishnyak's rejection. She sensed that the pleasures of the flesh were not for her and became increasingly contemptuous of all earthly pleasures. She read the Bible, Shakespeare, Nietzsche. She reread Heraclitus, whose *Fragments* and *Orphic Hymns* Nilender had translated. She shared many Heraclitian concepts of time, of the permanent flux in the universe, of the union of opposite elements.

In the poems of that period we see the coming together of many of her themes. Life on this earth did not satisfy her; her passionate nature carried her toward a higher destination, the world of the soul. Yet she reserved her most perceptive insights for human relationships. In combining the metaphysical with the erotic she reached the pinnacle of her art. Between destinations, always on the move but never arriving, Tsvetaeva felt driven by a powerful force. Turning more to introspection, she scarcely noticed the world outside. During her three years in Prague she wrote no topical poems. Instead she was enchanted by Prague's romantic beauty—its baroque buildings, its bridges, its old Jewish cemetery. One statue in particular—a young knight on the Charles bridge—caught her fancy. Slim and handsome, he stood guard over the river, the river of time, watching the flowing river of days. The Czech countryside also offered Tsvetaeva what she liked best: mountains and hills, forests and rivers. No wonder, then, that she was flooded with poems.

This emphasis on the superior power that inspired her was expressed in her two lyric poems "God" and "Poets," written in 1922 and 1923. Tsvetaeva's personal view of God contradicted the generally accepted Christian image of a loving, forgiving father figure. Instead God is faceless, severe, mysterious, and evasive. He rises "out of churches" and hides in forests. In the last stanzas of the poem "God" he appears:

> Oh, you will not limit him
> To presence and fate,
> In the settled slush of feelings
> He is a gray ice-floe.
>
> Oh, you will not catch up with him!
> God does not bloom
> In a household pot
> As a begonia on the window-sill!
>
> .   .   .   .   .   .   .   .   .   .
>
> Since he is speed—and he moves.
> Since the huge book of stars
> All of it—from Alpha to Omega
> Is only a trace of his cape.[10]

Here Tsvetaeva's image of the Genius/Rider in "On a Red Steed" fuses with her image of God. God, too, is defined by what he is not; God, too, is aloof and on the move; God, too, is inaccessible. Tsvetaeva even repeats the specific descriptions that she had used for the Genius/Rider: dressed in a cape,

God is "the ice-floe" just as the Genius "rides through the mountains of the blue ice-floes."

It is not surprising, then, that the poet in her cycle "Poets" is endowed with similar qualities: he, too, stands outside this world; he, too, is motion incarnate, unreachable. He "burns but does not warm, / plucks off, but does not cultivate." Unwilling to recognize the limits of reality, the poet is utterly destructive, knowing only the superiority of his world and feeling only contempt for the world around him. Tsvetaeva ends the poem with an appeal for understanding of the poet's special fate—which is her own:

> What shall I do, singer and first-born,
> In a world where the blackest black is—gray!
> Where inspiration is kept as in a thermos!
> With all this immeasurability
> In a world of measures?!

Tsvetaeva apparently lived a life of fanatical dedication to her craft and to her inspiration from above. But in looking closely at the poetic evidence, we find her self-love revealed. She endowed God, her genius, and the poet with her own characteristics. Little evidence of softness, love or compassion exists in these models. Severity to the point even of cruelty marks these "outsiders," these personifications of renunciation, aloofness, and total commitment. What she left out was the woman who required love and friendship in order to exist.

Tsvetaeva's letters of the time reveal her rising anger against anyone who criticized her and her fantasies of seeing them punished. "Do you believe in another world?" she wrote to Chirikova.

> I do. But in a terrible retribution! In a world where meaning reigns. In a world where the judges will be judged. This will be the day of my justification, no, that's not enough—of my exultation! I will stand there and exult. Because people won't be judged by their dress; mine, after all, was poorer than everyone else's, which made them hate me so in life. There people will be judged by that very essence, which hindered me here from paying attention to dresses.[11]

Several months after her arrival in Czechoslovakia, Tsvetaeva went back to her work on a long folkloric poem that she had begun in Moscow. She called it "The Swain" and dedicated it to Pasternak. By the end of 1922, she wrote to Pasternak: "I have just finished a major poem (one has to call it something), not a poem but a hallucination. I didn't finish it, it finished me. We parted as though torn asunder!" [12] Tsvetaeva again took the plot from a fairy tale recorded by Afanasiyev: a young girl, Marusya, falls in love with a vampire who kills her brother and her mother. Marusya conceals his crimes, but he still takes her life. Transformed into a plant, she is taken into the house of a rich man. On the stroke of midnight she changes back into her former self. The rich man surprises her, falls in love, and marries her. They have a son but the vampire comes back to claim Marusya. In the original story she chases the vampire by throwing holy water at him and making the sign of the cross. Tsvetaeva's heroine, though, leaves her husband and her child to soar upward with the vampire into the fiery blue.

> She—upwards
> He—closer:
> They merge,
> They soar:
>
> High heat into high heat,
> The surge into the surge!
> Home,
> Into the blue fire. [13]

This is a variation of the theme of "On a Red Steed": no price is too high for transcendence and self-annihilation. Once again the heroine sacrifices all her loved ones and herself, but this time the poem ends not with resignation but with the fiery fusion of passionate love. Tsvetaeva's knowledge of her own vulnerability to temptation fueled the poem. Vishnyak may have been only a "velvety mediocrity," but her passion for him had been real and uncontrollable. That is why Marusya, the poem's heroine, is so believable. Her scintillating gaiety reflects Tsvetaeva's own desire for the uncomplicated enjoyment of dance and song, of irresponsibility and lovemaking. But in her as in Tsvetaeva, we also hear the dark voice of frenzy.

Later, in her essay "The Poet on Criticism," Tsvetaeva explained that it was more love than fear that forced Marusya's submission.

> When someone says to me, do this and you will be free, and I don't do it, that means I am not particularly interested in freedom; it means that my non-freedom is more precious to me. And what is that precious non-freedom that exists between individuals? Love. Marusya loved the Vampire. That is why she never named him and so lost, one after the other, her mother, her brother, her life. Passion and crime, passion and sacrifice. [14]

Tsvetaeva often referred to this poem, quoted it, translated it into French—it was her own life's blood.

Because she was eager to have her Moscow diaries and essays published in book form, she sent them to Gul, who submitted them to Helikon on her behalf. Tsvetaeva wrote to him that Vishnyak had offered an excellent contract but wanted her to excise any mention of politics. She was outraged:

> Moscow from 1917 to 1919, what does he think I was doing, rocking in my cradle? I was twenty-four to twenty-six years old. I had eyes, hands, feet: with those eyes I saw, with those ears I heard, with those hands I chopped wood (and made notes), with those feet I walked from morning to night, from market to market, and from one end of the city to the other—wherever they would take me! There is nothing *political* in the book; there is *passionate truth*, a truth biased by cold, hunger, and anger, *by that year*. My younger daughter died from hunger in a children's home—that, too, is "politics" (it was a Bolshevik home).[15]

Tsvetaeva refused to "cripple" her book, which was never published in her version, although some excerpts appeared in journals.[16]

In that spring and summer of 1923, Tsvetaeva needed all her time for writing and often complained that her domestic chores exhausted her. Though Alya was a great help, daily life was primitive and demanded hard work: water had to be brought in from a well, the stove had to be lit. Cooking on a "primus" demanded patience, and shopping on their limited budget was always a problem.

Writing letters took a good deal of her time. First she wrote drafts into her notebooks, and then she copied them. As she explained to Pasternak, dreams were her favorite mode of communication, but letters were second best. "Neither one is ordered: we dream and we write not when *we* desire to but when they do: the letter wants to be written, the dream wants to be dreamed."[17] Indeed, dreams were Tsvetaeva's escape from criticism, from reality; similarly, her letters, most of them addressed to distant correspondents, allowed her full control. "I don't like meetings in life, foreheads clash," she wrote in the same letter to Pasternak.

Tsvetaeva's epistolary romance with Pasternak lasted for about fourteen years, with interruptions and ups and downs. Her letters were lost during the war, but drafts in her notebooks have found their way into print. Pasternak's letters are probably in the Tsvetaeva archive; only excerpts reproduced by Tsvetaeva's daughter are known. These suffice to give an idea of Pasternak's worship of Tsvetaeva. "Marina, my golden friend, my own miraculous predestination, my smoldering morning soul, Marina. . . . Oh, how I love you, Marina! So free, so inborn, so enrichingly clear. It suits the heart so well, nothing is easier!" [18]

According to her daughter, Tsvetaeva had great need of Pasternak's adulation. Besides "The Swain," which Tsvetaeva dedicated to Pasternak, about eighteen poems in her collection *After Russia* are addressed to him. Tsvetaeva's support was also crucial for Pasternak, who underwent a personal and creative crisis in the twenties. They commented on each other's books and manuscripts and shared what was most precious to them—the meaning of poetry, which was synonymous with the meaning of life. Tsvetaeva advised Pasternak in one of her first letters to write a big work. "This will be your second life, your first life, your only life. You will not need anyone or anything. You will not notice anyone. You will be terribly free." [19]

Pasternak had mailed Tsvetaeva his last collection of poetry, *Themes and Variations*, from Berlin. "The last month of this fall I have spent constantly with you, not with the book," she wrote back. She recounted how she had conjured him up early in the morning, in the still, dark station, as she awaited the train to Prague. "There was one place—a lantern post—without light. I called you there, Pasternak! And we had lengthy conversations side by side—as we ambled along." [20] Tsvetaeva became desperate when she heard that Pasternak was planning to return to Russia early in 1923. She pleaded with him in letter not to leave before seeing her. "Russia for me is . . . almost the other world. Were you to leave for Guadeloupe, the land of snakes, of convicts, I would not call you back. Russia is a different matter." [21] But Pasternak did not change his plans. Tsvetaeva wanted to come to Berlin before his departure, but she had a Soviet passport and needed special authorization or connections to obtain a visa. It didn't work out, and Pasternak departed on March 18. "Now my life is you and I have nowhere to go," she wrote, adding that she would live in the hope of meeting him in Weimar in two years, as he had suggested. [22]

In her poetry cycle "Wires," begun on the day of Pasternak's departure from Berlin and finished a few weeks later, Tsvetaeva expressed the pain of their separation. She invoked the passion of Eurydice and Orpheus; she used Ariadne's pain for the absent Theseus to convey her own passion, her own pain. She consoled herself with the thought that while waiting for their meeting, she would somehow find him in a dream. Tsvetaeva felt she had found in Pasternak not only a man she could love and a poet she could admire but a man who could respond to her as a poet and as a woman—exactly the kind of illusion that could be kept alive in letters.

What did Tsvetaeva know about Pasternak in real life? Obviously not much. When she realized that no meeting between them would take place, she wrote to Gul: "I know nothing about Pasternak and would like to know much (between you and me!). [ . . . ] I am always afraid of someone else's daily life. Mostly it saddens me. But I would like to know what [Pasternak's] wife is like . . . , what he was doing in Berlin, why he is leaving, who his friends were, and so on. Tell me whatever you know." [23]

Pasternak had come to Berlin with his young wife, Yevgeniya (Zhenya). Soon after he returned to Moscow his son Yevgeny was born. Neither fact affected Tsvetaeva's image of her poet-twin. She reached Pasternak in her poems, in her dreams—he belonged to her, she felt; he was her "brother in the fifth season and in the fourth dimension." [24]

In 1923, *Craft*, Tsvetaeva's collection of poetry, was published in Berlin and reviewed there by Aleksandr Bakhrakh, a twenty-three-year-old literary critic, whom Tsvetaeva had never met. In June she addressed to him the first letter of what would be a short, intense, mostly one-sided correspondence in which she shared with him her responses to many of her contemporary poets. Her tone, however, was confessional, reporting her most intimate feelings to him. At the outset she complimented Bakhrakh on his review and thanked him for calling her a "poet," not a "poetess." She finished by asking him to look for a publisher for her Moscow prose. By the next letter, she had begun to build him up into the image of the beloved stranger with whom "everything is possible, from whom everything is expected." [25]

Thus began another of Tsvetaeva's epistolary romances, this time with a correspondent utterly invented. The intensity of the letters reveals Tsvetaeva's lacerating need for human response. Pasternak had left, the correspondence with him was lagging, and Tsvetaeva did not feel like turning to Efron. She was drawn to Bakhrakh's favorable review as to a magnet. As she had many times before, she sought to introduce a mother-child pattern into this correspondence. Addressing Bakhrakh as "my child," she wrote: "Your voice is young, which makes me tender, and immediately transforms me into someone a thousand years old—some stony motherhood, the motherhood of a cliff." [26] A few days later she went on: "Motherhood is a question without an answer, or rather an answer without a question, a complete answer! In motherhood there is only one person: the mother. There's only one attitude:

hers."[27] This was the one-sided relationship for which she hoped: Bakhrakh was to be a son. She wanted to believe that she had found the ideal listener. She seemed to relish the fact that she had never laid eyes on him.

> I want from you, child, a miracle—a miracle of trust, a miracle of understanding, a miracle of renunciation. I want you with your twenty years to be an old man of seventy—and, at the same time, a little boy of seven. I don't want age, calculations, struggle, barriers.

> I have no idea who you are, I know nothing about your life, I am completely free with you; I speak to your spirit.[28]

Love and sex had disappointed her, she told Bakhrakh, because "the best, the finest, the most tender lose so much in the closeness of love; how vulgar and coarse they become." She claimed she had given up on sexual love and had retired into her own world, "an invisible world, where I am master."[29]

Now knowing that love and pain were inexorably linked for her, she wrote: "Returning to 'pain for pain's sake,' I confess to you one thing. Just now, walking in the forest, I wondered whence comes this eternal lament of the soul in love: Do hurt me! The thirst for pain—there it is! What do we want then?"[30] She probably knew very well that what she desired was self-annihilation in bliss or pain. And in her next letter she describes poetically and poignantly her need to forget herself, to become one with love, with hate, or with nature: "I write late at night after a stormy, windy, clear day. I have been sitting high in a birch tree, the wind was rocking both the birch tree and me; I hugged the white, smooth tree trunk, I felt bliss, I ceased to be."[31]

Tsvetaeva's invented passion inspired eight poems dedicated to Bakhrakh. In one, "The Seashell," she conveys her possessiveness:

> From the leper's hospital of lies and evil
> I have summoned you and brought you

> Into the light of day! From the dead sleep of gravestones—
> Into my hands, into both my palms,

> Shell-like—grow there, be quiet:
> You will turn into a pearl, within these palms![32]

Expressing a desire to meet Bakhrakh in Berlin, Tsvetaeva informed him in detail of her various phobias. She was extremely myopic, she wrote, but she didn't like to wear glasses and so was afraid of getting lost, afraid of cars, elevators, and subways.

Instead of a response, there was a month of silence. Bakhrakh was away and did not get her letter until his return to Berlin. Tsvetaeva's reaction was almost hysterical. "There was such a pain of loss, such a hurt for my living soul, such bitterness that—if it were not for my poetry—I would have flung myself at the first person I met: to forget, to quench, to drown."[33] In July she began to keep a special diary, calling it "Bulletin of an Illness," while she waited for Bakhrakh's response. Finally, at the end of August, Bakhrakh responded. Tsvetaeva sent him her "Bulletin" and went back to her confessional outbursts.

In August, the Efrons rented a room in a house in Prague, a house on a hill. At Sergey's insistence Alya was sent to a boarding school in Moravia. Tsvetaeva was becoming more aware that Alya needed something that she could not give her. As early as 1921, when Alya was spending a few weeks in the country, she had written to Lann that she noticed that Alya was better off with others than with her: "With others Alya laughs and with me she cries, with others she grows fat, and with me thin."[34] Now she wrote to Bakhrakh that her daughter was growing away from her:

> She is very lovely and very free, no embarrassment even for a second, directness itself. People will love her because she does not need anyone. Throughout all my life I have loved by *myself*, even more have hated by myself. From the moment when I was born I wanted to die; it was a difficult childhood and a somber youth. I don't see anything of that in Alya, but I know one thing: she will be happy—I have never wanted that (for myself).[35]

Although in her letters and poems to Bakhrakh Tsvetaeva claimed to have renounced the world, she was clearly hungry for a new passion. With Alya in boarding school and Efron in a sanatorium—he suffered a relapse of his tuberculosis soon after they moved into their new lodgings—she was alone. And on September 20, Tsvetaeva announced the big news to Bakhrakh:

> I love someone else—it cannot be said more simply, more crudely, and more truthfully. [ . . . ] My hour with you is over. What is left is my eternity with you! . . . How did it happen? Oh, my friend, how does it happen? I rushed toward him, he responded; I heard great words, there are no simpler ones, but I heard them perhaps for the first time in my life. [ . . . ] What will come of it—I don't know. I do know: great pain. I confront suffering.[36]

# 14. Great Love, Great Pain

*This kiss is without a sound:*
*Lips stiff*
*As you kiss the hand of — empresses*
*The hand of — corpses.*[1]

svetaeva's premonitions of pain and suffering proved all too accurate. With a new man in her life, how could it be otherwise? Even as she satisfied her own hunger for passion, she feared the inevitable end of the relationship. Her new lover was Konstantin Rodzevich, a former White Russian officer three years younger than she, and a close friend of Efron's; he was studying for his law degree at the same university and was active in local pro-Soviet politics. According to Alya, Efron loved him "like a brother."[2]

Tsvetaeva met Rodzevich soon after her arrival in Prague; he became her lover about a year later. In a few short months — from September to December 1923 — the relationship ran its course, though the two remained on friendly terms. Rodzevich's personality and his part in the affair remain rather undefined. Recently, though, he told Viktoria Schweitzer that they had been attracted to one another but that he had never courted her: "She was writing letters to her distant correspondent and lover, but she was searching for an intense attachment. So, it happened because I was close by."[3]

In the photos of the period, Rodzevich looks surprisingly like a coarser version of Efron — with the same large eyes, the regular, rather soft features — but he was shorter and his face broader. Tsvetaeva's contemporaries differed widely in their opinion of him. Alya, away at boarding school, did not know him at the time, but she met him later in Paris and was greatly taken by his charm and tenderness. She even saw in him what had been so dear to her mother: a sense of chivalry. Others were less impressed. Slonim wrote that he met Rodzevich only twice, but "he seemed to me cunning, somewhat foxy, not without a sense of humor, but rather dull, mediocre."[4]

Efron's friend Yelenev, who studied with both Efron and Rodzevich, was even less kind: "Marina paid dearly for having trusted a roguish man who was a liar by nature."⁵ Mariya Bulgakova, the woman Rodzevich married soon after the affair with Tsvetaeva had ended, also had little praise for him, calling him later "a total nonentity, a charming swine and immoral as well."⁶ In fact, all these characterizations are irrelevant. As Slonim wrote, Tsvetaeva "fell in love, not with Rodzevich as he was, but with him as she imagined him—with her own projection, with a dream."⁷

It is in Tsvetaeva's letters to Bakhrakh and in her poems of those months, even those not dedicated to Rodzevich, that we find the key to their relationship. This was not like her romance with Vishnyak, when, surprised by her own feelings of tenderness and femininity, she had exposed herself totally and had ended by becoming frustrated and bitter. Unlike Vishnyak, Rodzevich responded fully to Tsvetaeva's desire. As a result, she seemed to experience something of the same intensely sexual feelings for him as she had for Parnok. In the process, she probably came as close as she ever had to fulfillment since that time. She wrote to Rodzevich:

> For the first time I have felt the unity of heaven and earth. Oh! The earth I loved before you appeared and the trees! I've loved everything, I knew how to love everything except the other, the other who was alive. The other has always bothered me; it was a wall against which I broke, I didn't know how to live with the living. Hence my feeling that I was not a woman, but a soul. [ . . . ] You have simply *loved* me . . . I told you: there is a Soul. You said: there is Life.⁸

Shortly after her affair began, Tsvetaeva shared with Bakhrakh her anxiety and her hope:

> Woman. Yes, that, too, is in me. Not much, feebly, in spurts, in reflection, in reverberation. Rather a longing for—what? . . . Oh, I speak of something very specific—about sensual love in which any woman is stronger, more fulfilled and more passionate than I.

> This current hour may bring about a miracle for me—God willing—perhaps I will actually become a human being, become whole.⁹

Tsvetaeva was in turmoil, tortured by her own ambivalence. On the same day, she wrote a second letter to Bakhrakh: "Creativity and being in love cannot coexist. You live either there or here . . ."¹⁰ But the poems Tsvetaeva wrote during the affair with Rodzevich reflect her resurrected hope to be loved as a woman, not as a great poet. Rodzevich did not particularly like her poetry, but that only fired Tsvetaeva's passion. Everything seemed to augur full happiness. Yet from the very beginning the poems transmit Tsvetaeva's fear of the coming end—separation and death.

Her first poem addressed to Rodzevich was "The Ravine," dated September 10 and 11, 1923. The first section finds the lovers at the bottom of a ravine: "You'll lie down—and I'll lie down, / You have become a tramp with me." [11]

Everything is abandoned to the physical: "Oaths not needed." There is no guilt: "God / is for free! Like falling into an abyss." The second section, written the next day, continues the note of sexual abandon, "the quicksilver of painful delirium," but moves to associations with war, corpses, and graves. "Like bodies in the war—in harmony and in rows." The conclusion raises interesting questions.

> In this mad race of the sleepless trees
> Someone has been killed.
> Your victory—is the defeat of the *hosts*. —
> Do you know that, young David?

Are the "*hosts*" other lovers, the "traces of—storms not ours you kissed away"? Or is the "young David" vanquishing Tsvetaeva's poetic hosts? Has sexual pleasure been enjoyed at the expense of the poet's creativity?

Early in October, in "The Train of Life," Tsvetaeva focused on the conflict she perceived with Rodzevich—his acceptance of the conventional and her hatred of it. She uses the metaphor of a third-class railway carriage to reject the sham of women's lives when they consist only of curlers, diapers, crackers, and pillows.

> I do not want to wait for the hour of death
> In this box of female bodies!
> I want the train to drink and to sing:
> Death, too,—is outside of class. [12]

In another poem, untitled, passion means stepping not out of clothes, but out of one's body. Her passion allows her to transcend all limits of ordinary existence, to touch the divine. Her love is superior; it comes from on high, just like her poetic inspiration. Still she desperately needs physical tenderness and human warmth to fight off her anxiety, her fear of death. She begs her lover to rock her to sleep, "Not with words, but in the cradle of your arms: / With warmth, with safety." [13]

Rodzevich apparently soon tired of her constant demands, and her intensity. Both knew it was over. Tsvetaeva wrote an epitaph to their passion:

> You who loved me with the falseness
> Of truth — and the truth of lies,
> You who loved me to the ultimate!
> Beyond boundaries!
>
> You who loved me longer
> Than all time — Destiny raises her hand:
> You don't love me any more:
> That's the truth in six words.[14]

Mark Slonim understood that Rodzevich was "stunned and frightened by [Tsvetaeva's] impetuousness, which came down on him like a wave. He fled from the storm and the thunder to the calm refuge of bourgeois life and a conventional marriage. He was, of course, not up to Marina, especially when she began her mythologizing." [15]

To Bakhrakh, Tsvetaeva announced that she was not made for life:

With me everything is a conflagration! I carry on ten affairs at once (what affairs!) and I can persuade each one of them from my profoundest depths — that he is the only one. But the tiniest turning of the head from me — I cannot tolerate, I HURT, you understand? I am a person whose skin has been torn off, and you are in armor. You all have art, social concerns, friendships, entertainment, family, duty. I deep down, have NOTHING. Everything falls off like skin, and under the skin — raw flesh or fire: me, Psyche.[16]

Although she knew that she had loved Rodzevich as she had never loved before, she wrote, she had no choice but to separate from him. He had asked her for an ordinary life. He wanted a home, a wife, a marriage, while Tsvetaeva would never consider divorcing Efron to marry someone else. Now she begged Bakhrakh not to abandon her: "Friend, now you understand why it is a necessity for me that you love me (call it friendship, never mind!). Because I *am not*, only by being loved will I understand that I exist." [17] In fact, this was the end of the passionate correspondence with Bakhrakh. Later, when Tsvetaeva moved to Paris, they exchanged notes on purely practical matters, but the former intensity was gone. A meeting came to nothing.

Efron had to cope with Tsvetaeva's latest passion when he returned from his short stay in the sanatorium. He shared his misery in a letter to his friend

Voloshin. No longer could he deny to himself that he was facing a recurring problem.

> Marina is a creature of passions, much more now than before, than before my departure. Plunging headlong into a hurricane has become a necessity, the very air of life, for her. The person who unleashes the hurricane now — does not matter. Almost always (now as before) or rather always, everything is based on self-deception. A person is invented and the hurricane begins. As soon as that person's mediocrity and worthlessness are discovered, Marina gives into an equally hurricane-like despair, a condition that improves only with the appearance of a new love. *What* doesn't matter; only *how* matters. Not the substance, not the source, but the rhythm, the demonic rhythm. Today, despair; tomorrow, enthusiasm; then love, a new plunge, body and soul, and the day after, despair once again. And she does all this while maintaining her acute, cold (I'd almost say cynically Voltairian) intelligence. Yesterday's love objects are derided today (almost always accurately) with wit and cruelty. Everything gets written down, everything is quietly poured, with mathematical precision, into a formula.

> She's like an enormous stove that, in order to function, needs wood, wood, and more wood. The ashes are thrown away, the quality of wood isn't important. So long as there's a good draft, everything turns to flame. The bad wood burns quickly, the better wood takes a little longer. Needless to say it has been quite some time since I have been of any use in kindling that fire.[18]

Though "all Prague" was talking about the affair, Efron had found out about it by accident. He suggested separation to Tsvetaeva, but he was afraid she might attempt suicide when Rodzevich — whom he called a "little Casanova" — left her, as he inevitably would. When Tsvetaeva — after many sleepless nights — refused to leave him, Sergey understood that he was "at the same time her lifebelt and a millstone round her neck. To free her from that millstone is not possible without depriving her of the last straw she is grasping."[19]

Where once Tsvetaeva had meant life to Efron, living with her now, he wrote to Voloshin, was a "slow suicide." Totally blind to him, to his needs, she believed that by giving up her own happiness, she was giving him his. However, he could fool himself no longer. Now he remembered how hurt he had been in 1918 when he had come to Moscow to bid Tsvetaeva good-bye before rejoining the White Army: "I only want to tell you that on the day of my departure from Moscow after my short visit (you know what I was facing then), when I was looking at everything as if for the last time, Marina divided her time between me and someone else whom she calls now an idiot and a scoundrel."[20] The Rodzevich episode was traumatic for Efron. He saw clearly now what he had only suspected before: that Tsvetaeva's emotional pattern was something she would never be able to control. He also told Voloshin that he had come to believe that Tsvetaeva had lied to him when she blamed his sisters for Irina's death. Now he heard a different version, widespread in the émigré community, that Tsvetaeva had neglected Irina and refused his sisters' offer of assistance. He saw clearly now the extent to which she was unable to avoid self-deception if reality was too painful for her to bear—or too damaging to her self-image.

In 1924 Tsvetaeva wrote her two great poems, "Poem of the Mountain" and "Poem of the End."[21] "The Mountain" was written while the affair with Rodzevich was doomed but not over. As G. S. Smith writes in his brilliant analysis of the poem, it "is above all concerned to explore and define metaphysical essences or absolutes: the idea of love, the work of causation, the chosen status . . . conferred by heightened spiritual awareness, and the nature of the relationship between the individual so chosen and other human beings."[22] The "Poem of the End" is a much more personal narrative; both poems, however, are brilliant examples of Tsvetaeva's very special mixture of detailed reality and her private poetic world. In "Mountain" there is the objective matter-of-fact ("Do you remember that last house / of the mountain—at the edge of the suburb?") along with the subjective ("My grief began with this mountain. / It became my tombstone"). In the "Poem of the End" there is "The time is six" along with the outcry "Oh, with whom can I share my sorrow, my grief, / My horror, greener than ice? . . ." Tsvetaeva wants to pull readers into her psychological state of being and make them share both her pain and her longing for a better world beyond.

In "Mountain" she uses the similarity of sounds in Russian of *gora* (mountain) and *gore* (sorrow) to develop diverse meanings. The mountain stands for many things: it is not only the hill on which Tsvetaeva lived at the time, but also a symbol of the superiority of an independent life, of the passions over the commonplace world that held Rodzevich prisoner. Moreover, it is personified; it speaks to the lovers: it "threw us down on our backs, / It pulled us to itself: lie down!" Tsvetaeva was still angry when she wrote "Mountain"; her contempt is as infinite as her love. She has no use for "Happiness—*at home!*

For love without fantasy." For people who want a life of ordinary pursuits, she feels not only contempt but hatred. She curses those husbands and wives who would build their suburban lives on the ruins of her mountain; curses their sons and daughters. Here the persona is not the poet, but the woman inspired by divine transcendent passion and relieved of any responsibility.

"Poem of the End" on one level recounts the lovers' last meeting; on another level, it unfolds Tsvetaeva's inner world. Using colloquial language and stream-of-consciousness associations, it achieves such powerful authenticity that this personal drama takes on universal meaning. From the very beginning, a mood of anxiety pervades the poem. The narrator sees life as though facing death, and death remains a constant presence. On the surface the poem follows the lovers from their meeting place, across town, to the outskirts and on to their last adieu. Underneath it expresses the poet's vision of love and her hopeless defiance of the world around her. The most dramatic section is a dialogue between the lovers:

> "You don't love me?" "Yes, I love you."
> "You don't love me!" "I do, but I am tormented,
> Drained, exhausted."

And later:

> "No mountains have to be moved!
> Love means . . .
>                     —Mine."
> "I understand you. So what?"
> The drum beat of his fingers
> Grows louder (the scaffold and the square).
> "Let's leave."—And I: "I had hoped let's die.
> It would be easier!"

The lovers come to a bridge, the last bridge, a bridge that does not connect but separates. In the pit of her unhappiness, the woman seems ready to sacrifice her soul, her poetry, to become all body, all pain. She questions the very foundations of her life: perhaps she never had a soul, or perhaps she has been robbed of it by passion. She knows only that: "The body that once wanted to live / Wants to live no longer." Yet, just as she reaches the point of negating life, she rises beyond the walls of the city, beyond the borders of ordinary life, to assume the life of the outsider, the poet, the Jew. Transcending the notion of fate, she chooses a world beyond reality, the world of poetry: "Life—is a place where one cannot live, / A Jewish quarter." In full identification with the fate of the outcast, she concludes this section with the words: "In this most Christian of worlds / All poets are Jews."

In the final sequence, tears unite the lovers; their love is a ship sinking "without a trace / without a sound." Like the ship, their love has drowned.

There are two images of mother, one hidden, one direct, in the poem. Tsvetaeva's description of love—"Love—means a bow-string / Stretched back: bow-string: a parting"—recalls the dream she had described to Ellis in which mother is "straight like a bow-string on a bow." Later in the poem, when the moment of separation comes closer, the woman clings to her lover's body and tells him that she holds him as close as

> That woman—remember you called her
> Mother? Forgetting everything and everybody
> In the motionless triumph of
> Carrying you,
> Could not hold you any closer.

Pasternak was overwhelmed by the poem's impact when he read it. "This is the fourth evening that I have shoved a piece of nocturnal Prague into my coat pocket—hazy, slushy, smoky, misty—with the bridge in the distance and then, suddenly, just in front of my eyes—you. . . . What a great, a diabolically great artist you are, Marina!"[23]

In life, if not in her work, Tsvetaeva tried to play down the pain of Rodzevich's rejection. In a letter to Olga Chernova she described their encounter at one of the literary evenings in Prague, an encounter remarkable only for its uneventfulness. Tsvetaeva, looking back, seemed to feel that her passion, her suffering, her pain had been excessive: "How simple all this is! If only one could know it beforehand! They all left me like this, except for Boris Pasternak, whom I have not yet met—and from whom, consequently, I have not yet separated."[24]

# 15. Resignation and Birth of Son

*Pain as familiar as the palm to the eyes—*
*As the lips know—*
*The name of one's own child.*[1]

**W**ith the Rodzevich affair behind her, and her two great poems about it written, Tsvetaeva went back to her normal life: work and family. She discovered she was pregnant again early in the summer of 1924. Still in need of "a friend's shoulder, where one could hide, snuggle up and forget oneself," she looked to Slonim for solace.[2] Once, after reading him the "Poem of the End," she told him that although her feelings for Rodzevich were ebbing, "the wound has not healed, it still hurts and burns, the blood is already coagulating, drying—but now anger rises at the thought of having trusted again, again having been deceived, and I feel a desire to destroy that idol I created, thus punishing both him and myself."[3]

This was, of course, the pattern Efron had described in his letter to Voloshin. Slonim came close to suffering the same fate. Newly separated from his wife, he seemed to Tsvetaeva one in whom she would find the support and love she needed. But Slonim knew Tsvetaeva too well: "As usual, M. I. first built up an illusion about me: she saw in me an incarnation of spirituality and of all kinds of virtues, being totally ignorant of my private life, my tastes, my passions, my vices."[4] Slonim admired her, liked her, but did not respond to her advances. He called her feelings for him "love-hatred" and once told her that she was "a naked soul! Even frightening!" Now Tsvetaeva was bitterly disappointed by his rejection.

Fortunately, a pleasant surprise was in store for the Efrons that spring. While they were still living on the hill in Prague, a new neighbor—Olga Chernova—moved in. She had just separated from her second husband, a prominent Socialist Revolutionary and a former minister in the Russian Provisional Government. Olga and Natalya, her twin daughters from her first marriage, lived in Paris, but her younger daughter, Ariadna, lived with her. Chernova has described their first meeting in an essay published in 1970. On the day after she moved in, Tsvetaeva knocked at her door: "A young woman entered, her brown hair cut in bangs, her complexion smooth and sallow, her eyes light. Slim, almost unnaturally upright, her steely posture was striking, making her impetuous movements angular and somehow unfeminine. She utterly lacked softness."[5] Tsvetaeva came to get acquainted and to borrow some forks, knives, and spoons. When Chernova told her that all she could offer were two damaged silver spoons and "a Corsican dagger and a Corsican pen knife[,] both engraved on one side with the Corsican blazon of a Moor's head in a turban and on the other side with the inscription *vendeta Corsa*," Tsvetaeva was enchanted; to slice onions with a dagger appealed to her. When she found out that the name Ariadna was as dear to Chernova as it was to her, their friendship was cemented.

Tsvetaeva read her poetry to Chernova and her daughter and shared with them her love for Pasternak's poetry. In July 1924 when the Chernovs left for Paris, distance only enhanced Tsvetaeva's and Chernova's intimacy. Tsvetaeva's letters to her friend give details of the Efrons' daily life and, in their frankness, read almost like a diary. Slonim, whom both women called "the dear one" in their correspondence, was obviously very much on Tsvetaeva's mind. She reported to Chernova when she saw him, when she dreamed about him, what presents he gave her and Alya. In November, she wrote that she had "made up with the 'dear one'." Slonim had accompanied her home, where they discussed the Rodzevich affair, sang little songs, and parted friends.

But when Slonim went away for five days to rest, Tsvetaeva assumed he was with another woman and became angry and jealous. Her rage inspired one of her most powerful poems, "Attempt at Jealousy."[6] With her characteristic lack of restraint, she sent it to Slonim. She may also have had Rodzevich in mind when she wrote this scathing poem, in which the central woman character, though in pain, emerges triumphant. She sees herself as Lilith the seductress, not as Eve the wife. She has no doubt that she is "Carrara marble," while her rival is "plaster dust"; where she was her man's "Sinai," the peak of divine inspiration, the woman he now lives with is a simple earthling. The bitter questions she fires at him whip the poem into a frenzy of contempt, destroying both the lover and the memory of love. By controlling her own pain in order to inflict pain on the other, the speaker triumphs. Tsvetaeva wrote to Chernova: "Let it cut his heart a bit or lash his conceit. At least, for that evening his 'plaster trash' will be poisoned for him."[7] Tsvetaeva soon made up with Slonim; she realized that he was close to her, closer than most people she had met. They remained friends for the rest of her life.

§ In the fall of 1924 the Efrons moved to the village of Vshenory. Tsvetaeva wrote to Chernova: "My life is at home, a life I love and hate, something between a cradle and a coffin, but I have never been either an infant or a corpse!"[8] Alya, now almost twelve, had returned from boarding school and lived with the family again, but she did not attend regular school. Tsvetaeva tutored her and taught her French, but without much enthusiasm. She could not come to terms with the idea that she, a genius, was forced to spend her time cleaning house and worrying about money. Now that Alya was home, Tsvetaeva again forced her to help with the housework, though she also acknowledged Alya's wasted childhood. "Nothing but scrub pails and rags—how can she develop with that? Her only recreation is the gathering of fire-wood," she wrote to Chernova. She didn't want "entertainment" for Alya, but the joy and leisure of childhood, instead of "cleaning, laundry, corners, pails, food, studies, firewood, sleep."

> I feel sorry for her because she is unusually appreciative: she never complains, tries always to make it easier and is happy about little things. She renounces things too easily. But this is not right for an eleven-year-old, since by twenty she will become fiercely angry. Childhood (the ability to have pleasure) is irretrievable.[9]

Efron was not much help to the family. He came home from Prague exhausted, irritated, burdened. He wrote to Chernova:

> I rush and scramble around from the university to the library, to endless and innumerable meetings (which nobody needs), between Prague and Vshenory. I arrive home on a late train, drag myself through the mud, and barely make it to the house. After dinner, prepared by Marina, I fall into bed, my legs and my thoughts—gone. In the morning, at dawn, I run with kangaroo steps to the station! And the same every day. Dozens of people pass before my eyes daily but I see very few of them.[10]

Like Tsvetaeva, Efron, too, may have been looking for a "friend's shoulder" to lean on. In her letters to Chernova, Tsvetaeva often mentioned Katya Reytlinger, a young woman obviously attracted to Efron, whom Tsvetaeva was ready to manipulate to her own advantage. She told how one day Katya, full of enthusiasm and compassion, said: "Marina Ivanovna! What can I do for you? I would give half my life, my right eye, I would give my soul." [11] Tsvetaeva immediately asked her for three pairs of warm underpants for Alya and went on to specify the colors and patterns she wanted. She was aware of Katya's interest in Efron, but she didn't care. The extent of Efron's involvement is not known, but Katya remained part of the Efrons' inner circle in Prague until she married and left for the Soviet Union.

In addition to being exhausted by the demands of his schedule, Efron was also frustrated with his work. He was not particularly involved with his studies, and his attempts to write did not meet with much success. For a while he tried to revive his interest in the theater by producing one of Tsvetaeva's plays and performing in it. But he still felt unhappy and lost. He was eager to return as soon as possible to Russia, but he knew that it would take time because of his White Army past. Now in the process of reevaluating his political views, he was attracted to the pro-Soviet groups in Prague.

Tsvetaeva was far from isolated during these Czech years. Many Russian families lived in the villages around Prague, where they re-created a way of life that would have been familiar to her: the life of Russian dachas, with frequent visits, organized picnics, and many hours spent in the forest gathering mushrooms. The émigrés recited poetry together and put on amateur plays. Despite these simple pleasures, with friends around her and her exploding creativity, Tsvetaeva felt sorry for herself. "What have I seen of life besides dishwater and garbage and how can I, being of sane mind, love it?" she wrote to Chernova. "After all, my existence is just like my landlady's, with only one difference: while she has a secure roof, secure food, a secure corner, all this is up in the air for me. We are head over heels in debt, [ . . . ] even this stamp is borrowed." [12]

Then Tsvetaeva learned she was pregnant. She did not know how to cope with the practical problems involved:

I am scared of the free hospital. A public ward; instead of one infant, twenty; Czech physicians speaking Czech; smoking is forbidden. [ . . . ] The situation with my dresses also looks tragic: the only one I can use is your green one. [ . . . ] I have trouble squeezing into the blue one, and squeezing out of it is practically impossible; some day I will get stuck in it forever (as in an elevator). [ . . . ] Another problem is the need for a girdle. The corset is hopeless, all the bones have come out and it creeps up to my neck so that my stomach is free. A somewhat unnatural look. Of course, you cannot help me. I simply play Lazarus, I play Job, I complain. [13]

She reported ten days later:

> Finally I acquired a girdle. [ . . . ] My spirits lifted immediately; I hate shapelessness. [ . . . ] The weather, however, is lovely; no ice, not a snowflake—autumn with a warm wind—not even a raindrop! [ . . . ] Yesterday we went to the movies with Alya to see "The Niebelungen." A splendid show. And besides, there are poems.[14]

This is typical of Tsvetaeva's correspondence with women—complaints, begging, but still humor, nature, and "besides there are poems." However, those last months of her pregnancy added to her recurrent feelings of confinement and she was depressed. "I am afraid that the trouble (fate) is within me. I don't love anything, really, to the end. [ . . . ] I am unable to love anything except my own soul. I feel cramped in everything, in every person and in every emotion as I do in any room whether it be a hovel or a palace." [15]

In October, Tsvetaeva began to work seriously on her verse play *Ariadne*, the first part of a trilogy dealing with the Theseus legend. She had begun to plan the drama in 1923, but now the theme of carnal love versus immortality was uppermost in her mind. The play was inspired by the Greek legend of Ariadne, the daughter of Minos, who falls in love with Theseus and helps him find his way out of the labyrinth by giving him a thread that she holds. Theseus then deserts her on the isle of Naxos when Bacchus promises immortality for Ariadne if Theseus renounces their love and leaves her. No passion on earth can compare with the prospect of such an exalted fate. In Tsvetaeva's play, Theseus emerges as the tragic hero who sacrifices his happiness on this earth to secure Ariadne's immortality.

On February 1, 1925, Tsvetaeva's son was born. Tsvetaeva called on Dr. Altschuller, a Russian émigré physician who lived nearby, to deliver the baby. At first he had refused to get involved because he was not trained as an obstetrician, but now he came. He found Tsvetaeva alone, chain-smoking in bed, calm and smiling. The baby was already on the way. Altschuller looked around the room for something clean—a piece of soap, a handkerchief—but could find nothing. With the help of some of Tsvetaeva's women friends, he managed to deliver a healthy boy, although the child was two weeks premature and Tsvetaeva's labor was long and painful.

A son—this was Tsvetaeva's dream child! She had never forgotten that her mother wanted a son. When Irina died, Tsvetaeva had promised herself that she would have a son with Sergey. She fantasized about a son with Pasternak, with Rodzevich. A son would heal all her wounds, and would belong totally to her. Even before her son was born she wrote to Chernova that she knew she would be jealous of anyone he loved, and she was worried that he would be drafted into the army in 1946.

Now that her son had arrived, she dreamed of being on an island with him where there would be no one else for him to love. She followed his development day by day and described him when he was a week old as "generally a Tsvetaev." She had wanted to name her son Boris after Pasternak. But Efron for once objected, and the boy was named Georgy. Dr. Altschuller remarked that "she did not want to name her child—if it was a boy—after the husband or the boy's father." [16] He apparently believed the Prague gossip that Rodzevich, not Efron, was the father, although Tsvetaeva's affair was over by the time the child was conceived.

To Chernova, Tsvetaeva wrote: "By the way, the boy is definitely [named] Georgy. [ . . . ] It is easier to give in than to insist. And, besides, I don't want to introduce B. P. [Boris Pasternak] into the family, to make him common property. It would mean some lessening of my rights in him." [17] Tsvetaeva still fantasized about having a son by Pasternak, although she knew that she would never be able to leave Efron. She was unable, she wrote, to "transform love into *everyday* life, to fragment eternity into days. I am not to live with B. P., but I want a son by him, so that *he should live in him through me*." [18] She called her son Mur, inspired by E. T. A. Hoffmann's *Kater Murr*. The spelling differed, but she looked to her son for the qualities of Hoffmann's tomcat—"spirit, intelligence, and sharp claws." [19] She was well aware of her unconditional emotional involvement with Mur from the very beginning: "I was proud of Alya in her childhood, I even showed her off, but this one I love passionately," she wrote to Chernova.[20] She dedicated herself totally to the new baby: nursing, feeding, getting up at night, taking him out for walks.

But at the same time, she was exhausted by the additional burden and fighting a rising depression. She felt lonely, caged in, worn out. As always she needed the intensity of a new friendship to overcome her feeling of emptiness. She found it in Anna I. Andreyeva, the second wife of the Russian writer Leonid Andreyev, who had died in 1919. There was something of the Gypsy about Anna Andreyeva, who attracted Tsvetaeva precisely because she did not fit any mold. Tsvetaeva wrote to Chernova that she found her "willful, difficult, extravagant, impetuous, totally incomprehensible. She is attracted to me [ . . . ] by my strength, I assume. She is made of surprises. We have made some forays and swoops into each other's souls. I have never in my life met such directness: naturalness. [ . . . ] I understand why Andreyev fell in love with her. [ . . . ] I could fall in love with her, not love her."[21]

Every night, she wrote, "we walk around the sleeping village (Sergey half asleep watches the sleeping Mur). We tell one another horror stories about cats and corpses."[22] Their relationship was a purely emotional intoxication, a game with sexual undertones. Andreyeva loved "in her own way, in a burst when under pressure, but she loves. An animal of an alien breed loves an animal of a breed alien to all: me. [ . . . ] She doesn't bother me with her family; she gives herself to me—outside, only at night, in her hours. All this is precious. And I cannot exist (and how I cannot!) without another's love (a stranger's)."[23] The excitement of the flirtation soon came to an end. After six months Andreyeva had had enough and became irritated. Tsvetaeva wrote to Chernova: "I am not sad because I didn't love her [ . . . ] I think that, everything considered, she loved me more."[24]

In July, in her first letter to Pasternak after a long silence, Tsvetaeva summed up her life:

> I myself am the soup that has boiled constantly for the last eight years (1917–1925) on my primus stove. [ . . . ] I boil all day in that cauldron. I've been writing the poem "The Ratcatcher" for five months; I have no time to think, the pen does the thinking. Five minutes in the morning (just time to sit down), ten minutes during the day. The night is mine, but at night I can't give my writing the same attention. I have no friends. They don't like poetry here, and outside of poetry—rather, not poetry but what it is made from—what am I? An inhospitable hostess, a young woman in old dresses.[25]

In that same letter, she reassured Pasternak, who had hinted that he was losing faith in his own poetic powers: "That's where I cannot follow you. To abandon poetry? And then what? Off a bridge into the Moskva River? Well, it is the same with poetry, my dear one, as it is with love: as long as it does not abandon you, you will be a slave to the lyre."[26]

Tsvetaeva reached a new and higher level in her craft in these years in Czechoslovakia. Even the circumstances of her life were relatively favorable. Though the Czech subsidy was just enough to keep them sheltered and poorly fed, still it seemed to offer security. Yet restlessness was taking hold of her; she felt lonely and wanted change. She wrote to Chernova that summer:

I cannot stand another winter in Vshenory; I feel an icy rage in my spine just at the thought. I cannot take this narrow canyon, being squeezed and corked up and this loneliness of a dog (in a doghouse!). Always the same (indifferent) faces, always the same questions, issues. [ . . . ] When winter comes, I definitely want to be out of here! Away! Life here is too difficult, boring and black. Either to Prague, or to Paris.[27]

The Chernovs wrote from Paris, encouraging the Efrons to come and promising to organize a reading for Tsvetaeva. The idea was appealing. While the Efrons were in Prague, the center of the Russian emigration had shifted from Berlin to Paris. Tsvetaeva hoped for a broader audience there.

One of Sergey's friends, an actress, described a visit to the Efrons that summer of 1925:

I remember well my first impression. Marina Ivanovna: not very tall, good figure, attractive looks, with large eyes in a very tanned face, silver bracelets on equally tanned arms, her appearance slightly Gypsy-like. . . . Just as one always does at a first meeting, we talked of all kinds of things, including their intention to move from Prague to Paris. I remember exactly [Efron's] words: "We have to leave. Here Marina might become a cook." [28]

Efron was working on his doctoral dissertation and had developed asthma, but Tsvetaeva decided to go to Paris with the children in the hope that he would follow when he had fully recovered. It was agreed that they would decide, once in Paris, how long they would stay. She hesitated to leave Efron behind and it was difficult to borrow the money for the fare, but the decision was made. On October 31, 1925, Tsvetaeva, Alya, and Mur left Prague and set out by train for Paris.

# 16. Paris, Success and New Problems

*Every poet is essentially an émigré, even in Russia.*
*The poet is an émigré from the heavenly kingdom and*
*from the earthly paradise of nature.*[1]

T svetaeva left Prague committed more than ever to her calling as a poet, to her special destiny. The reality of her life—poverty, disenchantment in love affairs, the growing awareness that the cause of her unhappiness was within herself—made her see the world and her own body more and more as prisons from which she longed to escape.

In her last months in Czechoslovakia, Tsvetaeva had written most of "The Ratcatcher: A Lyrical Satire."[2] She finished the last canto in Paris. Her source was the well-known German legend, used by Goethe, Heine, and Browning, among others. For Tsvetaeva, this cruel tale proved a perfect vehicle for many of the themes she was grappling with at the time. The poem's strongest quality is the mixture of sarcastic wit and vitality with which the world of the rich, "fat" citizens of Hamelin is contrasted with the lyrical, pure "Beyond." This is Tsvetaeva at her best, transforming her joy and bitterness, love and hatred into superb poetry.

Canto I describes the "lovely" town of Hamelin, where life is cheap and death is serene. Happy spouses sleep together forever. "Both sweat together, both rot together." Only sin and souls are missing. Hamelin has no beggars; Hamelin has good manners and full barns. The abode of the healthy, of the righteous, it is "paradise." Neither too hot nor too cold, it lives by the clock, and everything is undertaken in moderation. In Canto II, Tsvetaeva introduces us to the psyche of Hamelin's burghers. In other towns:

> Husbands dream of
> Mermaids, wives of Byrons,

> Infants — of devils
> Maids — of horsemen.

In Hamelin:

> The husband sees his wife,
> The wife sees her husband,
>
> The infant — a nipple,
> The round-faced beauty
> Her father's sock she just darned.

With the introduction of the burghers, Tsvetaeva's loathing of the bourgeois world explodes, and she imagines building a hundred-domed temple to her hatred of it all. Only the mayor's daughter, who dreams of "fragrances, whispers," is exempt from her scorn. In her notes on the poem, Tsvetaeva wrote that the mayor's daughter personified the soul.

The satire of Canto III is so biting, the sounds and rhymes so vivid, that we see and hear the cozy marketplace with its contented citizens milling around, interested only in their food, their health, and their gossip. Their refrain in German is "*Zuviel ist ungesund*" ("Too much is unhealthy"). The rats come. They stand for those who rebel against hunger. They are the "revolutionaries," the proletariat, organized according to the Soviet model and using Soviet slogans. But they also succumb to the same vices as the citizens of Hamelin and the citizens of Moscow under the NEP: greed and vulgarity. They desecrate the Bible with grease and destroy the law books. Chaos reigns, and the new "rules" bring terror: "Whoever is not barefoot is a bloodsucker, / Whoever hasn't been beaten is a parasite." When a copy of the poem found its way to Moscow, Pasternak, who was living with the Communist bureaucrats, with the rats, wrote to Tsvetaeva: "If I had not read 'The Ratcatcher,' I would more easily reconcile myself to my present path of compromise (which has already become natural to me)."[3]

When the rule of the rats becomes unbearable, the mayor issues a proclamation offering his daughter's hand to anyone who will rid the town of this plague. At that very hour a man in green carrying a flute slowly enters the town. Canto IV is Tsvetaeva's hymn celebrating change and rebellion. The flutist's Ti-ri-li sings of the glory of breaking away, of leaving behind a comfortable bourgeois life. The flutist conjures up the beauty of an unknown land — the Himalayas, Hindustan, Paradise. The rats fall under his spell and the flutist leads them toward a pond where they will drown. He consoles them with Tsvetaeva's credo of a Beyond better than life. The canto's final image of circles in the water is cruel in its brevity.

In Canto V Hamelin celebrates the flutist's victory over the rats with food and music making. Soon, though, the members of the town council realize that they must make good on the Mayor's promise. But in their view it is simply unacceptable for a musician to marry the Mayor's daughter.

> —What is music? The twittering of birds!
> A joke! A child can do it!
> —What is music? A noise in one's ears.
> A marriage entertainment.

A long sequence follows in mockery of the councilmen's contempt as they face the musician, music, art. Music is anarchy, music is the Devil! Then one of the councilmen, the councilman "of the romantic," finds a new argument against the marriage of the flutist to the Mayor's daughter. Marriage is not for him. The flutist, he claims, belongs to those who live in a higher, better world.

So the councilmen decide to reward the flutist with something else, something practical: a fishing rod? a dozen cheap socks? a watch-case? a painting in oil of the Kaiser on horseback? a small briefcase? a cane? Finally, they agree upon a case for his flute. And not too expensive, either, because the main thing is to show him appreciation. A papier-maché case would be just the thing. Understandably, the flutist is outraged. In Tsvetaeva's voice, he extols the role of the musician and the poet: "The sound is not in the instrument— / But in us. Break the flute!"

Pasternak appreciated the next canto, Canto VI, most, calling it "a cruel chapter, terrible, to which one listens entirely with one's heart; it is all smiles and still it is cruel, terrible." It begins with the children's liberation from school, from the clock, from the parental home, from everyday life. The sound of the flute makes them throw away their school books and follow the flutist, who has "dolls for the girls, guns for the boys / and waffles for all." The rhythm of the lines reminded Pasternak of a funeral procession. Some doubters among the children have heard rumors that the flutist is leading them toward their death, but they cannot withstand the magic of his music. He tells them of the paradise where he is taking them—a paradise where all that matters is essence, meaning, hearing, sound. Attracted by this sweet music, the Mayor's daughter joins the group of children, and the flutist becomes even more enticing:

To live means to age
Steadily to age and to grow gray.
To live is for the enemy!
Everything eternal is on the other shore!

The last lines of the poem suggest in a few words the children's death. They die like the rats: "Mother, do not call to dinner! / Bu-b-b-les." Tsvetaeva refuses to see the suffering of these mothers. The poem is fueled by her rage. Her most powerful poems need the intensity of either love or hate, compassion or contempt. Her rage can best be understood by recognizing the pain and frustration that her nature actually invited. Her burning desire for absolute communication, absolute love, absolute merger could never be satisfied because they existed only in her imagination. She had to turn to the "Beyond" of her own making, and to reach it no sacrifice was too much. Of course, the poem also defines Tsvetaeva's own persona. She is the piper: proud and superior, but betrayed, misunderstood, insulted—in pain. She too inhabits the Hamelin of the poem; she has no tolerance for its citizens, and no compassion for the grief of its mothers. If anything, she longs to join the children in death.

"The Ratcatcher" was serialized in *Freedom of Russia* in Prague and thus addressed only a small Russian reading public; in the Soviet Union it was unknown. Emigré critics did not pay much attention to this original work. Only Dimitry S. Mirsky, a prominent Russian literary historian and critic, gave it a well-deserved review, emphasizing not only its poetic beauty but its political and ethical significance.


Olga Chernova and her three daughters, Olya, Natalya, and Ariadna, welcomed Tsvetaeva and her children to Paris on November 1, 1925. The family lived on the Rue Rouvet in a new building surrounded by factories, on the outskirts of the city. They gave one of their three rooms to Tsvetaeva and furnished it with a writing desk, a rare luxury for her. Tsvetaeva's letters from Paris to Teskova in Prague now replaced her correspondence with Chernova. Teskova, herself a writer and translator, was an admirer of Tsvetaeva's poetry; as the head of the Czech-Russian Society she had often invited Tsvetaeva to give readings. Now she became the listener to whom Tsvetaeva turned with all her many problems. Tsvetaeva's letters were full of complaints about her daily routine: the lack of privacy that did not permit her to write, the lack of time to see Paris or Versailles. Prague—now, even

Moscow—seemed better in retrospect. She hated the working-class neighborhood and was irritated because it took longer than she had expected to find a hall at the right price where her reading could take place. She begged Teskova to get her a dark dress for the reading from some "rich lady," a feat that Teskova managed to accomplish.

Tsvetaeva's letters to Olga Chernova had been overwhelming in their frankness and intimacy, but after less than two months of living together, Tsvetaeva began to refer to the Chernovas as her "landladies" in her letters. She never mentioned either their friendship or the hardships her presence imposed on the family, for whom she was the center of attention. All three daughters and their fiancés—Vadim Andreyev, Daniil Reznikov, and Vladimir Sosynsky—were intensely interested in Russian literature and admired Tsvetaeva's poetry. Natalya Chernova, who later married Reznikov, has recalled this period:

> Everyone in those years shared in the common poverty of emigration. Yet, this was not real poverty; there were potatoes, macaroni, soup from cubes, margarine, small cheap red apples. People always talk about that heartbreaking poverty, about hardship, but there was something else: common youth, daring, poetry, and the love of poetry. . . . There were still many good things in [Tsvetaeva's] life. Many understood and loved her poems. Everything was boundless in her, especially her talent. The tragic element was within herself.[4]

Tsvetaeva's awareness of this element appears clearly in her letter to Teskova of December 30, 1925: "I don't like life as such. For me it begins to have importance, to acquire meaning and weight only when transformed, for example, in art. If you were to take me across the ocean—into paradise—and forbid me to write, I would reject both the ocean and the paradise."[5]

She ends this letter with the chilling words: "I terribly dislike living."

Tsvetaeva's first poetry reading in Paris had been planned for January, but it proved too difficult to find a hall, sell tickets, and get a dress and shoes by that time. Finally, in early February, the reading took place in a packed hall before a tremendously enthusiastic audience. It was a total success. Encouraged by this response, the Efrons decided to stay in Paris for the time being, a decision made easier by the fact that they were still receiving their subsidies from Czechoslovakia.

Efron had joined the family during the Christmas holidays. Soon after he arrived, he found a new cause in the Eurasian movement, a political movement that had been founded in Sofia, but whose center had shifted to Berlin and then to Paris. Among the Eurasians were important historians and philosophers who believed that Russia was not only a European but an Asian country, and that as such it had to create its own civilization, its own political institutions. The Eurasians were opposed to any counterrevolutionary activity or foreign intervention in the Soviet Union. No wonder, then, that this group was suspected by many Russian émigrés of having pro-Soviet sympathies.

Together with Mirsky and Pyotr P. Suvchinsky, another prominent Eurasian thinker, Efron began working on the publication of a literary journal that took its name from Tsvetaeva's collections, *Versts*. They planned to publish works of high literary quality, whether the authors lived in the Soviet Union or in emigration. Tsvetaeva appeared in the pages of the three issues published in 1926–1928.

Tsvetaeva's first personal encounter with Mirsky probably took place at one of the Eurasian meetings. Mirsky had reviewed some of her poetry in 1922 and recently had praised "The Ratcatcher." Though he had reservations about her early collections, he caught the essence of her art:

> [Tsvetaeva's] poetry comes from the soul; it is willful, capricious, and terribly lively. It is very difficult to push Tsvetaeva into the chain of poetic tradition; she emerges not from the poets preceding her, but directly from under the Arbat pavement.* The anarchistic quality of her art is expressed in the extraordinary freedom and the variety of her forms and devices, as well as in her profound indifference to canonized rules and taste. She can write worse than anyone else, it seems, but when she succeeds, she creates things of inexpressible beauty, of almost incredible transparency, lightness, like cigarette smoke . . . and often with a merry challenge and mischief.[6]

He became a great admirer of her work, as well as a good friend. He was a professor of Russian literature at London University and divided his time between London and Paris. In March 1926, at his invitation, Tsvetaeva went to London for a couple of weeks, where she stayed at the house of a friend and wrote to Teskova how much she enjoyed the luxury of a "vacation." Mirsky became involved in pro-Soviet politics and joined the British Communist Party in 1931. He helped support the Efron family financially until he left for

---

*One of the main streets of Moscow.

the Soviet Union in 1932. He was arrested there in 1937 and died in a labor camp in 1939.

Before leaving on her London "vacation," Tsvetaeva mailed an essay called "The Poet on Criticism" to a new journal, *The Well-Intentioned One* (Blagonamerenny), published by Prince Dmitry Shakhovskoy in Brussels. Tsvetaeva's work was appearing in the most important émigré journals and newspapers in Prague, Berlin, and Paris. Such major critics as Slonim and Mirsky recognized her brilliance. She had a responsive audience, and she knew that she was admired in the Soviet Union, not only by Pasternak but by other young poets. But this was not enough for her. She was angered by reviewers who called her work complex and obscure, and she was frustrated because some of her manuscripts did not find publishers. She felt offended and so she hit back.

In "The Poet on Criticism" Tsvetaeva combined her theoretical views on the function of critics in general with attacks on specific critics who were either named or presented in such a way that their identities were not difficult to guess. In the appendix, which she called "A Flowerbed," she quoted from the writings of Georgy Adamovich, a poet and influential critic, to demonstrate what she saw as his incompetence, inconsistency, and lack of taste. He was her prime target, but not the only one. Her language was deliberately insulting when she wrote about other prominent critics: "the lamentable article by the academician Bunin," "the rosewater that trickles through the articles of Eichenwald," "the feigned perplexity of Zinaida Gippius," "Yablonsky's truly indecent article on Remizov," and so on. The article attacked both émigré and Soviet critics, but the main thrust of its offensive was directed against the émigré literary establishment.

Published in May 1926, "The Poet on Criticism" created a storm of reaction that descended on Tsvetaeva at the seashore at St. Gilles in the Vendée region, where she had gone with her family at the end of April. Writers and critics of the Russian émigré community rallied in their defense of Tsvetaeva's targets and criticized her almost unanimously for the content and the tone of her essay. The Russian émigré press was filled with vicious personal attacks on her. Peter Struve, a highly respected Socialist Revolutionary, published an article entitled "About Sterility and Insolence," attacking Tsvetaeva's poems as well.

It is typical of Tsvetaeva's aggressiveness that in this article she described her imperative need for money to enable her to continue writing poetry but deliberately alienated the influential people who might have helped her. But feeling entirely justified in her criticism, seeing her role as the lofty poet set upon by petty, ignorant critics, she was astonished and even wounded by the hostile reaction. She accused her friends Lebedev and Slonim of failing to come to her support. To Teskova she wrote, "*not one voice in my defense. I am totally content.*" [7]

## 17 . The Correspondence with Rilke and Pasternak

*Oh the losses into the All, Marina, the stars that are falling!*
*We can't make it larger, wherever we fling ourselves, to whatever*
*Star we may go!*
— Rainer Maria Rilke [1]

I t was almost preordained that Tsvetaeva would find the consolation she needed in her correspondence with Pasternak and Rainer Maria Rilke, which began in May 1926. Here were the only two living poets whom she considered her equals and who shared not only her emotional intensity but her opinion of the modern world. The correspondence was initiated in December 1925 with a letter to Rilke from Pasternak's father, Leonid Pasternak, the well-known painter. He had met Rilke during the latter's visits to Russia in 1899 and 1900 and now wrote to him on the occasion of the poet's fiftieth birthday. In his reply, Rilke not only expressed his delight at having heard from his old friend but mentioned, too, that he had read some of Boris's poems in translation in a French anthology and found them "very beautiful."

The news of this letter reached Boris Pasternak after some delay, arriving, coincidentally, on the same day, April 3, as a typescript of Tsvetaeva's "Poem of the End." Pasternak was wrestling with one of his depressions; Tsvetaeva's poem and the news about Rilke restored his creativity. Once Rilke's letter was finally in his hands, Pasternak wrote to him on April 12, sending the letter to his father in Germany with the request that he forward it to Rilke, who was living in Switzerland at the time. (Switzerland, unlike Germany and France, had no postal or diplomatic connections with the Soviet Union.) "Great, most beloved poet!" he wrote, "I am indebted to you for the fundamental cast of my character, the nature of my intellectual being. They are your creations." [2]

Hoping for a continuing correspondence with his adored master, Pasternak introduced Marina Tsvetaeva to him, not only because she was a great poet, but because letters could be forwarded from her Paris address; through Tsvetaeva, he anticipated a faster exchange of letters. He told Rilke how happy Tsvetaeva would be to receive an autographed copy of one of his books directly from him, adding that he, Pasternak, would know by the book's arrival that he might write to Rilke again.

So began the short-lived epistolary exchange between three great poets of our century: Rilke, gravely ill; Tsvetaeva, exiled and indigent; and Pasternak, depressed and restricted. Rilke had influenced both Pasternak and Tsvetaeva long before this correspondence. Both had responded to his nonreligious mysticism, his search for spiritual values, and his rejection of materialism and the world around him. Pasternak had translated parts of Rilke's *Book of Images*; they both knew of his "love affair" with Russia. Tsvetaeva's poem "Eurydice to Orpheus," written in Prague in 1922, echoes Rilke's interpretation of the myth in his "Orpheus, Eurydice, Hermes." Death and the "Beyond" appealed to both of them more than earthly existence. In both poems, Eurydice prefers the other world. "In Eurydice and Orpheus there is an echo of Marusya with the Swain," Tsvetaeva wrote to Pasternak. "Orpheus came for her [Eurydice] to live," she adds, "but the other [the vampire] came for mine [Marusya] not to live. That is why she (I) rushed to him. Had I been Eurydice, I would have been ashamed . . . to go back!"[3]

There was, however, a more personal emotional link between Tsvetaeva and Pasternak as well as between Tsvetaeva and Rilke. Tsvetaeva and Pasternak shared similar childhood memories—their mothers were talented pianists who had given up their professional ambitions because of the prejudices of their time. Tsvetaeva and Rilke were both poets of longing who felt that they had disappointed their mothers—Rilke's mother had hoped for a girl, had dressed him like a girl and called him "Miss" in their games;[4] Tsvetaeva never forgot that her mother wanted a son. This early feeling of abandonment by their mothers, the pain of early rejection, created in both of them a longing for a better world.

Pasternak treasured Rilke's messages. After his death, an envelope marked "The most precious" was found in a leather wallet tucked in one of the pockets of his jacket. It contained two light blue sheets of paper. One was Rilke's short undated note thanking Pasternak for his letter and informing him that the *Duino Elegies* and the *Sonnets to Orpheus* were already in Tsvetaeva's hands. On a second sheet of paper Tsvetaeva had copied sentences from a letter to her in which Rilke had referred to Pasternak: "I am so shaken by the fullness and power of his message to me that I cannot say more today, but would you send the enclosed sheet to our friend in Moscow for me? As a greeting." [5]

In her own way, Tsvetaeva made it equally clear how important the correspondence was to her. Not only did she insist in writing that it be published in its entirety after a fifty-year interval, but she took special care to keep the letters from falling into the wrong hands. After returning to the Soviet Union in 1939 and before being evacuated from Moscow at the beginning of the German invasion of Russia, she entrusted to Aleksandra Rabinina, an editor at the State Publishing House, all her letters from Rilke, some of his photographs and autographed books, and eleven letters from Pasternak. On the package she wrote: "Rilke and Pasternak, 1926." In 1975 Rabinina transmitted the letters to Pasternak's heirs. Tsvetaeva's letters to Rilke are in the Rilke archive; her letters to Pasternak were lost during the war but were reconstructed from her notebooks. The Soviet Rilke scholar Konstantin Azadovsky worked with Pasternak's son Yevgeny and his daughter-in-law Yelena to edit and annotate the correspondence, which has been published in German, French, Italian, and English.[6]

The pattern of the correspondence shows Tsvetaeva's central role. There is only one letter from Pasternak to Rilke and one note from Rilke to Pasternak, but there are eleven letters from Pasternak to Tsvetaeva (sometimes two in one envelope) and five letters from Tsvetaeva to Pasternak; six letters from Rilke to Tsvetaeva and nine from Tsvetaeva to Rilke. This imbalance was partly due to problems with the mail, but certainly Tsvetaeva's need for intense, exclusive relationships contributed to the odd pattern of the correspondence. Already, in her answer to Rilke's first letter, Tsvetaeva hints at her jealousy, mentioning that while the ocean reads his letter along with her, "I wonder if such a fellow-reader troubles you. There won't be any other; I'm much too jealous (zealous—where you are concerned)." [7] Eventually Tsvetaeva antagonized both Pasternak and Rilke.

Rilke's first letter to Tsvetaeva, dated May 3, 1926, was accompanied by copies of the *Duino Elegies* and *Sonnets to Orpheus*, inscribed to her. Books for Pasternak were to follow. Rilke's inscription on Tsvetaeva's copy of the *Elegies*—Tsvetaeva who had called herself the "winged one" in many of her poems—amounted to a meeting not only of minds but of spirits:

> We touch each other; how? with wingstrokes,
> With distances themselves we touch each other.

One sole poet lives, and now and then
The one who bore him, and who bears him now, will meet.[8]

Tsvetaeva had met the poet of her dreams. Pasternak was eclipsed.

At first, Pasternak, encouraged by Rilke's calling his poems "very beautiful" and inspired by Tsvetaeva's "Poem of the End," felt reborn. He was optimistic, even elated, and his letters to Tsvetaeva at the end of April and the beginning of May are filled with his exalted desire to join her. In a dream about her, he wrote, "I loved you as in life I had only dreamed of loving, long, long ago, loving to eternity."[9] Although he had been married since 1922 to Zhenya—a painter with whom he had been madly in love and the mother of his son—he called Tsvetaeva "his only legitimate heaven and wife." Now he wanted to join Tsvetaeva, to go with her to Rilke, but he hesitated, feeling that he ought to use his rekindled creativity to advance his work. Should he come to Paris now, he asked Tsvetaeva, or wait for a year? But she was not ready for a meeting. Five years later she recalled Pasternak's hopes of joining her. "Boris, after reading somewhere my 'Poem of the End,' was madly drawn to me; he wanted to come—I sidestepped the issue, not wanting a total disaster," she wrote to Teskova.[10]

Pasternak, no doubt hurt by Tsvetaeva's rejection and her failure to share Rilke's letters, was shocked when, early in May, Tsvetaeva asked him to assist Parnok, whose latest poetry collection, *Musica*, had been ignored by the Soviet press. She enclosed in her letter a poem from her cycle "Woman-Friend." Pasternak was appalled by the "pain, jealousy, tears and suffering" she expressed in evoking an old love—and a lesbian love at that—and refused to have anything to do with Parnok, with whom he had "never had anything in common."[11]

In early May, Tsvetaeva and Rilke exchanged letters in which they shared their deepest feelings about poetry and the role of the poet. Tsvetaeva wrote to Rilke: "You are a phenomenon of nature that cannot be mine and that one does not so much love as undergo, or (still too little) the fifth element incarnate: poetry itself or (still too little) that whence poetry comes to be and which is greater than it (you)."[12] To Rilke she expressed her hope that the three poets would meet. Tsvetaeva sent him her *Poems to Blok* and *Psyche*; he sent her a copy of his *Vergers*. She told him of her premonition about the delivery of the books he had sent her, one that seemed to confirm her sense of a special psychic tie between them. "The children were still asleep (seven A.M.)," she wrote. "I suddenly got up and ran to the door. At the *same* moment—I had my hand on the door handle—the postman knocked—right into my hand. I merely had to end my door-opening movement and from the same still-rapping hand receive the books." [13]

Tsvetaeva introduced Rilke to her family, and wrote about her appreciation of Pasternak. They exchanged pictures. After Rilke mentioned in his second letter that he had been living in a sanatorium since December, she asked him about his health. Rilke wrote about his broken marriage, his adult daughter, about the solitude he loved and his present threatening illness, which "the doctors *cannot* understand." [14] In his third letter (May 17) Rilke asked Tsvetaeva to forgive him if "all of a sudden I should turn uncommunicative," and he admitted that he had trouble understanding her poetry because his Russian wasn't as good as it should be. This was enough to break Tsvetaeva's sensation of absolute bliss.

As for her correspondence with Pasternak, the mail between Moscow and France was quite erratic, and it is in most cases difficult to know whether any one letter came in response to another. But her letter of May 22 to Pasternak was unmistakably a reaction to Rilke's letter of May 17 to her. She was depressed, irritated, sarcastic. Though she could not have been unaware that Pasternak longed for more contact with Rilke, she now included him in what she perceived as Rilke's rejection: "I tell you Rilke is overburdened; he doesn't need anything or anyone. [ . . . ] Yes, yes, despite the fervor of his letters, his unerring ear, and the purity of his attention—he does not need me, or you. He has outgrown having friends. For me this encounter is a great wound, a blow to my heart." [15]

Pasternak, meanwhile, was disappointed and deeply unhappy because Tsvetaeva had not shared Rilke with him—had not even added a few personal lines when she sent him Rilke's short note. Working on his *Lieutenant Schmidt*, which he dedicated to Tsvetaeva, he needed her reassurance. Now, on May 23, he was troubled by her attitude toward both Rilke and himself:

> I have a vague feeling that you are gently pushing me away from him. And since I see the three of us as a unit held in a single embrace, that means you are pushing me away from you, too, without openly acknowledging it. [ . . . ] I am not writing to Rilke at present. I love him no less than you do. It saddens me that you don't understand this. How is it that you didn't think of telling me how he inscribed the books he sent you, and how it all came about, and perhaps something from his letters? After all, you stood at the very heart of the explosion and suddenly—there you are, off to one side. His blessing is what gives me the strength to carry on. [16]

On the same day Pasternak wrote this letter, Tsvetaeva began one to him that she went on writing for three days. It was full of tenderness, of longing for Boris. She told him how she talked to him while pushing Mur's carriage on an unfamiliar road. She daydreamed about their being together some-where—in Moscow, in St. Gilles, in a dream. "Now I am here with you in the Vendée in May 1926, playing endless games, switching from game to game, collecting seashells with you, cracking open green gooseberries, the color of my eyes." [17] She recalled her childhood in Tarusa: "the Khlysty, five years old." [18] It is interesting that at a time when she felt rejected, she remembered the sect whose members loved her better than anyone else. Yet the figure of Rilke overshadowed everything: "Oh, Boris, Boris, lick my wound. And tell me why. Show me that all is as it should be. No, don't lick it; cauterize it." [19] She tried to accept the finality of Rilke's silence, but she could not help re-turning to it again in the letter: "I don't write to Rilke. It's too distressing. And fruitless. It upsets me, upsets my poetry." But then her anger and her pride surged in her: "I am no less than he is (in the future), and I am younger than he, many lives younger." [20]

On June 3, Tsvetaeva wrote to Rilke again. She wanted him to know that she had overcome the pain he had caused her; it was a letter of supreme, proud renunciation. Rilke answered almost immediately, on June 8, and sent her his "Elegy for Marina Zwetaewa-Efron" and five photographs. Their con-nection was restored.

Around this time, Tsvetaeva asked Ilya Ehrenburg, who was traveling from Paris to Moscow, to give Pasternak her "Poem of the Mountain," "The Rat-catcher," and some personal gifts. Shortly afterward she sent him copies of Rilke's first two letters to her. Pasternak was ecstatic. He had undergone a financial and domestic crisis and was burdened with doubts about his work. The uncertainties in his relationship with Tsvetaeva and Rilke weighed heavily on him. Now he was reassured and believed that all his doubts had been due to misunderstandings. He dreamed again of the three of them united in their love for one another. Still, he could not conceal in his letter to Tsvetaeva that he blamed her for having excluded him for so long and for criticizing Rilke unjustly. By mid-June he mailed to Tsvetaeva the first part of *Lieutenant Schmidt* and a collection of his poetry published in 1917.

But now that Rilke had reentered Tsvetaeva's life with his "Elegy," her hope for a special relationship with him was renewed. Pasternak's image began again to fade even as Tsvetaeva knew quite well that her behavior was hurt-ful to him. "Listen, Rainer, from the beginning, so you'll know. I am wicked. Boris is good," she wrote to Rilke. She felt no remorse and admitted freely that Pasternak was the injured party. "Boris has made me a present of you. And, having barely received you, I want to have you for my own. Ugly enough. And painful enough—for him. That's why I sent [him] those letters." [21]

That summer Pasternak was anxious and depressed. He still longed for Tsvetaeva. "How I do love you!" he wrote. "How deeply and for how long have I done so! It was precisely this impulse, this love for you, formerly un-identified, that gnawed at me from within and darkened and saddened me from without, that weighed down my hands and shackled my feet. It is pre-cisely because of the nature of this passion that I am languid and unsuccessful and just what I am." [22] Still, despite his anguish, he analyzed "The Ratcatcher" almost line by line, with enormous attention to its technical aspects. Carried away by the musicality of Tsvetaeva's verse, he wrote: "The privileges ac-corded rhythm in [the Cantos] "Exodus" and "Children's Paradise" are prac-tically limitless—a lyric poet's dream. Here we have the subjective rhythm of the writer, his passion, his ecstasy, his soaring flights of fancy—in other words, something that is rarely successful: art that makes itself the subject." [23]

Almost on the same day Tsvetaeva wrote to Pasternak analyzing *Lieuten-ant Schmidt*. She was very critical of this novel in verse, finding it inferior to the rest of his work. His hero, she wrote, was "a student not a sailor," and "the poem rushes past Schmidt. He is an obstruction." [24] Pasternak was disappointed: "To write something that turns out to be bad is an unex-ampled misfortune for the members of our brotherhood." [25] Tsvetaeva began her next letter to Pasternak: "I couldn't live with you, Boris, not because I don't understand you, but because I do." [26] His letters in that same month, though, kept their exalted, confessional tone and described his weaknesses, his anxiety, his uncontrollable lusts. He admitted that he loved his wife Zhenya "more than anything on earth." Tsvetaeva's reply showed little toler-ance for his human failings and even less inclination to share him with his wife: "I am speaking of the ancient, insatiable hate of Psyche for Eve. Eve, of whom there is nothing in me. Of Psyche—everything." [27]

Later in July, Tsvetaeva wrote to Pasternak that she felt their correspon-dence had come to an end. Pasternak accepted her decision. He assured her of his undying love, of his need for her friendship, and asked her never to leave him without her address. He begged her, however, not to write to him. "You know what torture it would be for me to get a letter from you and *not answer it*. Let mine be the last. I give you my blessing—you, Alya, Mur, and Sergey, and all who are near and dear to you." [28] It is not entirely clear who broke off the relationship. Pasternak wrote to his wife that it was Tsvetaeva, but Tsvetaeva wrote to Rilke that Boris had stopped writing to her. In any event, Tsvetaeva's jealousy of Pasternak's wife was unconcealed. When his wife went on a vacation with their son to France, Tsvetaeva wrote to Rilke that she did not like the idea at all of Pasternak's writing to both of them in the same country: "To sleep with her and write to me—all right; write to her and write to me, two envelopes, two addresses (in one France), to become *sisters* through the handwriting . . . him for a brother—yes, her—for a sister—no."[29] The Tsvetaeva-Pasternak dialogue, for the time being, had ended.

Now Rilke alone held Tsvetaeva's attention. He had written to her from Ragaz, where he had gone to meet friends, reminding her that although she was a "great star," it was Pasternak who had "placed the telescope in front of my sky for me." Tsvetaeva's eagerness, however, to go to Rilke was becoming difficult for her to control, to the point that she was unable to understand that Rilke was referring to his ill health when he wrote in that same letter: "But my life is so curiously heavy in me that I often cannot stir it from its place; gravity seems to be forming a new relationship to it."[30]

Tsvetaeva's answer of August 2 was a bitter confession of the struggle between the spirit and the flesh she had renounced in her letters to Pasternak and in many of her poems.

Rainer, another reason I want to come to you is the new Me, the one who can arise only with you, in you. And then Rainer, [ . . . ] don't be cross with me—it is me talking—I want to sleep with you, fall asleep and sleep. [ . . . ] Sometimes I think: I must exploit the chance that I am still (after all) body. Soon I'll have no more arms. And more—it sounds like confession (what is confession? to boast of one's blackness! Who could speak of his sufferings without feeling inspired, which is to say happy?)—so, to keep it from sounding like confession: bodies are bored with me [ . . . ]. Soul is never loved so much as body; at most it is praised. With a thousand souls they love the body. Who has ever courted damnation for the sake of a *soul?* [ . . . ]

Everything that *never* sleeps would like to sleep its fill in your arms. Right down into the soul (throat)—that's what the kiss would be like.[31]

When Rilke did not reply immediately, Tsvetaeva wrote again begging for a meeting. In his last letter to her (August 19), Rilke did not hide his fear of "the oddly persistent affliction I am going through and often feel hardly likely to get over." He would have liked to believe in a meeting with her, but he sensed that it was not to be. He expressed his distress that in some way he had come between Pasternak and Tsvetaeva since he knew by now that their correspondence had lapsed. "I still find you stern, almost harsh toward him [Pasternak] (and stern toward me, if you like, in that Russia must never and nowhere exist for me except through you)."[32] This last reproach was provoked by Tsvetaeva's assertion in her letter of August 2: "In Rainerland I alone represent Russia."[33] Tsvetaeva wrote to him once more on August 22 to tell him that she was returning from St. Gilles to Paris in October and hoped to meet him in November. Rilke did not respond.

It is true that when these great poets engage in shop talk—Pasternak's extraordinary technical analysis of "The Ratcatcher," Tsvetaeva's criticism of *Lieutenant Schmidt*, Rilke's understanding and appreciation of the other two poets—they are, as the editors of the correspondence put it, "initiates of the same myth."[34] But, on the other hand, it seems to me that reviewers, biographers, and Tsvetaeva scholars have often exaggerated the full understanding and harmony among the three poets. As we have seen, this was not really a tripartite correspondence (as it is often called) since Tsvetaeva successfully pushed Pasternak aside. Anna Tavis, primarily a Rilke scholar, has brought out the gulf between Rilke and Tsvetaeva. "Rilke was an accomplished dialogical letter writer," she points out, while, "narcissistically enveloped in her emotions, Tsvetaeva violated the most sacred principle of letter-writing, turning a deaf ear to Rilke's voice. . . . Tsvetaeva's deafness to the subtle undertones in Rilke's correspondence resulted from listening exclusively to the echo of her own voice."[35]

For Tsvetaeva this was another painful non-meeting. Vishnyak, Bakhrakh, Rodzevich had left her, in different ways, with an open wound. The émigré literary critics were attacking her mercilessly—not without her provocation, but it still hurt. She yearned for hope. She may have seen in the distant Rilke the Swain, may have wanted to soar with him into the spiritual realm they both knew. In her desperate quest for connection she followed her self-defeating route, demanding the impossible and ending with nothing for herself as a woman. Yet, despite the non-meetings—in life and in letters—between Tsvetaeva and Rilke, Rilke's poetic influence became even stronger in Tsvetaeva's work.

The two long poems that Tsvetaeva wrote in May, June, and July of that year, "From the Sea" and "Attempt at a Room," were inspired by Pasternak and are evidence of a move toward mysticism and into the freedom of new creative forms. "From the Sea," addressed to Pasternak and written on the beach of St. Gilles, was originally called "Instead of a Letter." Based on a dream described by Pasternak in a letter to Tsvetaeva, the poem begins in an almost playful mood. The meeting of the two poets in a dream allows the narrator to jump from her dream into his—reality is suspended. They play games with the sea, share memories of childhood and thoughts about time. The mood of the poem changes, however, from a feeling of liberation to one of dread before the huge sea. Tsvetaeva never liked the ocean, was even afraid of it: the only consolation is sleep and dreams.

"Attempt at a Room," written during her correspondence with Rilke, shows his growing influence on her work. Again it takes place in a dream, perhaps in a nightmare; it is a strange poem, steeped in anxiety and dread. The style is elliptical and difficult. The room of the title has only three walls; the persona is waiting for someone—originally it was to have been Pasternak; later, she would change the addressee to Rilke. The main symbol of the poem, the corridor, underscores Tsvetaeva's preference for being between destinations. But here it seems that there is nowhere to go; the world outside is as much in chaos as her own. There are executions, Pushkin's duel; everything is in flux. Véronique Lossky, the French Tsvetaeva scholar, translator, and biographer, says that it is "a world of objects without soul. . . . This world of inanimate objects is a vision of death." [36]

In August she also finished "Poem of the Staircase," which she had begun in January. In this poem, the working poor rush up and down the back stairs of a Paris tenement: the smells of cabbage, garlic, and dirt are the "Coty" of the poor; there is no time for tenderness, not even for a greeting. The dehumanized existence of the poor is seen in a collage of sharply observed images, given in short, staccato stanzas reminiscent of "The Ratcatcher." Then night descends on the staircase—a time of silence, of cleanliness, even of stars. Nightfall, the hour of redemption, brings some hope and introduces the rebellion of objects, which want to return to their original state—before man transformed wood into furniture and iron into railroad tracks. When a fire breaks out, caused by an accident with matches, it brings, as it so often does in Tsvetaeva's poetic world, both destruction and liberation. The fire's mission is to destroy things but to save people. All the same, a final stanza tells us that the next morning life goes on as before.

The summer of 1926 had begun with the news that the Efrons' Czech subsidy would be in jeopardy if the family did not return to Prague. Tsvetaeva believed that the Czech authorities might refuse to renew the subsidy because the Paris critics had attacked her in response to her article "The

Poet and Criticism." Convinced that the critics had been motivated by envy or frustration, she now worried that she might find herself out on the street with her children. She wrote to Teskova that she would love to return to Prague, but Efron would be unlikely to find work there. When they were informed that the subsidy would be reduced by half, but not canceled, they decided to stay in France.

The first issue of the journal Versts, which appeared in July, only added to the fury of Tsvetaeva's attackers. Pasternak, Yesenin, Babel, and Mayakovsky appeared in its pages, together with Tsvetaeva and Remizov. To publish Soviet authors was regarded as pro-Bolshevik, and as a result Tsvetaeva had even more trouble placing her new poems. The journal editors, Tsvetaeva wrote to Teskova, "are asking for poems of 'the former Marina Tsvetaeva,' that is, of the year 1916." [37]

Despite all these worries, Tsvetaeva's vitality and her ability to live on different levels at the same time were as evident as ever. At the seashore with Alya she went on tending the one-and-a-half-year-old Mur, who had begun walking. Efron was seldom there. As always, there were problems with the landlady, who threatened to call the police about damage to the furniture. There were many visitors: old friends like Slonim and Volkonsky, Balmont and Andreyeva with her children, the Lebedevs and Chernovs, as well as new friends, including the three fiancés of the Chernova sisters, whom people in Paris called "Tsvetaeva's three knights." She seemed to have been particularly attracted to one of them—Daniil Reznikov—whom she invited to visit: "I would be delighted if you would come this summer. [ ... ] We have a whole barrel of wine—I would treat you to it. The wine is young, not heavier than my friendship. [ ... ] What else to attract you? I would read you my poems." [38]

An intimate and important relationship was growing between Tsvetaeva and Princess Salomea Andronikova-Halpern, a well-known St. Petersburg beauty and a close friend of Akhmatova and Mandelshtam. Halpern lived in Paris, later in London, and Tsvetaeva's letters to her, published in 1983, reveal that in addition to friendship reinforced by distance, there was a strong erotic attraction. From St. Gilles, Tsvetaeva wrote to Halpern about her way of relating to people and about her present mood of withdrawal from the real world.

> When I love someone, I take him with me everywhere, do not part with him inside me, *make him my own*, slowly transform him into the air I breathe and in which I live—into the everywhere and into the nowhere. I am absolutely incapable of being with someone, it has never worked.

It could have if I could live nowhere, travel all the time, simply—not live. Salomea, people bother me, [ . . . ] You know where and how I feel good? In a new place, on a pier, on a bridge, nearer to nowhere, in hours that border on no-hours (they exist).[39]

Still, the rent had to be paid and the family had to be fed. At Halpern's initiative, friends formed a "Committee to assist Marina Tsvetaeva" to cover the basic budget of the Efron family. Mirsky, Izvolskaya, Halpern, Lebedev, and Slonim became the fund's main financial backers. In the fall, the committee rented an apartment for the Efrons in Meudon, a suburb of Paris. For a few months, though, the Efrons had to share an apartment with another family in Bellevue. Tsvetaeva wrote to Pasternak: "I live in terrible crowded conditions; two families in one apartment, a common kitchen, three in a room; I am never alone, I suffer."[40]

Though the summer in St. Gilles had not been easy, her correspondence with Rilke had made her feel special and superior; it had alleviated the pain she felt when she was attacked by the émigré critics. She had also written three major poems and begun working on *Phaedra*, the second part of her Theseus trilogy. (The third part was never written.) Now, however, she could no longer expect to hear from Pasternak, and Rilke seemed to have forgotten her. On November 7, she mailed him a postcard, with her new address and a few short lines:

> Dear Rainer,
> This is where I live.
> I wonder if you still love me?
>                     Marina.[41]

# 18. Spiraling Down

*In Russia I am a poet without books, here*
*I am a poet without readers.*[1]

The news of Rilke's death reached Tsvetaeva in Bellevue. He had died of leukemia on December 29, 1926, in a Swiss sanatorium and had been buried according to his wishes in a little cemetery at Rarogne. Slonim was the one to inform Tsvetaeva two days later, on New Year's Eve. Her immediate response was "I have never seen him; now I never will see him."[2] Although she had not heard from Rilke for four months, she had never given up hope of meeting him. What mattered to her most was that Rilke, through his letters and his poetry, had made her feel his equal. Now, she felt bereft.

She immediately began to write her long poem "New Year's Greeting," which she called a letter to Rilke, completing it on February 7, 1927.[3] In it, she faced her own mortality in an utterly personal way, imagining the crossing over from this world into "that world." She wanted to believe that only Rilke's body had died, but that *he* was somewhere else. She spoke not to the dead Rilke, buried in his grave, but to his soul in eternity — to the ideal listener. She made Rilke in death more her own than he had ever been in life.

The diction of the poem is extraordinary — mixing a conversational tone with philosophical probing. It lets the reader share Tsvetaeva's agony and her attempt to find a new meaning in life and in death. Even Tsvetaeva's punctuation speaks volumes, or rather, the volumes she cannot bring herself to speak:

> Happy New Year! (You were born tomorrow)
> Should I tell what I did when I found out about . . . ?
> Shsh. . . . I misspoke as usual.

> I have put life and death in quotation marks.
> For a long time, like some obviously empty talk.

As Svetlana Boym points out, Tsvetaeva "introduces the news of Rilke's death in the ellipsis, as if afraid to distort the tragic fact irretrievably by naming it. The poet's death can be easily trivialized with 'ordinary language.' In the next strophe she proposes a different typographic element for death—an asterisk."[4]

Though the poem greets Rilke as though after a trip, Tsvetaeva's feeling of loss, of loneliness, breaks through soon enough:

> What am I to do in that New Year's din?
> With this rhyme within me: Rainer is dead.
> If you, if such an eye has closed,
> Then life is not life, death not death.
> It means—it blurs, I'll understand it
> Better when we meet!—
> There is no life, there is no death—there is
> A third thing, something new.

In that "third thing" lay Tsvetaeva's concept of the afterlife she hoped she would find after death. It was the very intensity of her hope that inspired her poetry of the period. In describing the world where Rilke had gone, she uses irony to mask the anxiety that permeates the entire poem. "What are the mountains like there? / And the rivers? / Are views finer without tourists?" She even introduces the concept of different stages of paradise, perhaps taking her ideas from Rudolph Steiner's "spiritual science," called anthroposophy, to which Bely may have introduced her.

In Tsvetaeva's summing up of her relationship with Rilke, she seems to understand that it was only in her imagination that a reciprocity had existed: "Nothing happened between you and me." The poem ends with Tsvetaeva addressing the "letter" to Rilke:

> I shelter it with my palm not to let it be flooded
> Above the Rhone and above Rarogne,
> Above the obvious and absolute separation
> To Rainer—Maria—Rilke—into his hands.

What would flood the letter? Her tears? The image of flooding and sheltering makes this lament all the more personal and moving. In Joseph Brodsky's words: "Emotionally and melodically this last stanza creates the impression of a voice that has burst through tears and, cleansed by them, takes off from them. In any case, the voice chokes when reading it aloud." [5]

Tsvetaeva informed Pasternak immediately of Rilke's death, telling him of the unanswered postcard that she had sent Rilke. On the next day she wrote again, insisting that Pasternak meet her in London. In a note to Tsvetaeva, Pasternak did not respond to her demand and told her that he was resuming his silence. But it was a silence that Tsvetaeva refused to respect. In her reply, she urged him to continue their relationship, "underwritten by Rilke's death." [6] She told him that her poem "Attempt at a Room," which she had dedicated to him, Pasternak, "turned out to be a poem about him [Rilke] and me." She went on to develop her belief in reincarnation. "I live with him and by him. I am deeply concerned about the distance between our heavens — his and mine. Mine can be no higher than the third, whereas his, I fear, is the last, which means I have to come back many, many times and he not more than once. All my labors and concerns are now concentrated on one thing: not to miss that one time (his last)." [7]

In that same month, February 1927, Tsvetaeva addressed an essay, "Your Death," to Rilke, in which she spoke to him about the recent deaths of Alya's French teacher and a little Russian boy, Vanya. "Every death returns us to every other death," she wrote. [8] She spoke of her mother's and father's deaths, but neglected to mention the death of her daughter Irina. In May 1927, still influenced by Rilke, Tsvetaeva began writing "Poem of the Air." Lindbergh's crossing of the Atlantic sparked her imagery, but the substance of the poem has nothing to do with this event. It is a solitary monologue, a dream journey into the "seven spheres of air" in search of the essence of existence and the posthumous transformation of the self.

In the spring of 1927 the Efrons finally moved to Meudon, a suburb of Paris where many other Russian émigrés had settled; the apartment their friends had rented for them was now available. It consisted of three rooms and was very comfortable in comparison to their former living arrangements. Many of their neighbors were Eurasians, Efron's friends.

The best news for Tsvetaeva was that her collection of poems written in Berlin and Prague had found a publisher. Called *After Russia*, the book appeared in 1928. It would be the last collection published during her lifetime. By the late twenties, her readership was growing. While some of the editors of Russian-language publications held that their readers did not understand her poetry and others objected to her tolerance of Soviet writers, such a major

Paris journal as *Contemporary Notes* (Sovremennyye zapiski) published Tsvetaeva regularly. She also contributed to the main Russian dailies in Paris, *Latest News* (Posledniye novosti) and *Renaissance* (Vozrozhdeniye). Yet she did not find in Paris the acceptance she had known in Prague. Editors often cut and distorted her work; literary critics frequently ignored her and sometimes attacked her. Nonetheless, some of the most respected critics — Slonim, Mirsky, and later Khodasevich — placed her next to Pasternak and Akhmatova as one of the great Russian poets of her time.

Yelena Izvolskaya, the daughter of a former Russian ambassador, was her neighbor and admiring friend. She accompanied Tsvetaeva and Mur on their walks through the woods, and spent many hours in Tsvetaeva's kitchen, where neighbors and friends came to hear her recite and to be charmed by her personality. Here, as in Moscow, poverty did not prevent Tsvetaeva from attracting people of different political and religious persuasions and from creating a special atmosphere around herself. Efron was rarely home; Alya generally returned late from art school; Mur was usually asleep. According to Izvolskaya, Tsvetaeva was far from lonely. Yet, even this loyal friend noticed Tsvetaeva's pattern of using friends for a while and then discarding them.

> She liked people and people liked her. There was even a certain "sophistication" in her, if not coquettishness — a desire to shine, to amaze, to confuse, to charm. She had many friends. She often told me that she valued them, liked to communicate with them, but then, unfortunately, she lost them. Her desire, her thirst for friendship suddenly was cut short. "Then," she would add with a sigh of sadness or rather of liberation: "life hurls me back into my monastic cell, to my writing desk, to creativity." [9]

The life of the Efron family was growing more difficult with every passing year. Their Czech subsidy had been halved and the family was barely surviving. "We are being devoured by coal, gas, electricity, the milkman, the baker," Tsvetaeva wrote to Teskova. "As for meat, we've eaten only horsemeat for months, and only the cheapest parts: horse heart, horse liver, horse kidneys and so on." [10]

Their extreme poverty was painful and humiliating, but many émigré poets, writers, and artists of their acquaintance suffered similarly. For Tsvetaeva, the pain and humiliation were increased a hundredfold by the fact that so many émigré critics rejected her. "In Paris I have no friends and am not likely to have any," she wrote to Teskova. "There is the circle of the Eurasians — Suvchinsky, Karsavin, and others — who like me as a poet but do not know me . . . Now conversation, my main—no, my only—pleasure with people is gone. I have settled for good in my notebooks."[11]

Pasternak was still the one to whom she turned when she needed understanding and friendship:

> Oh, Boris, Boris, how often I think of you, how I turn toward you—for help. You don't know how lonely I am. I have finished a big poem ["Poem of the Air"], read it to some, read it to others—complete silence—not a syllable, an indecent silence as far as I'm concerned. Certainly not from an excess of feelings! From a total nonreaching, from incomprehension. . . . That is why I am washed toward you, a a board toward the shore.[12]

They continued to admire one another. Pasternak was concerned about Tsvetaeva's difficult life; he dedicated poems to her and tried to understand her on the human level by transforming her into the fictional heroine in Spektorsky, his novel in verse begun in 1924 and published in 1931. The early passionate intensity, however, never returned.

In August of 1927 Tsvetaeva awaited a visit from her sister. Maxim Gorky had invited Asya to spend a month in Sorrento with him, and she had decided to use the occasion to see Tsvetaeva in Paris. Tsvetaeva wrote to Gorky, thanking him for providing an opportunity for the sisters to meet again after five years of separation. Yet she couldn't keep from criticizing Asya in a letter to Gorky even as she cloaked her criticism in kind words: "If Asya should irritate you, don't get angry, be patient. She is uniquely good."[13]

When Asya arrived in the first days of September, Efron met her at the station because Tsvetaeva had to stay home with the children. The reunion was emotional, happy, noisy. To Asya, her sister seemed changed—aged, tired. Her complexion had grown sallow, making her eyes look lighter than Asya remembered. And for the first time Asya met Mur: he was two and a half, very big for his age, stocky, with Tsvetaeva's coloring and eyes. Alya, fifteen, now looked more like her father. Most of all, though, Asya noticed Tsvetaeva's gentle ways with Mur, so different from the outbursts of harsh impatience toward Alya that Asya remembered well from their Moscow days.

The sisters chatted until late into the night, with Tsvetaeva lying on a narrow sofa smoking one cigarette after another. She spoke of their poverty, of Efron's illness, of her isolation among the émigrés and her alienation even among Efron's friends, the Eurasians. With tears in her eyes, she complained:

Please understand: how can I write when in the morning I have to go to the market and buy food with painstaking care, so I'll have enough money to pay for it. We buy, of course, only the cheapest. Then, after doing all that, I drag myself home with my shopping bag knowing that the morning has been wasted. Then, I have to clean and cook while Alya takes care of Mur. When everyone has been fed, everything has been cleaned—I lie down exhausted, as I'm doing now, all empty, not one line! And again next morning how I try to get to my table to write— and so on day in and day out.[14]

Soon after Asya's arrival, Mur, Alya, and finally Tsvetaeva fell ill with scarlet fever. Asya's presence seemed a godsend, yet nursing the family left little time to reestablish the already complicated relationship between the sisters. Unfortunately, this would be their last meeting.

When, upon her return to Moscow, Asya told Pasternak about Tsvetaeva's difficult life, he wrote to Gorky, asking his help in arranging Tsvetaeva's return to Russia. "The immense talent of Marina Tsvetaeva is of urgent and personal importance to me, as is her unhappy and hopelessly entangled fate."[15] Gorky, however, was very candid in his response:

I perceive her as a person who values herself too highly, whose opinion of herself is wrong and who is too morbidly self-preoccupied to be able to or to wish to understand other people. . . . It is difficult for me to agree with you in your high evaluation of Marina Tsvetaeva's talent. Her gift seems to me shrill, even hysterical. She is not a master of language. Language is her master.[16]

After Asya's departure, Tsvetaeva slowly recovered from her scarlet fever— and life continued with its chores, its worries, and its slanders. Tsvetaeva dreamed of having Teskova come to Paris or of visiting her in Prague; she dreamed of having some time for herself, for her work. But there was no peace for her, as she wrote to Teskova:

Did you read about the harassment of the Eurasians in *Renaissance*, *Russia* [*Rossiya*], and *Days* [*Dni*]? "Reliable information" that the Eurasians received *huge amounts* from the Bolsheviks. Naturally, no evidence (since there can't be any); those writers know the emigration! Denials will soon appear—how sordid to have to deal with notorious liars—but it cannot be avoided. I am far from all that, but even my indifference to politics is shaken. It is as though they were accusing *me* of having taken Bolshevik money! Just as clever and as likely. Sergey naturally gets up-

set, and because of it his health suffers. His earnings: he works from
5:30 a.m. to 7:30 or 8 p.m. as a movie extra for 40 francs a day, of which
5 francs are spent on transportation, 7 francs on his meal—coming to
28 francs a day. And there are two days like that, at best, in a week. There
they are, the Bolshevik sums! [17]

Two years earlier Tsvetaeva had come out in print expressing her admiration
for Soviet writers who wrote "with censorship deletions, under the threat of
literary denunciation." She proclaimed, "One can only marvel at the heroic
ability to survive of the so-called Soviet writers who write as the grass grows
from under prison slabs—with disdain and defiance." At the same time,
however, she believed that if a writer went to Russia, it would be only to be
silent or to "speak within the walls of the Cheka." [18]

Tsvetaeva had no illusions about the fate of the writer in Soviet Russia, but
Efron felt otherwise. For the time being he satisfied his longing for a role in
the political and cultural destiny of a new Russia by working with the Eurasians and by editing Versts, but he had taken a different turn of the road than
Tsvetaeva. It is difficult to know how much the Eurasians, and Efron in particular, were already playing along with the Bolshevik organizations abroad.
Even Tsvetaeva's genuine remoteness from politics was suspect to the émigrés, while Efron was plainly attracted to the Soviet Union. Their circle of
friends was increasingly limited to Eurasians. Welcoming 1928 with them,
Tsvetaeva felt alienated and bored. The movement made sense to her, but
"honestly, I have been a stranger in any circle, all my life. Among political
activists as among poets. [ . . . ] That is why on New Year's Eve I felt as if I
were in a desert," she wrote to Teskova. [19]

This was the beginning of a new stage in the growing conflict between
Tsvetaeva and Efron. She withdrew more and more into her own world,
while he became increasingly active in his support of Soviet Communist
organizations.

# 19. Growing Isolation

*Above the world of husbands and wives —*
*That Optina emptiness,\**
*Which has given up — even bells.*
*The soul without layers of*
*Feelings. Naked as a fellah.*[1]

T svetaeva's "Poem of the Air," written in 1927, had celebrated the mind, "the full dominion of the forehead." The end of the poem indicates that now the poet's ultimate aim is to reach not so much the realm of the spirit and the soul, but of the mind:

> Upwards! Not into the realm of souls —
> into the full dominion
> of the forehead. Is there a limit? Force it![2]

Now, in December, she wrote to Teskova about the costs of dependency on the mind:

> In these long years (1917–27) not my mind but my soul has been blunted. An amazing observation: it is precisely for feelings that one needs time, not for thought. Thought is lightning, feeling is the ray of the most distant star. Feeling needs leisure, it does not live under fear. Simple example: while I roll three pounds of small fish in flour I can think, but feel — I cannot. [ ... ] Feelings, obviously, are more demanding than thought.[3]

In 1928 Tsvetaeva finished writing *Phaedra*, a verse play, the second part of the Theseus trilogy she had planned when she wrote *Ariadne*. "My Theseus is conceived as a trilogy," she wrote to Teskova:

> Ariadne-Phaedra-Helen; but out of superstition I haven't announced it yet — I need time to finish at least two parts first. Did you know that all

*The Optina monastery was a revered Russian spiritual center.

the women of all time fell to Theseus's lot? Ariadne (the soul), Antiope (the Amazon), Phaedra (passion), and Helen (beauty). Yes, the famous Helen of Troy. At the age of seventy Theseus abducted her as a seven-year-old girl, and perished as a result. So many loves and all of them unhappy.[4]

The trilogy was never completed, but *Phaedra* was published in 1928 in *Contemporary Notes*. Emigré critics reviewed it unfavorably; yet it was produced in Moscow recently with great success.

The psychology of the play is interesting. Tsvetaeva left the basic pattern of the classical Theseus myth unchanged. After Theseus's second wife, the Amazon queen, is killed in battle defending their son, Hippolitus, Theseus marries his third wife, Phaedra, the younger sister of Ariadne. The child Hippolitus is sent to Theseus's birthplace, where he grows up hating women, particularly Phaedra, who has taken his mother's place. When, as an adolescent, he joins Theseus and Phaedra, Phaedra falls in love with her handsome stepson, but she still loves her husband and feels deeply loyal to him. When Theseus leaves for a journey, Phaedra's nursemaid makes her admit her passion and persuades her to try seducing her stepson. But Tsvetaeva's Hippolitus responds to Phaedra's declaration of love with one word — "Vermin!" In reaction, Phaedra hangs herself, leaving an explanatory letter. When Theseus returns, he curses his son and banishes him without reading Phaedra's letter. Soon after, Hippolitus meets his death on the road and his body is brought back. It is at this point that Theseus reads Phaedra's letter and realizes that hers was a tragic, unconsummated love. With his blessing, Phaedra and Hippolitus are buried together under a myrtle tree.

In her notes to the drama, Tsvetaeva played with a number of different versions.[5] Her comments reveal how hard she tried to understand her protagonists' psychological motivations. She went so far as to ponder whether Hippolitus was the son of a happy or unhappy marriage; whether it was women or love itself he hated. She clearly tried to understand and to use some of the themes that she knew well from her own past: the conflict between loyalty and passion her mother had faced; the erotic attraction between Tsvetaeva's mother and her mother's stepson Andrey; Tsvetaeva's own weakness for handsome young men, mixed now with her awareness of aging. As in *The Tsar-Maiden*, Tsvetaeva empathized with the sexually aggressive female, not with the self-centered, cold Hippolitus.

Especially interesting is the character of Phaedra's nursemaid. She stands at the center of the drama, sensing the secret passion of the young woman and encouraging her to seek the fulfillment of her natural sexual needs. Her milk has nurtured Phaedra, and her feelings for her are as strong as any mother's blood-tie. She knows that Phaedra loves Hippolitus and warns her not to let precious time elapse:

> In the myrtle bushes
> Lips to lips!
> Yes, do not delay. Yes, today!
> Phaedra![6]

When Phaedra speaks of the shame that frightens her, the nursemaid reacts with a violent temper. Tsvetaeva may have remembered the stories that she had heard about her own Gypsy nursemaid, who had trampled a gift of earrings into the ground. Phaedra's nursemaid, as Tsvetaeva created her, is obviously the opposite of her own mother. Perhaps she was the mother Tsvetaeva wished she had had.

In the end, Phaedra emerges as a moving, tragic human figure unable to evade what Tsvetaeva saw as woman's fate: rejection by a cold, unfeeling male.


Tsvetaeva had hoped to find in Paris a broader audience, had hoped, if not for fame, at least for recognition, for understanding. Now, in 1928, her hope was fading. When *After Russia* came out in February, the publisher, a private patron, sold twenty-five subscriptions. Slonim had placed a few more, and Tsvetaeva tried to sell still more, but the critical response was disappointing. There was one favorable review by Slonim, but Adamovich and Khodasevich were critical. In her frustration, the thought of returning to the Soviet Union crossed her mind, but she knew that the country was closed to her. "I choke from the thought alone," she wrote to Teskova.

In her despair, she began to dream of a reading in Prague and of a reunion with her friend Teskova there and in the "Beyond":

> I want to go to you and I want — to say it simply — to *love*. I haven't loved anybody for a long time. I love Pasternak but he's far away; only letters, no sign of *that* world, probably not of this one either! Rilke was torn out of my arms. I was supposed to visit him in the spring. I won't speak about the family. That is another love, with pain and concern, often muffled and distorted by life's demands. [ . . . ] You do know that sex and age have nothing to do with that. I want to come home to you:

ins Freie, into a foreign land, outside the window, and—oh, what enchant-
ment in that—"ins Freie"—it feels good, safe; one can live in it. A cloud
on which one can stand. Not that world and not this one—a third one:
of dreams, of fairy tales, mine.[7]

Yet there was some consolation. Financial relief arrived unexpectedly in
May from Raissa Lomonosova, the wife of a prominent Russian railway
engineer who had held important government posts before and after the
Revolution. Lomonosova had traveled frequently with her husband in Western Europe and the United States. Chiefly interested in literature, she wanted
to promote better understanding between East and West by having contemporary literature translated and distributed across political boundaries. She
could afford to act as a patron for literary translations and in this connection
had begun a correspondence with Pasternak. In the mid-1920s, the Lomonosovs had decided not to return to the Soviet Union and settled in London.
It was Pasternak who had asked Lomonosova to help Tsvetaeva, whom he
called "the greatest and the most innovative of our living poets." Lomonosova immediately mailed some money to Tsvetaeva by express mail. Tsvetaeva
thanked her benefactress, ending the letter with a postscript: "Yes, Pasternak is my close friend in life as well as in work. And the best thing about it
is that you never know who is greater in him, the poet or the man? *Both are
greater.*"[8] This was the beginning of a lively correspondence that lasted until
1931. Lomonosova explained to Pasternak in 1933 that Tsvetaeva had charac-
teristically misinterpreted as rejection a strain on the Lomonosovs' finances,
which forced her to suspend her contributions.

Another friendship that helped blunt Tsvetaeva's pain was with a young
poet, Nikolay Gronsky. The handsome eighteen-year-old son of one of the
editors of the newspaper *Latest News* was a mountain climber and a poet. He
and Tsvetaeva met in the spring of 1928 in Meudon, where his family lived,
and were immediately attracted to each other. Tsvetaeva considered him an
original, promising poet who, though he belonged to the new generation,
was rooted in Russian poetic language; for his part, Gronsky was ready to be
her pupil. At the time, Tsvetaeva was organizing one of her yearly readings
to earn enough money to spend the summer on the coast with the children.
That summer, in Pontillac, on the Atlantic Ocean, she exchanged letters with
Gronsky and awaited his visit. On the day he was supposed to arrive, she
went to the railroad station, only to find that he had not come. She returned
home and found his letter explaining that he had to cancel his visit because

of problems between his parents. "I was so happy," she wrote to Teskova, "and then — as always — what? — the *non-happening*." [9]

In the same letter Tsvetaeva found solace in the idea that she could have forced Gronsky's visit if she had wanted to, but had chosen renunciation instead. She claimed that she no longer yearned to be someone whom men loved, for whom they sang, and for whom they died. "All my life I have behaved with the young and the old as a mother," she wrote. "I am the Loving-one, not the Beloved." [10] But was she as resigned as she tried so hard to sound? Whether or not Gronsky offered more than a literary flirtation, she seemed ready to put him on a pedestal, to make him a "son," perhaps to make love to him. Life, however, interfered, and they drifted apart. Gronsky fell in love with a young girl his age, and he and Tsvetaeva saw less and less of one another.

Nothing exciting happened that summer in Tsvetaeva's life or her work, and she dreaded the winter in Meudon. She complained to Teskova that although she was surrounded by Eurasians and other Russian friends, she felt lonelier than ever. Her mood was heavy as she prepared to close the summer house: "Ahead is the threat of departure: the moving of my belongings, the returning of the housewares to the landlady, unforeseen expenses, the final chord (a dissonance!). I am scared of such things — I am depressed, miserable. What is money for? Not to be tormented emotionally — for a broken pitcher." [11]

Because *Latest News*, a regular source of Tsvetaeva's literary income, was interested mostly in her early poems, she asked Teskova to get her the manuscript of *Juvenilia* from Slonim. Meanwhile, Efron was working on the publication of a new weekly paper, *Eurasia* (Yevraziya). A short statement by Tsvetaeva in the first issue was to cause her great harm. After Mayakovsky gave a poetry reading in a Paris café on November 7, she recalled that on the eve of her departure from Russia she had met him and asked him for a message for Europe. " 'The truth is here,' " Mayakovsky had answered. Now, Tsvetaeva said, "The power is there." [12] It didn't help that this statement appeared in Efron's pro-Soviet paper. Serious repercussions ensued. Although she meant the power of Soviet poets, many of the émigrés interpreted her remark politically, seeing it as an indication of her support for Red Russia. *Latest News*, which had been preparing a separate volume of her White Army poems, immediately stopped publishing her and was closed to her for four years.

But even if Tsvetaeva had known the consequences of her declaration, she would not have changed it. Her support for a man who had never shown any support for her but whose power and authenticity had made him a great poet was typical of her. The truth she defended time and again was not the evanescent truth of politics, but the more enduring truth of poetry. Whether in Moscow, where she stood before a crowd of Red Army sympathizers to read her White Army poems, or in Paris, where she faced the intolerance of the émigré press on which her livelihood depended, Tsvetaeva never hesitated to challenge established opinion.

After the Mayakovsky debacle, the pressures on Tsvetaeva intensified. Her break with *Latest News* had reduced the Efrons' meager income, and Sergey's small salary at *Eurasia* was never secure. Their only regular income came from the Czech subsidy—always in question—and from some small grants by émigré literary associations, friends like Lomonosova, and from Tsvetaeva's regular spring poetry readings. Meanwhile, the campaign against Efron was becoming more bitter and personal. The Eurasians were splitting up, deeply divided on the issue of Bolshevism. Tsvetaeva wrote to Teskova that among others Professor Nikolay N. Alekseyev, a leading member of the group, "asserts that Sergey is a Chekist [member of the Soviet Secret Police] and a Communist. If I should meet him—I can't answer for myself. . . . Professor Alekseyev is a scoundrel; believe me, I don't speak lightly. . . . [Sergey] is the only moral force of the Eurasian movement. [ . . . ] They call him 'the Eurasian Conscience.' Professor Lev Karsavin calls him 'the golden child of the Eurasians.' " [13]

In January 1929 Slonim, aware of Tsvetaeva's difficulties, introduced her to the painter Natalya Goncharova and her husband, Larionov. Tsvetaeva became excited from the very first mention of Natalya's name, associating her with Pushkin's wife, also Natalya Goncharova. Goncharova invited Tsvetaeva to her studio, offered to give painting lessons to Alya, and volunteered to illustrate the French version of Tsvetaeva's poem "The Swain." Using their talks, Tsvetaeva wrote a long "biographical" study of the painter. Yet Goncharova was really a pretext for Tsvetaeva to discuss the role of Pushkin's wife in his life, for writing about other lives, the conditions for creativity, and for personal remembrances. Tsvetaeva was never much interested in painting and did not feel a real connection to Goncharova the painter or the woman. "Natalya Goncharova: Her Life and Art" was one of Tsvetaeva's least successful literary portraits, perhaps because of her preoccupation with her own problems at the time.

Tsvetaeva had never liked summer in Meudon, but the summer of 1929 was even more difficult than usual. Alya had gone to visit friends in Brittany and Efron was rarely home. Mur, meanwhile, had no friends. Tsvetaeva felt sorry for him, though he often embarrassed her by his loud, wild behavior, which set him apart from French boys. In a letter to Lomonosova in September 1929, Tsvetaeva tried to give a picture of her life and family to her new friend: "I get up at 7 A.M., I go to sleep at 2 or even 3 A.M. What is in between? Routine: laundry, cooking, walks with the boy (I adore the boy, I adore walks, but I cannot write while walking), dishes, dishes, dishes, mending, mending, mending." Efron she described as "the *heart* of the Eurasian movement. The newspaper *Eurasia*, the only one in emigration (and in Russia as well) is his initiative, his child, his burden. His joy. He resembles Boris [Pasternak], [ . . . ] mainly with his conscience, his sense of responsibility, the profound seriousness of his being, but he is more virile."

Just to get away, Tsvetaeva decided to organize a reading in Brussels and then to go to Prague, where she expected to find beauty, friendship, peace. She went to Brussels, but Prague had to be postponed when Efron became seriously ill. His tuberculosis flared up again, undoubtedly, Tsvetaeva thought, because he was exhausted. His doctors recommended that he spend the next several months in a sanatorium, but the family could not afford it. Again friends came to their aid. In December, Efron left for the Savoy.

In these years, 1928 and 1929, Tsvetaeva's creativity diminished. She had written about eighty-five short poems and three long poems ("The Swain," "Poem of the Mountain," and "Poem of the End") in Czechoslovakia between 1922 and 1925, and in 1926 and 1927 she had finished "The Ratcatcher" and had written three long poems and "New Year's Greetings." Now she faced a crisis, which she ascribed to poverty and a lack of time, but there were other, less obvious, reasons. In creativity as in love, Tsvetaeva wanted exclusiveness and adoration, not just acceptance. Although her public readings were crowded and most of her poems were published, she resented it that many critics considered her poetry opaque, and she was deeply disappointed by the poor response to the publication of *After Russia*. Her correspondence with Pasternak and Rilke had made her believe that the two greatest poets of her time were her listeners. Now both were silent; Rilke was dead and Pasternak was not corresponding with her.

She was beset by family problems as well. Efron's growing commitment to Communism was one that she could not share. She was doubly alarmed when Alya began to follow in her father's footsteps. As far as she was concerned, the family was falling apart. Seeing Efron attacked by the emigration as a Bolshevik sympathizer, she felt solidarity with other victims who had suffered for their beliefs. But her victims were not of the left: her old heroes of the White Army returned. She had never entirely left behind the romanticism her mother had bestowed on her. Now she bridged two worlds — the romanticism of the nineteenth century and the revolutionary rhythm of her own. As she would write in 1932, "There is not a single important Russian poet of the present whose voice hasn't shaken and grown since the Revolution."

She wrote two long poems: "Little Red Bull" (1928), inspired by the death of the son of friends who had been a volunteer in the White Army, and, the longer and more important "Perekop" (1929), most of it based on Efron's Civil War diary. It sang the glory of the last stand and temporary victory of the White Army under Wrangel. Tsvetaeva wrote to Teskova: "I am writing a big thing — Perekop (the defeat of the White Army) — I write with great love and pleasure, incomparably greater than with Phaedra." [14] This was a return to some of Tsvetaeva's deep identification with doomed heroic men, a lyrical memorial to their courage. Yet it was rejected by all major Russian publications and remained unpublished until 1967. [15] Efron, of course, was actually opposed to its publication since his allegiance was elsewhere. Tsvetaeva told Teskova that she could not find a publisher. "For the rightists, it is leftist in its form; for the leftists, rightist in its content." [16]

In the same year, 1929, she began "The Tsar's Family," another major poem, even more provocative than "Perekop." Until she completed it in 1936, she was engaged in prodigious research for this project. "It is a huge work: a mountain. It gives me joy. [ . . . ] But nobody needs it. Here, it will not be understood because of the 'leftism' (of its form, in quotes because of the nastiness of these words), there, it will simply never arrive physically, like all my books." [17]

One short chapter of the poem, "Siberia," has appeared in print. The rest of the poem was among the manuscripts Tsvetaeva left with friends before her departure for the Soviet Union. When the war broke out they were sent to the International Socialist Archive in Amsterdam for safekeeping, but they were destroyed by air raids during the German occupation. In 1981, however, Yelena Korkina found notes and chapter headings as well as fragments of the text in one of Tsvetaeva's notebooks. They show that the poem was a detailed account of the painful last journey of the Imperial family from Moscow to Ekaterinburg, offering portraits of the Tsar, his wife, and their entourage.[18]

Tsvetaeva gave a reading of the poem in 1936 to her friends in Paris at the home of the Lebedevs. Slonim recalls his impression that much of it was powerful, bold, and tragic—impressive as a poem. Yet when Tsvetaeva asked him whether he would publish it if he still had a journal, he replied that he would have to make some changes because the poem would be perceived as a political statement. Tsvetaeva, however, insisted that "the poet ought to be on the side of the victims and not of the executioners and if history is cruel and unjust the poet has to oppose it."[19] Lebedev went even further than Slonim, concluding that, intentionally or not, the poem turned out to be a glorification of the tsar. " 'You all know I am not a monarchist,' " Tsvetaeva told them. " 'And Efron and I are accused of being Bolsheviks.' " Political labels were meaningless for her.

The seven years of work on "The Tsar's Family" reflect Tsvetaeva's resistance to Efron's growing desire to return to the Soviet Union. She depicted the tsar's family as emotionally and spiritually united in their time of troubles even as her own family was falling apart. By 1936, along with the drafts of "The Tsar's Family" found in her notebooks, she would write:

> Given the choice—*never* to see Russia or *never* to see my workbooks—for example this one [ . . . ]—I would not think twice. Right away, *clearly* [I would say] that Russia can do without me, my workbooks cannot. I can do without Russia—I cannot do without my workbooks.[20]

# 20. Hitting Bottom

*Solitude in the heart.*
*Solitude: Go away*
Life!* [1]

**I**n 1929, as a new era of economic crisis and political unrest began, the mood among Russian émigrés in Paris darkened. The kidnapping of the prominent White Russian general Kutepov increased the tension between the émigré groups in Paris. Soviet organizations were suspected, but nothing was proven. Still, Tsvetaeva lived in her own world. As Slonim's brilliant biographical essay describes her:

> She had made no place for herself in émigré society with its salons, both political and literary, where everyone knew one another. As I have said, "we sat around the same table set for tea" where, despite differences of views and situations, we felt we were "in the family." She, however, was a loner, a stranger, outside all groups, outside personal and family relationships, standing out sharply by the way she looked and talked, with her worn dress and the indelible stamp of poverty.[2]

In her private life, too, there was little happiness. Many contemporaries have noted Efron's absence in Tsvetaeva's life. From Efron's letter to Voloshin after the Rozdevich affair it is clear that no real closeness between them was possible; he was too deeply disappointed and saw clearly the destructive pattern of Tsvetaeva's emotional involvements. If a basic friendship between them never died, Efron—handsome, attractive, intelligent—was rumored to have other women in his life. It was known that Tsvetaeva and Efron often lived separately, but a recently published letter of April 1930 from Mirsky to Suvchinskaya, the wife of one of the editors of *Versts*, throws more light on Efron's relationships:

I have found out everything about Efron's young girl friend. Her name is Lery Rabin. She is Swiss, from Kazan. Her father is a millionaire and a former consul. . . . Efron says that his frenzy is beginning to cool and he doubts whether she is the right one for him. I asked him, what did you tempt her with? To which he replied: "That is not so difficult to understand, but what did she tempt me with?" . . . Nevertheless, it turns out that he intends to stay in Meudon. Apparently he still wants some clarifying talks with Marina.[3]

We know of another short-lived affair, even in the early years of their marriage. There is gossip of many more in their Paris years. It would seem from Mirsky's letter that there was a certain pattern. Both Efron and Tsvetaeva—for different reasons—had a strong commitment to their relationship, but they had different needs and felt free to indulge them.

Increasingly Tsvetaeva saw herself as outside her time, her society, outside life itself. She wondered about her destiny. There was no doubt in her mind that she was a poet, an inspired poet, but she was unable to reconcile herself to the lack of recognition of her work. "I could have been the premier poet of my time," she wrote to Lomonosova, "I know that, since I have *everything*, all the potential, but I do not love my time. I don't recognize it as mine."[4] Or, she explained to her distant friend, she could simply have been a wealthy and recognized poet either in Russia or in the West, if she had accepted compromise. That, however, was beneath her dignity. She had never considered it.

In April 1930 Mayakovsky committed suicide in Moscow. The émigré community was split into two opposing groups: one that mourned the poet's suicide, and another, comprised of most of the prominent writers and critics of the day, that signed a letter of protest expressing their belief that all of Mayakovsky's poetry had been inspired by the Communist Party and the Soviet government. Tsvetaeva, of course, did not belong to either camp. Instead, she wrote a poetry cycle, "To Mayakovsky," in simple, declarative, slangy language that heralded a change in her poetic style. Gone were the obscurity and complexity of her long poems. Mayakovsky's death seemed to force Tsvetaeva to return to this world.

"To Mayakovsky" was a tribute not only to the poet she admired, but to a man whose suicide note had registered the superiority of love over ordinary life—"The love boat has smashed against the everyday." Tsvetaeva responded to Mayakovsky's tragedy, the tragedy of a poet defeated by "the many." Her poem echoes Mayakovsky himself when she attacks their common enemy, the philistine. She succeeded in bringing Mayakovsky to life as he had been—

not the Communist singer he yearned to be, but the romantic hooligan poet he was. Death brought Tsvetaeva and Mayakovsky closer than they ever could have been in life.

During the summer of 1930 Tsvetaeva went to the mountains with the children to be near Efron, who was still in a sanatorium. There she finished her translation of "The Swain" into French. She hoped the poem, with illustrations by Goncharova, would bring in some money, but it was never published. By the time the whole family returned to Meudon in the fall, their situation had worsened. "Life is hard," Tsvetaeva complained to Teskova:

> Sergey is without work; *Eurasia* has ceased publication and no factory will take him. Actually, who can speak about a factory when in eight months he has gained only five kilos, of which he has already lost two. He's a sick man. He has registered at a school for cinematic techniques which will allow him, upon graduation, to be a cameraman. I have been finishing my [translation of] "The Swain," my only hope to make some money, but one has to wait; one can't give it away for nothing. Six months of work. We live on credit in the store and sometimes I don't have one franc and 14 centimes to take the train to Paris.[5]

They were again rescued by Lomonosova, who sent them money. Tsvetaeva put all her efforts into selling the translation of "The Swain." Besides urgently needing the money, she hoped that success would open the French literary journals to her. Friends tried to introduce her to French editors and literary salons, but without success. Her friend Izvolskaya has recalled a reading she arranged at the home of the famous Natalie Barney, the Amazon of Paris, whose home was a meeting place for Paris writers and artists.

> I accompanied Marina and hoped very much that she would find there help and recognition. Marina read aloud her translation of "The Swain" into French. It was received in dead silence. Alas, the Russian swain did not fit into the snobbish atmosphere that reigned in that house. I believe that in other Paris circles they might have appreciated her, but after the fiasco of that reading, Marina withdrew into her loneliness.[6]

Tsvetaeva sensed that her poetry was not reaching her audience, that people wanted her poems to be, as she wrote to Teskova, "1. simpler 2. more cheerful 3. more elegant."[7] Tsvetaeva felt abandoned, humiliated, rejected. Her letters to Teskova and Lomonosova in February 1931 were cries for help, for love. To Teskova she wrote: "Everything is pushing me out into Russia, where I *cannot go*. Here I am not *needed*, there I am *impossible*." [8] Old wounds opened up: she felt that she had never been loved as she deserved. "People did not love me much; they came to me with something else, for something else — from childhood on to this very day," she wrote to Lomonosova. "My mother admired me, but she *loved* my younger sister. It didn't cross people's *mind* that one could (one should) love me!" [9]

In March, Tsvetaeva learned that Pasternak had left his wife because he loved someone else, a married woman. The news came as a shock to Tsvetaeva, who heard about it when she was invited to meet Boris Pilnyak, a Soviet writer recently arrived from Moscow. He assumed that she had already heard the news. Deeply upset, she wrote to Teskova:

> Now I feel empty. I have no one to seek out in Russia. A wife, a son — that I respect. But a *new love* — I step aside. Do understand me correctly, dear Anna Antonovna: this is not jealousy. But — to do without me! I felt for Boris that if I were dying — I would call him. Because I perceived him, despite his family, as utterly alone: mine. Now my place has been taken [ . . . ]. I do not feel a sharp pain. Emptiness . . . [10]

In the summer of 1931 Tsvetaeva's spirits reached a new low. Efron was out of work, and with unemployment rising in France, he had little hope of finding any. The Czech subsidy was often delayed, and it had been halved. *Freedom of Russia*, the émigré publication that had always accepted Tsvetaeva's work and paid decent fees, was starting to fold. Tsvetaeva's only reliable literary income came from her yearly spring poetry readings, but that was barely enough to cover the family's basic expenses. At the same time, some of the Efrons' friends could no longer be counted on: Izvolskaya had left for Japan, Mirsky was leaving for the Soviet Union, others were affected by the economic crisis. Tsvetaeva sold some of her rings and a few silk dresses given to her by wealthy patrons. Reduced to smoking cigarette butts that she had saved, she could no longer afford to buy medication for Efron's cough. "I walk around and cry, not from humiliation, but from the coughing spells I will hear all night. And from the awareness of life's injustice." [11]

She spent the summer of 1931 alone with Mur in Meudon. Efron and Alya had been invited to visit friends — he in the mountains, she at the seaside. Mur was a "difficult" six-year-old, very big for his age, loud and active. Tsvetaeva worshipped him without understanding his needs and made him awkward and demanding. While she had long felt that Alya's needs had to take second place to her poetry, she wrote to Lomonosova that "he should not suffer because I write poems, — let the poems suffer instead (as it actually happens)." [12] Her patience, however, began to wear thin. She wrote to Halpern:

> Alya is in Brittany. My summer has been somewhat like forced labor, all day long either heavy work or walks with Mur in the rain with the uninterrupted accompaniment of his chattering about a car or cars, about stamps, speeds, and so on. At six years of age he has jumped ten years (in the direction I hate). When he's sixteen, I hope he will have outgrown it (will have talked his fill! Since he is not silent for a second . . . ).[13]

At this point, Tsvetaeva was close to a breakdown. The family's financial situation was desperate, and life at home was uncomfortable and lonely. Alya was more and more involved with her studies. Tsvetaeva's relationship with Efron was increasingly strained, and her doubts about being able to publish any of her work were driving her to consider even the Soviet Union as an option. But returning to Moscow was an alternative she dropped almost as soon as she began to consider it. "After all, I cannot go to Russia, can I? There they will have the pleasure of — one, two, three — finishing me off. I will not survive there, since outrage is my passion (and there is enough to be outraged about!)," she wrote to Halpern.[14]

When Nikolay Yelenev, Efron's old friend in Moscow and Prague, met Sergey in Meudon, he agreed to drop in to visit Tsvetaeva, who would be "delighted" to see him, Sergey assured him. Yelenev was shocked. Tsvetaeva's complexion was sallow, her posture painfully erect, her lips sealed. She was unfriendly and unresponsive: "Marina's silence was the silence of a person who has no way out. Here, everything was mute despair. Here was the expectation of doom." [15] Tsvetaeva herself was the one who understood her predicament best:

> People around me see me as hard and cold; it may be so: Life, in sharpening the mind, hardens the soul. And then, you know, according to medical opinion, repressed emotion — for instance, grief or joy — is a strong thing which, if you do not allow it to come out — eventually makes the person quite ill: either breaking out into a bad rash or showing some other outward sign of trauma.
>
> Thus my entire adult life: *force refoulée, désire créateur* — refoulé [power repressed, creative urge repressed], what else do I do in life than *not*

write—when that's all I have ever wanted to do every morning of my life! Fourteen years in a row. That, too, makes you cold and hard.[16]

Exhausted and depressed as she was that summer of 1931, Tsvetaeva wrote a cycle of poems to Pushkin, as well as an "Ode to Hiking." She knew, however, that her poems now were "a rare luxury," that "the path is overgrown from one time to the next." [17] She had already admitted as much in her poem "Conversation with My Genius," written in the summer of 1928. There she confessed that she could no longer sing, that she felt "empty, dry," that she had nothing to sing about. In reply her genius insisted that she had to sing to spite the enemy:

> "Sing I cannot!"
> "Sing about that!" [18]

Now, in September 1931, in "The House," she did sing about the depression she was fighting.

> From under knitted brows
> A house—as though a day of my youth,
> As though my youth
> Were meeting me: Hello, I!
>
> So consciously familiar is the
> Forehead, hiding under the cloak of
> Ivy, fusing with it,
> Ashamed to be so high.
>
> Not in vain had I—Do carry! Do haul!—
> In the never dry mud of
> The slums destined to me
> Sensed my forehead as a pediment.
> The Apollonian rise
> Of the museum pediment was my forehead.
>
> Far from the street,
> Deep in my poetry, I'll end my days—
> Deep in the elder tree's branches.
>
> Eyes without warmth,
> The greenness of old glass,
> That have gazed into the garden, for a hundred years—
> Deserted—for a hundred-fifty.

Glass dense as a dream
Window whose only law:
"Don't wait for guests.
Don't reflect the passer-by."

Not having surrendered to dailiness,
Eyes which have remained, yes,
Mirrors of themselves.

From under knitted brows—
Oh, greenness of my youth!
That—of my garments, that—of my beads,
That—of my eyes, that—of my tears . . .

Surrounded by huge buildings—
The house—a vestige, the house—an aristocrat,
Hiding among the lime trees.
A maidenly daguerreotype
Of my soul . . .[19]

The poem radiates despair and loss; it renders a self unable to find its place in its time, in reality—a mere "vestige," an "aristocrat." The eyes, devoid of warmth, know the futility of looking outside for human connection: "'Don't wait for guests, Don't reflect the passer-by!'" How well the speaker knows her defeat: "Eyes which have remained, yes, mirrors of themselves."

Tsvetaeva had not forgotten her father's museum pediment or her mother's romantic garden. The hundred and fifty years of the deserted garden bring us back to the eighteenth century glorified by her mother and herself. There is no reaching out in the poem—no lips, no hands, no movement—only a high forehead, unseeing eyes, and a soul. Here was the defeat of a woman whose only joy was to communicate. Tsvetaeva had reached bottom.

# 21. Alienation and Self-Analysis

*The emigration makes of me a prose writer.*[1]

I n the early thirties, Tsvetaeva turned increasingly to writing prose, perhaps because it came more easily to her under pressure than poetry. Or perhaps she hoped to improve her chances of getting published by turning away from her "incomprehensible" verses. In August 1932 she heard that her old friend Voloshin had died. She immediately set to work on "A Living Word about a Living Man," an essay about his meaning in her life. It was the first in a series of brilliant portraits. For the next few years her prose—dense, original, poetic—became her main mode of expression. In her Moscow years, her prose had dealt mostly with life around her, interspersed with reflections and descriptions. Now most of her writings were either reminiscences about other poets or autobiographical essays. Magically weaving together past and present events, they mythologized the past and looked forward into an unknown future; they probed for the meaning of events, the essence of people and emotions. As in her poetry, Tsvetaeva searched for "the truth" and talked directly to her reader about what mattered to her. She could shift from narrative to monologue, from descriptions to interpretations. As Karlinsky writes:

> Whether Tsvetaeva's prose dealt with her mother and family, famous poets or theories about art, it remained at all times the prose of a poet—not necessarily because it was written by a poet but because in her prose Tsvetaeva consistently employed the lexical and stylistic and structural devices which she had developed in her verse. Except for meter and rhyme, the texture of her prose was the same as that of her verse. Here, too, she employed her play on verbal stems (paranomasia), alliteration

and anaphora, and used the ellipsis of verbs and nouns, which is typical of Russian colloquial speech, but rare in conventional "literary" prose.[2]

Still, prose never supplanted poetry in her heart. Later she wrote to Vladislav Khodasevich, a fellow poet: "One shouldn't grant life, or the emigration, or Vishnyaks, or 'bridge-parties,' or all of them—that triumph: [ . . . ] To force a poet to do without verses, to make of a poet—a prose-writer, and of the prose-writer—a corpse. You (we!) have received something which we have no right to drop."[3]

In a long letter to Teskova, Tsvetaeva summarized her ten years abroad: she had never liked France; she had found no real friends there, only short-lived relationships. Her only friend, Izvolskaya, had left for Japan. "In the seven years in France my heart has grown infinitely cold," she wrote. Only Mur, for the time being, still needed her. She made no mention of Efron, but offered a sarcastic description of the French milieu: "Salons, crowds of people, conversations with a neighbor, always met by chance, sometimes interesting talk and good-bye forever. [ . . . ] I sense that everyone knows and understands everything, but is utterly involved with himself—in literary circles (of which I am writing)—with his own current book. I feel that I have no place there." But she felt as alienated among the émigrés: "From the Russians I am separated by my poetry, which nobody understands; by my personal views, which some take for Bolshevism, others for monarchism or anarchism; by my different opinions on education (everyone is secretly blaming me for the way I bring up Mur); and then again—by all of me."[4]

Efron was now well on the way to turning his sympathy for the cause of Communism and his nostalgia for his homeland into active support of the Soviets. If his work on *Versts* and *Eurasia* had permitted him to bridge his pro-Soviet views with those of some of the émigrés, now the split between the left and the right in the Eurasian movement, which had widened since 1928, forced a decision. Together with some of his friends, he joined in 1932 the "Union for Repatriation," a notorious front-organization for the NKVD (Soviet secret police), which recruited spies among White Russian émigrés who wanted to return to Russia. As Tsvetaeva wrote to Teskova: "Sergey Yakovlevich has submerged himself totally in Soviet Russia, does not see anything else and sees only what he wants to see."[5] She felt isolated in her own family. Alya was growing away from her, siding with her father in his desire to return to Russia. She was torn by deeply conflicting feelings; what would become of Mur? "Should I go to Russia?" she asked Teskova. "There they will take Mur away completely and whether that will be for his good, I don't know. And not only will they shut me up there by not publishing my things, they won't even let me write them." [6]

Still, Tsvetaeva's unhappiness in France had grown by this time to such a degree that she was determined that Mur would not, must not, become a Frenchman. She had tried as hard as she could to alienate Mur from the surrounding French culture and society. He was "her" Mur and had to grow up in her culture: "Didn't I push into you / All Russia with an air pump!" In "Poems to My Son" she advised him to return to his own country, making a clear distinction between her generation and his:

> Go home, my son, —forward—
> Into *your* country, *your* century, *your* hour—from us—
> Into Russia—of yours, into the Russia—of the masses.[7]

The poem reads almost like a farewell to Mur, but also, through him, like a renewed hello to her native soil.

In the spring of 1932, the Efrons moved to smaller, cheaper quarters in Clamart, another Paris suburb. Their new home had no bathroom and no separate room for Tsvetaeva, who slept in the kitchen. Understandably, the crowded living conditions increased family tensions. "My nerves are in a terrible state," Tsvetaeva wrote. "At the slightest provocation, my tears come flooding and a lump rises in my throat. [ . . . ] I relax only when I write or when, miraculously, I am alone in the street, if only for five minutes. Then everything passes. If I am ill, it's only from this communal living." [8]

That summer of 1932, Tsvetaeva, driven by the need to think through, to analyze, to define, also wrote two major theoretical essays: "The Poet and Time" and "Art in the Light of Conscience."

In "The Poet and Time," Tsvetaeva considers a personal problem: can the poet, can she herself, stand outside her time? She had often written that she had been born too late, that she hated her own time, but now she came to understand that "I cannot love my century more than the preceding one, but neither can I create any other century than my own: one cannot create what has been created already and one creates only forward!" [9] From a purely psychological point of view, it is interesting that the image of mother and children surfaces even here in an entirely different context: "Verses are our children. Our children are older than we are because they will live longer and farther." [10]

For Tsvetaeva "there is something more important in poems than their meaning—their sound." [11] She demonstrates by recalling someone who had asked her if "The Swain" was about the Revolution, failing to understand that the poem "is it, the Revolution, its footstep." [12] But Tsvetaeva saw the poet as something higher than the voice of his time: "He is fated instead to lead his time." [13]

At the heart of the longer and more elaborate essay, "Art in the Light of Conscience," is the concept of the artist—more specifically, the writer and the poet—as ruled by different laws from those that govern uncreative people. Tsvetaeva used examples from Pushkin, Goethe, Tolstoy, Blok, Gogol, and others to convey what art meant to her. The poet's spiritual mission in life could be discussed only on the highest level. "Therefore, I insist, what I say is addressed exclusively to those for whom God—holiness—*are*." [14] Tsvetaeva had not turned religious, but her poetry served a higher power. Poetry *was* her religion.

But this poet, for whom moral values were of the highest importance, saw the ethical dilemma of the artist as follows: does he have to follow his calling, regardless of the human consequences, or is he limited by his sense of responsibility? "Here the law of art is the direct reverse of the moral law. An artist is guilty only in two instances: refusing to create a work of art and creating an inartistic work. Here his lesser responsibility ends and here begins his boundless responsibility as a human being." [15]

The two basic elements of creativity were inspiration and will, and of the two, inspiration was more important. Where inspiration was concerned, there were three categories: the significant poet, the great poet, and the lofty poet. Again, the image she uses incorporates her lifelong longing: even the loftiest poet is held in the hands of a higher power, conjuring up the image of an infant in the secure hands of a mother.

> For the merely significant poet, art is always an aim in itself, that is, a mere function without which he cannot live and for which he is not responsible. For the great and lofty poet, it is always a means. He himself is a means in someone's hands, as indeed the merely significant poet is, too—in other hands. The whole difference, apart from the basic difference of which hands, is in the degree of consciousness the poet has of his being held. The spiritually greater the poet, that is, the loftier the hands holding him, the more powerfully conscious is he of this "being-held" (his being in service). [16]

For Tsvetaeva, the poet creates "under a spell," bearing his or her own truth, outside the ordinary categories of good and evil. This certainly was Tsvetaeva's truth: "To be possessed by the work of one's own hands is to be held in someone's hands," the absolute union which gave her safety and superiority, the only such union possible for her in this life. She knew the price she had to pay for her dedication, for her willingness to separate herself from ordinary people with ordinary goals. "Therefore, if you wish to serve God or man, if you have any wish to serve, to work for the good, then join the Salvation Army or something like that—and *give up poetry*." [17] She recognized that, from the human point of view, the doctor and the priest are more necessary than the poet. Yet, she chose to be a poet and accepted that she might be judged—and found wanting—for her choice. Still, she felt confident that one day she would be redeemed. "If there is a Judgment Day of the Word," she wrote, "at that I am innocent." [18]

In the summer of 1932 Tsvetaeva literally dreamed up a new passion, this time for Salomea Halpern. The two women often met, but they also exchanged letters since Halpern had an apartment in Paris, while Tsvetaeva lived on the outskirts and spent many summers outside the city. A letter of August 12, 1932, throws a powerful light on Tsvetaeva's desperate attempt to break out of her isolation. It describes a dream in which she had seen Salomea "with such love and such yearning" that, on awakening, she wondered why she had not understood before that she could still love so much. [19] In the dream she saw Salomea in all her beauty, surrounded by many others, and wondered when she could be alone with her "since I wanted to crash down into you, as from a mountain into an abyss." She went on to describe Salomea's appearance:

> You were in something white, wide, loose, flowing, in a dress that was all the time being shaped by your body: the body of your soul. The memory of you in that dream is as of seaweed in water, its movements. You were quietly swayed by some sea which was separating you from me. There were no events, I know only that I loved you to such a degree of frenzy (wordlessly), wanted to be with you with such self-oblivion that now I am completely drained (overflowing).

More than ever, Tsvetaeva escaped from reality into a dream where she felt safe. "The dream is myself in full freedom (of inevitability), that air necessary for me to breathe, my weather, my light, my hour of the day, my season of the year, my longitude and latitude. Only in the dream I am I. The rest is incidental." Despite all her cerebral attempts to renounce desire, to deaden her sexual instincts, Tsvetaeva needed to blot out her pain in a sexual passion that promised oblivion:

> If I were now with you, near you, I would surely—notwithstanding either the seven-year-long acquaintance or the obvious nonsense of a dream in the light of day—I would, for sure, knowing myself—bury myself in you, I would dig myself into you, would cover myself with you from everything: the day, the century, the light, from your eyes and my own, no less merciless ones.

Tsvetaeva's passion, as we have seen, could flare up for men or for women. The dream about Halpern seemed at first to have originated simply from her need for human response, as she herself admitted: "Tonight you were exactly the face of my yearning, which for so long has had no face, —neither a man's, nor a woman's." But then she went further: "Since to love so much, so, so much as I loved you in my dream of today (so much is impossible), I could never have loved—what him?—not a single him, no him in reality. Only a woman (my own essence). Only in a dream (in freedom). Since the face of my yearning—is a woman's face." The letter ends on a note of utter sadness, Tsvetaeva's perception that reciprocal love does not exist: "In the dream you haven't really loved me that much (to love like that, the two of us, is impossible, there is no space for it)." It gives dramatic evidence of Tsvetaeva's anguish, her deep homosexual longings, and her entrapment in her own world.

This "dream experience" may have rekindled the memory of another fire that in real life had consumed Tsvetaeva: her love affair with Sofiya Parnok. Inspired by the reliving of the passion and pain of that unique relationship, Tsvetaeva wrote in French her *Letter to an Amazon*, a reply to Natalie Clifford Barney's *Pensées d'une Amazone*. The manuscript bears a note: "Clamart, finished in November–December 1932 (Recopied and revised in November 1934, with a little more gray hair. M. Ts.)"[20] In this essay, Tsvetaeva's own loneliness, her fear of growing old, is manifest in her portrayal of an aging lesbian, deserted by lovers who had chosen to bear children.

> She would die alone because she is too proud to love a dog, too full of memories to adopt a child. She wants neither animals nor orphans, not even a companion. [ . . . ] She does not want paid warmth, borrowed

smiles. She does not want to be either a vampire or a grandmother. [ ... ] She would never be the poor relation at the feast of other people's youth. Neither friendship nor respect nor even that other abyss which is our own goodness—she would substitute nothing for love. She would not renounce that splendid blackness, with its round, black burn-mark of the fire of joy of yesteryear.[21]

## 22. Indigence and Autobiographical Prose

*My loyal writing table!*
*Thank you for walking*
*Beside me on all my roads.*
*You protected me — like a scar.*[1]

I n the spring of 1933 Georgy Ivask, a poet and literary critic who lived in Estonia, became interested in Tsvetaeva's poetry and began a correspondence which lasted until 1939, when he moved to Paris. Tsvetaeva's responses to Ivask's questions clarify some of her more complex poems. But in her first letter she also described her life. "You cannot imagine the poverty in which I live. My only income comes from my writing. My husband is ill and cannot work. My daughter is earning five francs a day by crocheting little caps. I have a son, Georgy, who is eight years old. The four of us live off that money. To put it differently, we are slowly dying of starvation." [2] Tsvetaeva wanted Ivask to understand that she lived not only outside Russia but outside the émigré community, and although she hated the Bolsheviks as much as the émigrés did, hers was a different hatred:

> No, my friend, I am not with these and not with those, not with the third ones or with the hundredth ones; nor am I with the politicians or even the writers. I am with no one, alone all my life, without [my] books, without readers, without friends, without a circle, without a milieu, without any protection, without any belongings — worse than a dog, but instead — instead — I have everything.[3]

Tsvetaeva wrote mostly prose now, but she constantly had to battle with publishers and editors: first to have her work accepted, then to protect it from deletions and distortions. Prose would never offer her the same gratification as her poems. She was a poet. As she wrote to Teskova:

I hardly write any poems and this is why: I cannot limit myself to one poem—they come to me in families, in cycles, as in a funnel or even a whirlpool in which I find myself, and consequently the problem is time. I cannot simultaneously write the usual prose and poetry, I couldn't have done it even had I been a free person. [ . . . ] The emigration is making a prose writer of me. Of course, the prose is also mine, and the best in the world after poetry. It is lyrical prose, but still—*after* poetry.[4]

Tsvetaeva followed her Voloshin essay with "A Captive Spirit," a superb portrait of Bely, written immediately after his death in 1934. She also wrote "An Otherworldly Evening," a moving memoir of a literary evening in St. Petersburg on the eve of the Revolution that was an impressionistic evocation of the dying world of the writers and poets of that tragic period. However, her autobiographical pieces are the most significant writing of the years 1933–1936: "My Father and His Museum," "The House at Old Pimen," "Mother and Music," "The Devil," "My Pushkin," "Pushkin and Pugachev," "Mother's Fairy Tale," and "The Khlystovki." The themes of these autobiographical "prose poems" were the themes of her life: love and pain, renunciation and pride. And in the center stand Marina and her mother, as we have seen.

The news of her stepbrother Andrey's death in Moscow, in 1933, may have triggered Tsvetaeva's return to the past, as Jane Taubman suggests.[5] Or perhaps it was the twentieth anniversary of the opening of her father's museum. Whatever it was, she needed to leave her present misery behind and to go back to her "secure" childhood, to understand what had brought her to her present state. Her autobiographical essays are a form of self-analysis and a mythology of a lost world: "I want to resurrect that entire world—so that all of them should not have lived in vain, so that I should not have lived in vain," she wrote.[6]

In 1928, as she tried to mobilize goodwill among the émigré community, either to obtain a subsidy or to sell tickets to one of her readings, Tsvetaeva had met with an unexpectedly warm response from Vera Bunina, the wife of Ivan Bunin, who later won the Nobel Prize for literature. Tsvetaeva disliked Bunin and knew that the feeling was mutual, but Vera Bunina became one of her favorite correspondents. She had been a close friend of Tsvetaeva's stepsister Valeriya, and had known not only Tsvetaeva's family and home, but the entire family of Valeriya's mother, her father's first wife. Vera Bunina's maiden name was Muromtseva, and the Tsvetaevs, Ilovayskys, and Muromtsevs had been close for at least two, if not three, generations. According to family lore, the man with whom Tsvetaev's first wife had been in love was either Vera's father or her uncle. Now, in 1933, Tsvetaeva was grateful for this link to the past. She addressed long lists of questions to Bunina, pressing her to recall the season of a certain event, the specific statues in her father's museum and other details of the past. Bunina, in turn, sent Tsvetaeva her essay about the Ilovaysky house, material which Tsvetaeva used in her own way. Tsvetaeva remembered everything "emotionally"; she saw more than eyes alone could see. She wrote to Bunina that the forces in childhood were stronger than any other in life, for they represented the roots of one's existence.

> Listen. You know that all of that has come to an end, to an end forever. Those houses—are gone. Trees (our poplar trees of the Three Ponds house, especially the one, a giant, planted by my father with his own hands the day of the birth of his only son), these trees are gone. *We, as we were*—we are no more. Everything has burnt down to ashes, has sunk to the bottom and drowned. Whatever remains, remains inside: in you, in me, in Asya, and in a few more. Don't laugh, but aren't we the last of the Mohicans? And I am proud of the contemptuous "vestige," as the Communists call us. I am glad to be a vestige, because all that I represent—will outlive even me (and them!).[7]

Tsvetaeva began by writing about her father, writing shorter pieces that she wanted to combine under the title "My Father and His Museum." (Later she wrote additional sketches about him directly in French, hoping to make some money in French journals, but they never appeared.) She portrays her father nostalgically, idealizing his dedication to the museum that he created. She stresses his lack of vanity, but says little about his love of art or his feelings for his wife or children. Against the background of the museum's white marble and the cold sculptures, we see a man striving for achievement for achievement's sake. Even so, the pomp of the museum's opening, with the tsar in attendance, impressed the young Marina as a symbol of her father's success. Still, he remains as distant in these mature reflections as he was in her childhood.

While she was working on the essays about her father, Tsvetaeva turned to the next part of her family saga, "The House at Old Pimen," in which she let her memory and her imagination wander as freely as they did in her dreams. Andrey's and Valeriya's grandfather Ilovaysky lived in that house, along with his second wife, Aleksandra Aleksandrovna, and their three children: Sergey,

Nadya—whom Tsvetaeva had adored in her childhood—and Olya, who vanished when she married a Jew. Marina and Asya visited the house only once, but it was a perfect setting for Tsvetaeva to bring to life the themes she was contemplating: that of a young woman married to an older man she does not love; that of a mother's envy and control of her daughters, and, finally, the idea of all-powerful fate.

To Aleksandra Aleksandrovna Ilovayskaya—A. A.—Tsvetaeva could attribute some of the feelings she perceived in her own mother, although in this essay the two women are seen in contrast. A. A., the beautiful young woman who had married an old, powerful man, became, then, the personification of many suffering women. She lived in servitude to a man whose principles belonged to a different time, who was rigid and frightening and whose effect on A. A. Tsvetaeva must have witnessed:

> When you know that never . . . nowhere . . . you begin to live right here.
> This way. You adapt to fit the enclosed space. What from the threshold
> seemed madness and arbitrariness, becomes the measure of things—
> while the jailer, seeing submissiveness, softens a little, gives in a little,
> and there begins a monstrous alliance, but a real alliance of the pris-
> oner with the jailer, of the unloving with the unloved, the molding of
> her in his image and likeness.[8]

Reacting to the frustration and bitterness of her "monstrous marriage," A. A. controlled her daughters with endless prohibitions. If she had buried herself alive in that house, she would also prevent her daughters from enjoying happy, fulfilled lives:

> And there you have it, the *subconscious* (I underline this three times) re-
> venge on her daughters for her own ruined life. [ . . . ] She squeezed
> them with a steely hand and did not allow any freedom so that her
> female offspring too would not be happy. [ . . . ] But did she really
> know that she was exacting revenge? It was a knowing inner nature
> inside her that exacted revenge, that avenged the self that had been
> trampled down.[9]

In a letter to Bunina, Tsvetaeva wrote of A. A.: "In her lived the suppressed, the *crushed* youth. All that had been frustrated went to war against the life of her daughters (*Subconsciously:* 'I have not lived—and *you* ought not to live!'). All that is in the deepest core of women's being (NON-BEING)." [10] This was neither a realistic description of A. A. nor a picture of Tsvetaeva's own mother, but a composite sketch of the mother-daughter relationship as Tsvetaeva herself had subconsciously absorbed it. There was, however, also a son in the Ilovay-sky family and Tsvetaeva makes a clear distinction: "She [A. A.] was a mother to her son, not to her daughters. [ . . . ] And can you—I am only raising the question—do you inevitably and thus immutably love a child from a man you don't love, maybe a man you can't stand? Anna Karenina could, but that was a son, a son like her, a son of hers, an ego-son, the son of her heart." [11] There is no better description of Tsvetaeva's feelings toward Mur.

Unfortunately, Efron and Alya saw in Tsvetaeva the mother she depicted in "The House at Old Pimen." In a letter to Bunina written in November 1934, Tsvetaeva described overhearing them whispering in the kitchen. Alya was speaking about her with haughty disdain, but when Tsvetaeva turned to Efron and asked him what he felt when he heard such talk, he replied, "Nothing." She added, "And in Alya's presence he says that I am a living A. A. Ilovayskaya and that is why I described her so well." [12]

Once Tsvetaeva had finished her essay on Old Pimen, she resumed fighting with her editors, especially Vadim V. Rudnev, the senior editor of *Contemporary Notes*, who had substantially cut her Voloshin essay and published only half of "Art in the Light of Conscience." Tsvetaeva's efforts to have her work published without cuts, deletions, or corrections at a time when she needed every franc to pay her rent or buy food were heroic. She always remained polite in her letters to editors, but in letters to her friends she often expressed her anger, sometimes quoting the ignorant letters of her detractors. For her, to whom every comma was of the utmost importance, the poor copyediting in the journals was a curse she tried to avoid by asking friends to copyedit her work for her. She pleaded with Georgy Fedotov, one of her Eurasian friends and an admirer of her poetry, to speed up her fee because "they came to put a lien on our belongings, for the first time in our life." And in May, she apologized because she could not keep an appointment with him when the sole of one of her shoes—the only pair she had—fell off. [13]

Part of her reminiscences about her father appeared in *Latest News*. In the fall of 1933 she offered "The House at Old Pimen" to *Contemporary Notes*. Rudnev expressed his doubts, but asked to see the manuscript, which she submitted in October. In December she answered his offer to publish an abridged version of the piece:

I have worked for too long, too zealously, and too meticulously on "Old Pimen" to accept any deletions. A poet's prose is a different work from the prose of a prose writer; its measuring unit is the effort (the diligence)—not the phrase, but the word, and often even—the syllable

[ . . . ]. In these years I have eaten and drunk too much bitterness. I have been published since 1910, [ . . . ] and now in 1933 I am still considered *here* either a beginner or an amateur—a guest artist. I say *here* since in Russia my poems appear in anthologies as models of conciseness.[14]

Tsvetaeva asked to have the manuscript returned to her, but Rudnev gave in and in 1934 "The House at Old Pimen" appeared in its entirety in *Contemporary Notes*.

In March 1933 the Efrons had moved to a more spacious apartment, also in Clamart. Tsvetaeva was happy to have a room of her own, but her life continued under a cloud. Efron had applied in 1932 for a Soviet passport. Tsvetaeva wrote to Halpern that "his passport has not come yet, which makes me very (deeply) happy." She also wrote that she had received letters from some of those who had left for the Soviet Union. Clearly, they did not have enough to eat and needed money, even in St. Petersburg. So her decision was made: "I am definitely not going, which means that we must separate, and that (as much as we fight) after twenty years of life together—is hard." [15]

The marriage, always a complex, unconventional relationship, was in trouble. Tsvetaeva did not share the political work in which her husband was totally submerged. Yet she continued to present him to others as an idealist whose integrity, dedication, and intelligence she admired. And she went on seeing him as a gifted writer. "The main channel I am steering him into is, of course, writing," she had written to Lomonosova in 1931:

He can become one of the best theoreticians [on film, which Efron had studied]. He has the ideas, interest, training. In Czechoslovakia, he wrote many purely literary pieces and some were published. Good pieces. If he were in Russia, he definitely would be a writer. A prose writer (and a man of *his* type, with a strong public and ideological orientation) needs a *circle* and a *base*: everything we do not have and will not have here.[16]

In fact, Efron was quite unsuccessful as a writer, and it was not enough for him to be just "Tsvetaeva's husband." He probably looked for compensation in his political work as he dreamed of returning home and building a new life. By 1933 his political views were in sharp conflict with Tsvetaeva's.

Finally the entire family became ill. Tsvetaeva turned to Teskova:

At home—things are not too good. First of all, even if nobody is sick (seriously), nobody is well, either. Mur has an inflammation of the liver, needs a special diet, he has lost a lot of weight—both from the liver and from the idiotic French school. Alya is losing weight all the time, she is transparent, listless, evidently highly anemic. Six years of [art] school, for the time being, for nought. She makes some money— not by drawing, though, but by doing odd jobs, such as stuffing toy animals. Now, perhaps, she will get a job as an assistant to a dentist's assistant—because we have *nothing* to live on. She is also much changed inwardly. . . . It is dirty and cold in our place (coal and its absence). In Vshenory [Czechoslovakia] it was also dirty, but there was a big, cozy oven, the forest was outside the window, there was the *coziness of poverty* and the diversion of *real nature*.[17]

The year was 1933; Hitler had come to power in Germany and, despite Tsvetaeva's absorption in her private world, political events could not be entirely ignored. The world was in a crisis that would lead to World War II, and Tsvetaeva's husband and daughter were becoming politically committed. But Tsvetaeva refused to understand her husband's needs, or Alya's or even Mur's. She complained to Bunina that "my family lives with different things, in time and with time. Nobody wants a dream while awake (and—what's more— someone else's dream)." When she wrote about Efron and Alya, it was with a certain aloofness; she seemed to accept their distance. However, Mur's lack of sensitivity and his indifference to her must have stung her: "My son (eight years) lives totally not in the current day, but in tomorrow's, the coming one—with plans, promises, future joys—[ . . . ] and he listens to me even with some superiority (Poor Mama, how strange you are. You seem to be *very* old.)." Perhaps the most revealing passage in this letter shows Tsvetaeva's dismissal of the events around her and the contempt she felt for people who took them seriously. "Besides, there are events, wars, Hitlers, Herriot, Balboa, Rossi, and whatever else their names—that is what really grips people in life: the newspaper, which bores me to death."[18] It was not that she was unaware of the rising tide of totalitarianism, but that she had to see it in her own terms; only her own experience mattered. Early in life, her need for freedom had instilled in her a fear of any collective society, which she identified with the rise of totalitarianism. "I am not afraid of my future, but of 'theirs,' when I will be no more," she wrote to Bunina.

In childhood (when I was about thirteen) they took me once to an ideal children's home, a "settlement," where the children did everything themselves and did everything together. And there to the question: "How did you like it?" I answered the teacher laconically, as I used to talk then: "Well enough to hang myself." The future *in the best case* [ . . . ] is a "settlement." [19]

Physically and emotionally drained, Tsvetaeva wallowed in self-pity. Slonim has described her hopelessness: " 'I am totally alone,' she kept repeating. 'Around me is a void.' It seemed to me that she was not only painfully affected by her isolation, but was even ready to exaggerate it. . . . And she added: 'My faith is ruined, my hopes have disappeared, my strength is exhausted.' I never felt as sorry for her as on that day." [20] In a letter to Teskova, Tsvetaeva expressed the same despair: "They don't accept my poems anywhere. I write little and without any hope for them ever to be published. I live as though in a convent or in a fortress, only without the grandeur of either. I have never lived in such isolation and servitude."

Tsvetaeva's self-pity was transformed in May 1934 into one of her most moving poems, "Homesickness."

> It doesn't matter among what faces
> I am to bristle like a captive lion,
> Or what human crowd will
> Push me — without fail —
>
> Into myself, into my own feelings
> Like a Kamchatka bear without an ice-floe.
> *Where* not to fit in (and I am not trying)
> Or *where* to be humiliated — I do not care.

The rowanberry — mountain ash — which figures prominently in Russian folklore, and which is one of Tsvetaeva's earliest self-images, appears at the very end of the poem. Perhaps the creative process of writing "Homesickness" had revived, if only temporarily, her sense of belonging somewhere. Bitterly rejecting throughout the poem an attachment to any home, she cannot sustain the denial:

> Every house is strange to me, every temple empty,
> Nothing matters, everything is the same.
> But if along the road a bush
> Does rise, especially a rowan . . . [21]

Returning to poetry helped Tsvetaeva pull herself out of her depression, and her letters from Elancourt, a village near Paris where she stayed with Mur in the summer of 1934, convey a calmer mood. In the fall, the family moved to Vanves, another Paris suburb. For once, she loved their new place, an old stone house, almost a ruin, where she had a large room for herself, on a street lined with chestnut trees.

Tsvetaeva had expected to have regular outlets for her prose in *Latest News* and *Contemporary Notes*. Yet, though they published her longer autobiographical essays and her literary portraits, the shorter pieces she submitted could not bring in the income she needed. When some of her work, first tentatively accepted, was returned, she felt personally victimized. In one such case, she finally turned to Bunina, asking her to have her husband intervene: "Last time when the rent was due, Vera, there was quite a scandal: suddenly in the editorial office, a gush of tears and my own voice speaking without my will (and I listen: 'If tomorrow, gentlemen, you hear that I have applied to return to Soviet Russia, you should know that it is *you*: your lack of interest, your ill will, and your contempt')." In the same letter, Tsvetaeva asked her friend not to judge her if she should hear that she had really applied to return to Russia. But she ended with the words: "Yet, I'll still wait. I DON'T FEEL LIKE IT!" [22]

The yearly poetry readings that Tsvetaeva organized were an important source of income for her, but they were less well frequented than in her first years in Paris. One of her friends described such a reading:

> Marina Tsvetaeva did not enjoy great popularity, but still people came. Her dress was modest, worn, thin bangs on her forehead, her hair an indefinable color—ash blond with streaks of gray, her face pale, slightly sallow. Silver bracelets and rings on her work-worn hands. Her eyes were green, but not mysteriously green, and not strikingly beautiful, looking straight ahead like the eyes of a night bird blinded by the light. She obviously did not see those who had come to look at her or to listen to her. Marina Tsvetaeva recited her poems in a loud voice, stressing individual words and cadences as though she were issuing a challenge. She didn't seem to care about the impression she was making. I have never met a performer who was freer from the desire to please the public. [23]

Tsvetaeva reported to Bunina that someone, asked to buy tickets for one of her "evenings," had said: " 'Tsvetaeva is causing much harm to herself by her silver rings: *let her sell them first*.' " He was not the only one to reproach Tsvetaeva for her constant "begging." [24]

Then, November 21, 1934, "Another sorrow: mine. Pure and sharp like a diamond," she wrote to Teskova. Nikolay Gronsky, the young poet whom Tsvetaeva had considered her pupil, was killed in an accident in the Paris Metro. His last poem, "Belladonna," was published posthumously. His parents showed Tsvetaeva their son's notebook with a number of his unpublished poems, and she was saddened to discover that some of those he had written for her during the year of their friendship were now dedicated to his fiancée. Her article about the young poet, "A Posthumous Gift," initiated by Gronsky's father, was considered for a long time by *Latest News* and finally rejected as too intimate. She organized an evening to discuss Gronsky's poetry, but it was not very successful. So it was in a cycle of poems, "Gravestone," that she expressed her reawakened feelings for Gronsky. Her attitude toward death had changed since "New Year's Greeting," when she had spoken to the dead Rilke, whose soul seemed immortal and whose fate in heaven seemed assured. Now she mourned Gronsky, but she knew no consolation; death was loss and only in memory could the dead survive: "Your face, / Your warmth, / Your shoulder—where has it gone?" she wrote. "You've gone, you've gone forever."[25]

In 1935 Tsvetaeva enrolled Mur in a private school, incurring new expenses. She was criticized for this "extravagance," since he could have attended a public school. She explained her reasons to Bunina:

> Because my father sent students abroad at his own expense, paid for so many high school students and when he was dying, left—of his personal money—20,000 rubles for a school in his native village, I am entitled to have Mur study in a good school (if only because there are 15 and not 40 students in the class). That is, I am entitled to pay for him from my own pocket and when it is empty—to ask for it.[26]

This was Tsvetaeva's general attitude toward money: she was "entitled to it." And nothing could stand in the way of Mur's needs. Unusually tall for his age, stocky and not particularly attractive, he was always with his mother. Tsvetaeva's devotion to him knew no limits. Since his birth, she had sacrificed hours of her precious time to him and had never refused him anything. But many of her friends remarked how rude he was to her in return. She wrote to Teskova:

> As long as I live—Mur has to be happy, and happy means first of all he has to be alive and well. This is, as I see it, my most sensible decision

and even not a decision but my simplest instinct: to protect him. Please reply to that, dear Anna Antonovna, because my taking him to school and my walks with him (one hour in the morning, two—in the afternoon) are considered *crazy*. Give me a garden or a good person to replace me or leave me alone! Nobody judges the wealthy who have governesses and baby nurses, or the *fortunate ones* who have grandmothers. Why do they judge *me*? And they all do.[27]

Still, Tsvetaeva never experienced with Mur the closeness that she had shared with Alya. Alya had worshiped her mother, whom she saw as a great poet, while Mur fought back with cynicism and rudeness. Tsvetaeva "invented" her son as she had "invented" her "lovers." She dreaded ever losing him. She wanted to see in him an extension of herself. No wonder, then, that in her descriptions of Mur she stressed again and again how much he looked and acted like her, while in the photographs we see no such resemblance. She wrote to Halpern:

Let's start with Mur, i.e., with something pleasant: He is a brilliant student (and don't forget that he has learned French all by himself! Nobody taught him a word!); he is intelligent, fairly kind (that is, highly sensitive); he is an activist, a philosopher, he is like me, but with beauty and with gaiety; he is like me—without the catastrophe. (But, of course, his own will come.) He is very gifted, but nothing of a *Wunder-kind*.[28]

She sent a photograph to Teskova:

And here is my wonderful Mur—handsome? Anyway—looks like me. And looks more like Napoleon's son than Napoleon's son himself. I knew that since he was three months old: one has to know how to read features. And in response to his photograph when he was six months old, Boris Pasternak wrote to me: "I look and look at your Napoleonid." Since I was eleven years old I have loved Napoleon. My entire childhood, adolescence, and youth was in him (and his son) and this went with me and lived in me without fading, and with that I will die. I cannot see his name indifferently. And now *his face* is Mur's. Strange? Or not strange, as with any organic miracle.[29]

A small incident seems to epitomize Mur's attitude toward his mother. After school one day, he told her: "I looked today at my teacher and I wondered: 'After all she has some reputation, she is known in society, but Mama—she writes well, doesn't she?—but nobody knows her because she

writes abstract things and now is not the time to write abstract things. So—
what should you do? You cannot write other things, can you? No, you had
better write in your way.' "[30]

How different from Alya's acceptance of an idealized Marina! Mur, obviously, was more contrary and certainly more critical. It would not be surprising that the very bright Mur was aware of his mother's money problems.
The Czech subsidy had finally been canceled in 1932; *Freedom of Russia* had
ceased publication in 1933; neither of his parents had a secure income then.
It is more surprising that Tsvetaeva does not mention in her correspondence that Efron had been contributing financially to the family since 1934,
when he became a major actor in the NKVD establishment and had a decent
salary. Halpern, in the introductory notes to her letters, mentions that she
had stopped her assistance to the Efrons in 1934 "when things were financially improving for Marina."[31] Slonim set the date a year later: "From 1935
on Sergey Efron became a paid worker of the 'Union of Repatriation,' but
Marina didn't, of course, even suspect that the money he was bringing home
came from a special fund of the Soviet Secret Police."[32] New material about
Efron's activities continues to surface. In 1992 Alen Brossa wrote in an article
published in a special Tsvetaeva centennial edition of the *Literaturnaya gazeta*
(Literary Gazette) that Efron's " 'work' (from 1934) was so decently paid that
for the first time he could—finally!—support his family. For the first time in
his life Efron was earning a good salary and had a permanent position."[33]

How much did Tsvetaeva know or guess about the kind of work in which
Efron was involved? Many of her friends and admirers insist that she was
totally ignorant. Others, however, assert that his source of income and his
political activities were general subjects of conversation in their circle and
that Tsvetaeva must have known. Alya, who was close to her father, was no
doubt fully informed. Yet Tsvetaeva was altogether capable of denying the
obvious to herself, if she so desired.

She could not deny the break in the family that occurred when Alya moved
out in February 1935. She reported to Bunina that she had been scheduled to
give a lecture, but when she asked Alya to pick up a prescription for Mur as
a favor for her, Alya procrastinated. Tsvetaeva became angry, telling Alya that
it was a disgrace to behave like that on the day of her lecture. Alya replied
" 'You are disgraced anyway.' " One sharp word led to another and when
Alya said " 'You've gone far enough. Everyone knows you're a liar,' " Tsvetaeva slapped her twenty-three-year-old daughter. Then, she wrote, "Sergey,
enraged (against me), told her she should not stay a minute longer and gave
her money for her expenses."[34] The letter acknowledged that it was wrong

to slap a grown-up daughter, "but I would have slapped anyone, including the President of the Republic, who said such a thing [ . . . ]. My daughter is the first person to hold me in contempt and she certainly will be the last, unless her chldren follow suit." [35] Alya left, and "with her, such help as she gave me (under compulsion the last two years). Also gone are all her unbearable resistance and ridicule." Alya stayed with friends and moved back some time later, but the strains in the family continued.

In 1935 darkness began to descend on the world in earnest. The year saw Germany incorporating the Saar, Italy invading Abyssinia, the onset of the Nuremberg Laws against Jews, and the beginning of the Stalin purges. Tsvetaeva's private world was just as dark, with the fateful decision about returning to Russia hovering over the family.

# 23. Further Withdrawal

*The eyes wide open into the blue sky —*
*As you exclaim: A storm is coming!*

*Looking up at a passing rascal —*
*As you exclaim: Love is coming!*

*Through the indifferent gray mosses —*
*So I exclaim: Verses are coming!* [1]

By 1935 Efron was secretary general of the "Union of Repatriation"; Alya worked for *Our Country* (*Nasha Strana*), published by the Soviet Trade Commission; Mur had begun to side with his father and sister. Tsvetaeva, meanwhile, was rethinking, re-creating her past. She wrote to Teskova that she had discovered how, subconsciously, she had never left her Moscow house, never wanted to leave it: "I *never* had a light in the corridor in any of my apartments. And, suddenly not long ago I understood: Well, in our home at Three Pond Lane there was a dark corridor, and I, oh my lord, always shut my eyes tight to have it even darker. . . . You see — I am *restoring*." [2] Tsvetaeva was hiding from "modernity," from the new forces that were rising all around her: Communism, Fascism, Nazism. Thus she could not understand the world from which, in June 1935, Boris Pasternak suddenly arrived. He had undergone a deep personal crisis and was in a sanatorium for treatment of insomnia and depression when Stalin ordered him to Paris as a delegate to the International Congress of Writers for the Defense of Culture. Inside Russia there was a growing recognition of Stalin's terror, but in the West many saw the choice as between Nazism and Communism.

Tsvetaeva met Pasternak in the halls of the conference, but this was hardly the dramatic encounter about which both had been dreaming and writing. "What a non-meeting!" Tsvetaeva wrote. She reported to Teskova that Pasternak had whispered to her: " 'I didn't dare not to come, Stalin's secretary came to see me, I got scared.' (He hated to go without his beautiful wife, but they put him on a plane and sent him off )." [3] Tsvetaeva's tone conveys utter contempt for such lack of "fearlessness." Years later Yelena Fedotova, the wife of the religious philosopher Georgy Fedotov, recalled Tsvetaeva's telling her that Pasternak had whispered to her, " 'Marina, don't go to Russia. It's cold there; everywhere an icy draft is blowing.' "[4]

During his stay Pasternak visited the Efrons in Vanves. Though Pasternak would recall in his autobiographical sketch that Tsvetaeva's husband was "a charming, refined and steadfast man, and I grew fond of him as if he were my own brother,"[5] surely he must have realized that Sergey was a Soviet agent. Pasternak's biographer Lazar Fleishman points out that

> the vehemently expressed political passions of her family and the crisis tormenting Pasternak precluded any candid discussion of whether Tsvetaeva should go back to her native land. . . . And in her home Pasternak felt himself an even greater prisoner of his false official status, "premier Soviet poet," than he was in Moscow or even at the Paris congress. The people who were closest to him in Paris were much more pro-Soviet than he was, and to tell them about what was plaguing him, to transmit his doubts about the regime, with the arrests and deportations (including news about Mandelshtam, with whom Tsvetaeva had had a love affair before the revolution) was simply beyond his powers.[6]

Tsvetaeva herself had an uneasy feeling about Pasternak that she expressed in a letter to Nikolay Tikhonov in July 1935. She quoted Pasternak as comforting her: "You will love the collective farms!"[7] She who had always hated communal living. Pasternak's irony becomes even more obvious when we read Olga Ivinskaya's retelling of what brought about Pasternak's depression in 1935. He had gone on a trip to see the new collective farms and had told her: " 'There are no words to describe what I saw there. It was such an inhuman, unimaginable misfortune, such a terrible calamity. . . . the mind could simply not take it in. For a whole year I couldn't sleep.' "[8] Before returning to Russia, Pasternak stopped over for two days in London. Raissa Lomonosova wrote to her husband that he was "in a horrible moral and physical state. . . . He's not even able to read the newspapers. To live in constant fear! No, it would be better to clean latrines."[9] Pasternak had evidently conveyed to Raissa Lomonosova how much life in the Soviet Union had changed. Tsvetaeva had not understood his cryptic remarks.

In October 1935 Tsvetaeva wrote a bitter letter to Pasternak. She had encountered a different Boris Pasternak from the one in her dreams, her letters, her poems—not the real Pasternak, but a Pasternak who had disappointed and hurt her. She now responded by attacking. How could he have gone through Germany on his trip home without stopping in Munich to see his mother? But while accusing Pasternak without knowing his state of mind or his health, she defended herself against Rilke's remark in his last letter that she had been "too harsh" to Pasternak. Her "harshness," she wrote, was only her self-defense against Rilke's and Pasternak's softness, which covered up their egotism, their evasion of responsibility, of duty. She herself had strength left only for "communication, for service, for useless sacrifice." [10]

In July, Tsvetaeva left with Mur, who was recovering from an appendectomy, for La Favière, a small beach town in the south of France. Alya was in Normandy, and Tsvetaeva made no mention in her letters of any visits from Efron. She stayed alone with Mur in a small attic room, and her mood was gloomy. The room was hot, there was no table, and it was hard to write poems. Moreover, the resort atmosphere of the place annoyed her. She enjoyed nature and liked simple people, old houses, old streets. Here, everything was filled to overflowing with new boarding houses and vacationers. She felt ostracized and left out. So it was "Mur and I; I and Mur, the seashore and I; Mur, the primus and I; Mur, the ants and I (there is an invasion here!)." [11] Mur had no one to play with and irritated her with his constant questions, typical for a lonely ten-year-old.

At the end of August, she shared her despair, her fear of a breakdown, with Bunina. She had lost hope that her long poems would be published. Although she had turned to prose to bring in some money, poetry was her love, her life. Poetic lines still rose in her, but usually they vanished, leaving her with fragments of poems. "And what if I die? What will remain of these years? (What did I live for??) And—another fear: what if I have lost the ability? That is, if I am already incapable of writing a whole thing: of completing it. And what if until the end of my days I am doomed to fragments?" [12] Tsvetaeva did complete some poems that summer, but more often than not she spent hours looking for the right word, which she could not always find. In her anxiety, she began to think that she might lose her mind and end up a suicide as Schumann had. "Vera, there is such a thing as brain fatigue," she wrote to Bunina. "And I am a candidate. [ . . . ] But, please, say nothing to anyone! In any case, I am coping *for the time being.*" [13]

In the meantime Tsvetaeva had begun a new correspondence with a young Russian woman, Ariadna Berg, whom she had probably met at her friends'. Berg was interested in poetry, wrote some poems in French, and admired Tsvetaeva's "The Swain." On September 2, 1935, Tsvetaeva wrote her a long letter that shows how the appearance of a young man, who could become an admirer, would change her mood. He began visiting her at night when

Mur was asleep. They would read poetry sitting on the stairs — she higher, he lower. But then Alya arrived and the young man called on her instead. Tsvetaeva was outraged but she wrote: "I am reporting to you about that simply because I still am on top of the stairs and do not intend to descend. [ . . . ] The situation was clear: she is twenty, I am forty. [ . . . ] And she has the instinct of a cat to repulse — unnoticeably — with her little paw. [ . . . ] Don't think that it was a wound. My word of honor: not even a scratch. *Perhaps* — a tiny scratch, which is best treated with iodine." [14]

By the end of the summer, Tsvetaeva told Teskova that she had made two new friends: Else Mahler, a professor of Russian language and literature at the University of Basel, to whom she would give her manuscripts when she left for Soviet Russia, and the eminent philologist Boris Unbegaun. She also mentioned a new long poem that she had begun and she described "her marvelous mulatto tan, similar to our Crimean tan," as one of her achievements. "People think that I 'got younger' — I did not, but I have washed myself and dried out in the 40 to 50 degree sun." [15] Well aware that people responded to her charm, Tsvetaeva felt her vitality restored, for at least a little while.

When Tsvetaeva and Mur returned to Vanves in the fall, nothing had changed: Sergey and Alya spent little time at home, and Tsvetaeva understood that they would decide on their own whether to return to the Soviet Union. What was best for Mur? For her that was the burning question. She needed to see herself as a mother, and she needed his dependence on her. Still, she was aware that he was different from her, less emotional, more cerebral. He was highly intelligent, well-read, serious, but "he doesn't know longing, doesn't understand it at all," she wrote to Teskova. But she understood his dilemma: "Mur lives torn between my humanism and the near fanaticism of his father." [16] In her New Year's greetings to Teskova, Tsvetaeva described how she was sitting at home alone at night, with Mur asleep, knitting to the point of "torpor," dreaming about the lamp in her parents' house in Moscow. A month later, she told Teskova that in her hopeless situation only a good fortune-teller could advise her. "Everything is reduced to one thing: to leave or not to leave (if it's to leave — then it's for good)." [17]

Her strongest argument in favor of leaving was that her family was eager to return to Russia. Moreover, the threatening world situation and the hostility of the émigrés frightened her. She saw no future for Mur in France. As for herself, in Moscow, at least, she would find her sister Asya and writers who admired her. On the other hand, she was concerned that if the family moved,

Mur would no longer belong to her. "Here after school he is mine, with me—there he will belong to them, to all of them: Pioneer Groups, working brigades, children's courts, and in the summer—camps, all of it with temptations: drumbeats, physical culture, clubs, flags, and so on and so forth." [18]

She also understood enough of the Soviet political climate to know that with her "fearlessness" she "wouldn't be able to keep quiet, wouldn't be able to sign a congratulatory address to the great Stalin, since it was not I who named him great and even if he is great—this is not my greatness and—most important perhaps—I loathe every triumphant official church."

While Tsvetaeva agonized over her decision, Efron had become totally committed to Soviet intelligence. He occupied a responsible position in the Paris spy network, following orders from the NKVD. Old hands, rotating between Paris and Moscow, were increasingly aware of the danger they might face on their next return. [19] But Efron was politically naive and believed the obsolete slogans of the Communist Party. He was recruiting émigré volunteers for the International Brigade in Spain. What did he know of the fate that awaited some of them at the hands of the NKVD? According to new NKVD orders, many of them were not allowed to fight Franco because they were considered unreliable, and they were liquidated in Spain or, instead, sent to Russia. Tsvetaeva wrote to Teskova in March 1936: "I cannot hold Sergey here any more. And I'm not holding him. He'll not leave without me; he's waiting for something (my 'seeing the light'), not understanding that I will die as I am." She wanted Efron to take upon himself the responsibility for this grave decision. She did not want to return, but she felt that alone with Mur she would perish. She ended the letter with one of her dreams of finding peace and love, safety and nurture: "More than anything I would like to come to you in Czechoslovakia—forever. I would find companions, I would walk across all of Czechoslovakia, I would see castles, old small towns. . . . And—the forest!! and—You!! The friendship with You! (No one loves me really.) I'd love a lair—to the end of my days." [20]

In May, Tsvetaeva went to Brussels at the invitation of Princess Zinaida Shakhovskaya, sister of the editor of The Well-Intentioned One, who in 1926 had published some of Tsvetaeva's poetry, Efron's essay, and Tsvetaeva's controversial article "The Poet on Criticism." An admirer of Tsvetaeva's work, Shakhovskaya was trying to arrange for some of her French pieces to be published in Belgium. Tsvetaeva's stay in Brussels, where she gave a public reading of "My Father and His Museum," was financially quite successful. She continued to correspond throughout the year with Shakhovskaya, who tried without success to find a publisher for Letter to an Amazon. Tsvetaeva, however, had gone to Brussels with the secret hope of establishing a closer friendship with her. She returned "with empty hands of the soul." As she explained to Teskova, "I still need to be loved: to be allowed to love people: to be needed *like bread.*" [21] Shakhovskaya sensed Tsvetaeva's expectations, but despite her admiration for her, could not respond. She wrote in her reminiscences: "Yes, how greedily she searched in others (perhaps in me, too) for that loyal and basically compatible friend, her alter ego—and clearly did not find it." [22]

As always, Tsvetaeva had taken Mur along on the trip. She was shocked to see that people felt sorry for her because her son was so rude. Yet she was sure that because of his intelligence, he would outgrow his bad manners.

When she returned from Belgium, Tsvetaeva finished "Autobus," a poem on which she had worked sporadically since 1934. The first part describes an outing in a shaky bus. It is springtime: "Oh Lord, how green it is, how blue it is, how azure!" The season's beauty takes her mind off aging, off disturbing thoughts, making her leap up with joy. When the travelers on the bus arrive at the gates that open up into Happiness, Tsvetaeva realizes once more that she is not destined for happiness: "I searched for it on all fours in the field of four-leaf clover, when I was four years old!" [23]

In July 1936 Tsvetaeva went with Mur to Moret-sur-Loing, a small medieval town near Fontainebleau. Alya was invited to spend the summer with friends, but Tsvetaeva hoped that Sergey would join them for a while. Soon after her arrival, a young Russian émigré poet, Baron Anatoly von Steiger, sent her a book of his poems. Steiger, twenty-six or twenty-seven, was one of the poets of the "Paris School," a friend of Tsvetaeva's "enemy" Georgy Adamovich, whose attack against her in the wake of her "Poet on Criticism" had been the harshest. She had met Steiger briefly at one of her poetry readings, but she really didn't even remember what he looked like, and she didn't particularly like his poems. But once Steiger wrote to her from a sanatorium for tubercular patients in Switzerland, she was captivated. He was a young poet, he was of noble descent, he was ill and lonely— she let herself go in a whirlwind of emotions and illusions.

This new epistolary romance was based on a misunderstanding from the start. Scheduled to undergo a serious lung operation, Steiger was facing a physical and emotional crisis. A homosexual, he had enjoyed friendships with older women who offered warmth and sympathy, but he could not have expected that his first letter—in which he told Tsvetaeva about himself and intimated his need for affection — "had touched off a volcano." [24] It is less clear why he allowed the correspondence to continue for so long. Tsvetaeva, starved for affection, disappointed by her latest attempt at intimacy with her Belgian patron, Shakhovskaya, was flooded with hope. In her answer to his first long letter, she let him know at once that hers would be a love unlike any other he could have known. Not surprisingly, she assumed the role of "mother," but an aggressively domineering mother who addressed him as "my child," "my little one."

> And if I said *mother* — I did so because this word is the most spacious and the most embracing one, the fastest and the tiniest — taking away nothing. A word compared to which all, all other words are — limits.

> Whether you want to or not, I have already taken you to the place inside myself where I take everything I love without having the time to look at it closely, seeing it already inside. You are my annexation and my catch. [25]

Tsvetaeva informed Steiger that she would soon return to Vanves and would go from there to an old chateau in the Alps, where she would feel even closer to him. The Chateau d'Arcine was a center of Efron's friends of the Union for Repatriation and of the NKVD. Efron was there working with a group of people who shadowed suspected defectors and who were plotting against Trotsky's son Lev Sedov. It is not clear why Tsvetaeva went there: in her letters to Steiger she speaks only about the romantic atmosphere of the castle.

When Steiger informed her about his forthcoming lung operation she interpreted this as "son-like" behavior and wanted to know all the details of his illness. She promised an answer to a sixteen-page letter by Steiger in which he probably had tried to correct her mistaken notions about his feelings for her; she kept putting it off. Instead, she fantasized a total merger with him: "Sometimes I think that you are me." [26] On August 21, she finally answered this letter, which she called "as important as a declaration of war or peace," but her letter was less a response than a demand for his submission to her. [27] Her love was a mother's love, meaning a love that lived forever. Its only limit was her "duty" to Mur:

> Having given birth to my children (I speak of my son; of Alya I will tell you another time), I must, as long as he needs me, give him preference over everything: poetry, you, myself, all the expanses of my soul. [ . . . ] I buy with that (have bought all my life) my inner freedom —

my immeasurable freedom. Only because of that do I have such poems. In that freedom we will live and be, you and I. Our kingdom is not of this world.[28]

Though "their kingdom was not of this world," Tsvetaeva now began to insist on a meeting. Steiger would come to Paris in September or she would visit him in Switzerland. His silence awakened her fears that she had again been "too much." "Do convince me that you need me. (Oh, God, that is all that matters). [ . . . ] Then everything will be good, because then I can perform miracles."[29] But he failed to convince her, and there were no miracles. He wrote back that she had misunderstood him and that, after being discharged from the hospital in November, he would come to Paris to see his friends, the very same Russian poets she despised. This hurt badly. In her reply, she tried to cover up her wound with anger and pride. Finally, she understood that he really wasn't interested in her. "Yes, I had believed that someone needed me like bread," she wrote to Teskova. "And I found out that not bread was needed, but an ashtray with cigarette butts: not I, but Adamovich and Company. It's bitter. It's stupid. It's a pity."[30]

In 1938, while "Poems to an Orphan," a cycle of six poems written for Steiger, was being prepared for publication, Tsvetaeva added a popular ditty as an epigraph:

> A little boy walked down the street,
> Blue and shivering away,
> An old woman he chanced to meet
> Helped him find his way.[31]

This added just the ironic twist she desired.

In November, Steiger came to see Tsvetaeva. Despite her pain, she tried to help him by putting him in touch with Ivask, to whom she wrote, "he is worth corresponding with and, in any case, you should answer him. He's of a very high quality. [ . . . ] And don't forget—he's gravely ill."[32] Though hurt and disappointed, Tsvetaeva behaved less aggressively than she had before in similar situations. Perhaps she was too weary. She wrote to Ivask: "You can give only to the rich and help only the strong—this is the experience of my whole life and of this summer."[33] She never saw Steiger again.

# 24. A Fateful Year, 1937

*Black thoughts, a black fate, a black life.*[1]

After Steiger's rejection, Tsvetaeva saw herself in a short lyric as "that distinctly yellow, definitely rusty / leaf at the top—forgotten."[2] She may have been thinking of the line in Pushkin's poem "I've Lived to Bury My Desires": "Alone upon a branch that's bare / A trembling leaf is left behind."[3]

With the Pushkin centenary coming up in 1937, Tsvetaeva submitted "Verses to Pushkin," a cycle she had written in 1931, to *Contemporary Notes*, which, to her surprise, accepted them. "They are terribly sharp, terribly free, and have nothing in common with the canonization of Pushkin but are the opposite," she wrote to Teskova. "*Internally* they are revolutionary."[4] She also translated some of her Pushkin poems into French.

In her prose essay "My Pushkin," Tsvetaeva returned again to her childhood and, as in the other prose pieces of this period, she tried to understand the forces that had formed her. Khodasevich aptly described it as a study in child psychology. The essay starts with the image of the poet, as personified by Pushkin and first encountered in a picture on her mother's bedroom wall showing his fatal duel with the Count d'Anthes. But as far as Tsvetaeva is concerned, Pushkin was killed not by the insignificant count but by "all of them." At the age of four, then, her poetic self was born: "From Pushkin's duel a certain self was born, *the sister*."[5]

Tsvetaeva next encountered Pushkin when she was taken for walks almost daily to the Pushkin Monument, near her home. Since Pushkin's great-grandfather was of Ethiopian origin, Tsvetaeva declares her allegiance to Pushkin as the Negro, the outsider: "The Russian poet is a Negro, the poet—is a Negro and the poet was struck down." [6] In this essay she writes: "I loved the Pushkin Monument for its blackness—the reverse of the whiteness of our domestic gods," [7] probably her father's white statues. It was "a living proof of the baseness and deadliness of the racist theory, a living proof of its exact opposite. Pushkin is a *fact* that overturns the theory." [8]

Tsvetaeva also recalls how she had secretly read Pushkin's *Gypsies* in Valeriya's room, how "Pushkin infected me with love. With the word *love*." And she recalls how, when she was not yet six, she saw a scene from *Evgeny Onegin* at a Christmas festivity. Tatyana had become, as for many Russian women, her mother's model—the passionate, proud, controlled Tatyana. And Tsvetaeva recognized Tatyana's impact even on her own life when she wrote, "if there had not been Pushkin's Tatyana, I would not have come into existence." [9] Yet by then she knew what price the children had paid for this "sacrifice" when her mother had married "to the children's misfortune." Here, as elsewhere, we hear echoes of her mother's youthful diary entries. But in spite of her insight Tsvetaeva remained unable to break the chain. She, too, wanted to control her children to compensate for her emotional frustration. "That first love scene of mine foreordained all the ones that followed, all the passion in me for unhappy, unreciprocated, impossible love. From that very minute I did not want to be happy, and thereby pronounced the sentence of *non-love* on myself." [10] Who knew better than Tsvetaeva that "people with this fatal gift of unhappy love—one-sided love—all taken upon themselves—have a positive genius for unsuitable objects"? [11]

Pushkin's poem "To the Sea" was, Tsvetaeva writes, one of her childhood favorites. As a child she had misunderstood its very first line: "Farewell, free element!" Because of the similarity of the Russian words "element" (*stikhiya*) and "verse" (*stikhi*), she had read the line as farewell to verse instead of farewell to the sea. Then and now, the word "farewell" pierced her: "But why farewell? Because when you love you always bid farewell. It is when you bid farewell that you love." [12] She knew full well why Pushkin's persona remained on the shore, despite his longing for the sea. She wrote in her notes:

> He was enchanted by an overpowering passion; he desired so much that he couldn't move from the spot; he loved so much that he was rooted. I knew this by virtue of all my childhood longings, beginning with the favorite pastry that I always passed up, and ending with Serezha Ilovaisky, to whom I would never admit my love. But in not taking the pastry, in not confessing love to Serezha Ilovaisky, in not getting on the ship— how much happier we are than You! [13]

The essay focuses on control through renunciation—loneliness in life, loneliness in love, and the unrelieved pain of longing for merger. Tsvetaeva could identify with Pushkin's feelings because of "all the things of my life that I loved and kept on loving through parting, and not through meeting, through pulling away, and not through coming together, not unto life but unto death." [14] At the end of the essay, Tsvetaeva circles back to the beginning and points to her only fulfillment: "The illiteracy of my childish identification of the element with the element of poetry proved to be prophetic insight: 'the free element' proved to be poetry, and not the sea, poetry—that is, the one element from which there is no parting—ever." [15]

The year 1937 was the most fateful in Tsvetaeva's life. All her decisions from then on derived from the events of that year. The purges in the Soviet Union, intensified in 1936 under the direction of the new head of the NKVD, Yezhov, were becoming public knowledge—the show trials of the old Bolsheviks and the executions of Marshal Tukhachevsky and other Red Army generals. Among Soviet agents abroad there was growing fear and disaffection: old-time Bolsheviks were horrified by the Stalin terror. Among the Russian émigré community in Paris it was common knowledge that a new Stalinist power group had taken over; Trotsky had been exiled; repression and executions were the order of the day. In Russia, people were snatched from their homes and mothers, wives, and husbands waited in long lines at the prison gates. No one was safe. Russia was in the throes of a nightmare. [16]

How much of this nightmare was known to Efron and Alya is uncertain. Those aware of the terrifying events were often afraid to talk. The organization Efron had joined in the early 1930s, the "Union for Repatriation," had changed its name to "Union of Friends of the Soviet Fatherland" and was thoroughly infiltrated by Soviet agents, who found among the former White Russian officers many who were willing to work for the NKVD. To be sure, Efron and Alya were not alone in their hope that the Soviet Union would stand up to the growing threat of Nazism and Fascism. The French government, the Front Populaire, was an alliance of the left, including the Communists. Many believed that if Franco, with the help of the Soviets, was defeated in Spain, all of Europe would see better times.

Once Alya received her passport, Tsvetaeva reported to Teskova,

She began immediately to equip herself. Everyone helped her, beginning with Sergey (he spent his last cent on her) and ending with my women friends, including one who had never met her. All of a sudden she had everything: a fur coat, lingerie, bed linens, a watch, suitcases, and a cigarette lighter—and everything of the best quality, some of the things in great quantity. [ . . . ] I have never seen in my life so many new things at one time. It was a real dowry. [ . . . ] I gave her my last presents in the train compartment: a silver bracelet and a brooch—a cameo, and also a little cross to wear around her neck just in case. Her departure was cheerful—one leaves like that only for a honeymoon— in fact, not all honeymooners get such a send-off! She was all dressed up in new things, very elegant, running from one person to another, chatting, joking.[17]

Tsvetaeva's description seems to hold an undertone of envy, but she may have felt some foreboding when she gave Alya a little cross "just in case." For Alya this must have been one of the few happy days in her life: she was twenty-five; she thought she was starting a new life, a life of her own.

That same year Tsvetaeva wrote another essay, "Pushkin and Pugachev," to which she had alluded in "My Pushkin."

But I will speak about myself and the Guide, about Pushkin and Puga-chev, separately, because the Guide would lead us far off, perhaps even farther than Lieutenant Grinyov, into the very thickets of good and evil, to that place in the thickets where they are inseparably entwined together and in the intertwining, make the shape of real life.[18]

In 1834 Pushkin had written a factual history of the peasant rebellion of 1773–75 against Catherine II led by Pugachev, who called himself Tsar Peter III. Two years later, Pushkin wrote *A Captain's Daughter*, a romantic novella set against the background of the same uprising. In her autobiographical prose and in some personal letters Tsvetaeva has repeatedly countered reality with the deeper truth of poetic vision, and in her treatment of the Pushkin novella she returns to it. Pushkin knew that the historical Pugachev was an imposter, a cruel coward who betrayed his lover, his friend, and his faith. He created his Pugachev as "the retort of the poet to the historical Pugachev. The lyricist's retort to the archive." Tsvetaeva had been working on her long poem about the assassination of the Russian imperial family; she, too, had been steeped in research. Unfortunately this *poema* has not survived, but from her comments on Pugachev we can clearly see that hers, too, must have been a poet's interpretation of historical facts. For Tsvetaeva, "a deception that elevates us is dearer than a host of low truths."[19]

The plot of *A Captain's Daughter* is simple: Grinyov, a young nobleman, is sent by his father to join the army; he and his servant lose their way in a snowstorm and are saved by a stranger, the "Guide," who is actually Pugachev. An immediate affection springs up between Grinyov and Pugachev, and when they part the next morning Grinyov gives Pugachev his own warm hareskin jacket. At the fortress, Grinyov falls in love with Mariya, the daughter of the commanding officer, Captain Mironov, but soon this idyll is interrupted when Pugachev and his troops storm the fortress. The captain is immediately hanged by Pugachev; his wife dies too, but Mariya hides in the priest's house. This brings about the second important confrontation between Grinyov and Pugachev. Pugachev recognizes Grinyov, remembers his gift to him, but demands that he kiss his hand in recognition of his self-appointed status as tsar. Grinyov refuses out of loyalty and a sense of duty. All the same, Pugachev lets him and his bride go free. Once the rebellion and the imposter are defeated, Grinyov is accused, because of his friendship with Pugachev, of having collaborated with the insurgency. He is, however, acquitted by Catherine II, while Pugachev is condemned to death. Grinyov is present at his execution.

For Tsvetaeva, the main character in *A Captain's Daughter* is neither the pale, sweet Mariya nor her noble lover Grinyov. It is Pugachev, evil and powerful. She is fascinated by the love between Grinyov and Pugachev, not by the love between Grinyov and Mariya. It is Pugachev who casts his spell on her because he represents the rebel, the sinner, the wolf, the Devil. He is responsible for the death of Mariya's parents, but was Tsvetaeva "indignant at Pugachev [ . . . ] for their execution? No, because he was *supposed* to execute them—because he was a wolf and a thief. [ . . . ] Pugachev didn't promise anyone to be good—just the opposite: without promising, promising the opposite, he proved to be good. It was my first encounter with evil and evil proved to be good. And after that I always suspected it of good."[20]

Tsvetaeva as a child had known a "good" mother by whom she had felt abandoned, and now she understood that "a child hated only treachery, betrayal, a broken promise, a violated agreement."[21] In Pushkin's Pugachev she found the personification of her ideal: "An outlaw, a cannibal, a gray wolf who once loved someone, who killed off everyone, who loved one, and this one, in the person of Grinyov—is ourselves."[22] But if Tsvetaeva from early on identified with the outsider, the outlaw, she never accepted evil in authority. She had written to Teskova only a year earlier of her opposition to Stalin worship. It was the rebel and the lost cause that inspired her writing.

In *A Captain's Daughter*, Pugachev remains the hero to the very end. It is not Grinyov's marriage to Mariya that is the climax of the drama, but Pugachev's nodding to Grinyov, at his own execution, "a minute before his lifeless, bleeding head was held up before the people." [23]

Tsvetaeva adds to Pushkin's Pugachev: the spell—her romantic notion of the irrational, uncontrollable power of love, that power of the Devil, the vampire, the genius. It is not Pugachev's gratitude for Grinyov's gift of his warm jacket in a snowstorm or Grinyov's gratitude to Pugachev for granting him life that ignites Tsvetaeva's imagination. It is the emotional intensity of their mutual attraction, and for that, "the secret heat," no sacrifice is too great.

There is another important undercurrent in this work. If Pugachev is a reincarnation of Tsvetaeva's Devil, who is Grinyov? At that time Tsvetaeva was living under the daily pressure of having to decide whether to return to Russia. She must have begun to suspect that her husband was involved in more than recruiting for the Spanish Loyalists. And though no real parallel can be drawn between the conflict that we see in the essay and the situation facing the Efrons, it seems to me that Tsvetaeva tries in the person of Grinyov to justify her husband's loyalty and unquestioning service to the Party. The image of Efron she wanted to preserve appears clearly in the scene between Grinyov and Pugachev: "A confrontation of Duty and Revolt, of Oath and Lawlessness, and a brilliant contrast: in Pugachev, the outlaw wins out; in Grinyov, the child—the soldier wins out." [24] Tsvetaeva remained faithful to her basic romantic credo: passion, the *spell*, but also the non-freedom of duty. She knew all these contradictory, conflicting emotions and she would keep on seeing Efron as Grinyov. [25]

In early July 1937, Tsvetaeva went with Mur to the ocean; she expected Efron in August. Her letters to Teskova are filled with details about the landscape, their little rented house, the books she was reading, her work. When she heard from Alya that Sonechka Holliday had died in Russia, she immediately began writing *The Tale of Sonechka*, a two-volume account of that friendship. "I have never loved anyone so much," she wrote to Teskova on September 27, 1937. [26]

Evidently Tsvetaeva had no idea of the momentous events that had taken place during that same month. On September 1, for no special reason, her sister Asya had been arrested in Moscow. Some surmised that after Gorky's mysterious death, Asya remained without a protector. She may have been taken as a hostage, should Efron not live up to his superiors' expectations.

It is still impossible to reconstruct exactly the events of September 1937. One thing seems clear: since it was apparently not unusual for the Efrons to be separated for weeks without hearing a word about one another, one can safely assume that Tsvetaeva at that time knew nothing of Efron's role in the assassination of Ignace Reiss. Born Ludwig Poretsky and operating under the code name Ludwig, Reiss was a prominent figure in the Soviet European spy network. A veteran agent, he had once been a dedicated Bolshevik, but after his last trip to Moscow he had become disillusioned and frightened. Stalin and Yezhov were the new ruthless rulers, and Reiss refused to serve them. After writing a letter to that effect to the Central Committee of the Communist Party, he went into hiding in Switzerland with his wife and child. He had arranged a meeting with one of the leaders of the Belgian Socialists, hoping through him and Trotsky's son to find a new life. But his letter was opened at the Soviet Embassy in Paris and immediately the hunt for him began. Efron participated and seemingly directed the operation.

In the first week of September, the Swiss police found a bullet-ridden corpse of a man on a road near Lausanne. His papers gave the name "Hans Eberhard," since the murderers had schemed to conceal his identity. Reiss's wife and son were supposed to have been poisoned with candies filled with strychnine. But the German Communist Gertrude Schildbach, an old friend of the Reiss family, had lost her nerve at the last moment and had not given the candies to Reiss's wife. Now the widow identified the body and the Swiss police arrested another conspirator, a Swiss Communist sympathizer, Renate Steiner, who panicked and named her accomplices. Among them was Sergey Efron.

Efron was interrogated in Paris at the request of the Swiss police and released for lack of evidence. But then General Miller, president of a Russian officers' association and a well-known figure in the Paris White Russian community, was kidnapped on September 22 and disappeared. The French police suspected correctly that the same group that had carried out Reiss's murder was implicated. When the police came to arrest Efron, however, he was nowhere to be found. Instead they took Tsvetaeva to the police station for interrogation.

Tsvetaeva was shocked and horrified. To all her interrogators' questions she responded only with statements about her husband's integrity. Then, apparently for no reason, she began to recite French poetry, her translations of Pushkin and "The Swain." The officials, beginning to doubt her sanity, finally gave up and let her go.

According to an article by Natalya Reznikova, a close and reliable friend of

Tsvetaeva's, Tsvetaeva and Mur accompanied Efron on his escape by car from Paris. "When they arrived at Rouen from Paris, it was already dark," the driver told Reznikova. "Something scared Sergey and he left the car brusquely without saying good-bye to his wife and son."[27] He may have wanted to cover his tracks. In any case, he left for the Soviet Union on a Soviet ship.

Now the harassment of Tsvetaeva began in earnest. An anonymous letter in a major Russian-language newspaper, *Renaissance*, appeared on October 29, naming Efron as one of the leading members of the Union of Repatriation who, under orders of the NKVD, took part in the "liquidation of undesirable elements of the emigration."[28] Tsvetaeva was attacked, too; the writer claimed she was fully informed about her husband's Bolshevik commitment. She, however, kept repeating in her letters and in person that she trusted Efron and that he could not have participated in such a bloody business.

Nobody knows exactly when Tsvetaeva found out about her husband's political activity, or how much she knew about it. Most of her friends believed that she was utterly ignorant of the facts until the French police questioned her. Whatever she knew, she had her own world and in that world Efron remained heroic and courageous. Although Slonim, the Lebedevs, Fondaminsky, Halpern, Bunina, and a few other friends refused to desert her, Tsvetaeva, who had always felt isolated even when surrounded by friends, now felt entirely forsaken. Slonim met her at the Lebedevs in October:

> She looked terrible; I was amazed to see how she had suddenly aged and had somehow dried up. I embraced her and suddenly she began to cry, softly and silently; it was the first time I had seen her in tears. . . . I was shocked by her tears and by the absence of complaints against fate, as well as by some hopeless certainty that it made no sense to fight, that one had to accept the inevitable. I remember how simple and routine her words sounded: "I would like to die, but I have to live because of Mur; Alya and Sergey Yakovlevich don't need me any more . . ." When asked about her plans for the future, she said she would have to return to Russia and would apply for a Soviet passport because "anyway, it's impossible for me to stay in Paris without money or any way to be published, and the émigrés will hound me; already mistrust and hostility are everywhere."[29]

In January 1938 Tsvetaeva decorated her last Christmas tree for the Russian Orthodox Christmas, trimming it for Mur with gilded fir-cones that she had brought from Czechoslovakia. No longer in school, Mur studied with a tutor; he had no friends, and no chance for fun. Life for both of them was cold, tedious, poor. In February, Tsvetaeva wrote to Teskova: "I haven't written anything this last winter. Of course, life is difficult, but when was it easy?"[30] Inwardly, Tsvetaeva was already saying good-bye to her house in Vanves, the only home she had come to like in France. She had grown attached to it. Now it, too, must be left behind. She had already applied for a Soviet passport. As she reviewed the manuscripts that she wanted to leave in the West, she came across the diary entry written in the early days of the Revolution, when she did not know where Efron was, or whether she would ever see him again: "If God will perform a miracle — will keep you alive, I will follow you like a dog." Now in the margin she added: "And now I will go — like a dog. M. Ts., Vanves, June 17, 1938 (21 years later)."

That summer Tsvetaeva moved with Mur to a small hotel in Paris on the Boulevard Pasteur. It was the summer of the Munich crisis. Hitler was stepping up his attacks against Czechoslovakia, and the fear of war permeated Europe. Russia promised to come to Czechoslovakia's aid, but the Western allies — France and Great Britain — vacillated. Now Tsvetaeva began to read newspapers, to be interested in political news. On September 24, when war seemed imminent, she wrote to Teskova that she believed Russia would save Czechoslovakia. After the Munich betrayal of Czechoslovakia and the German occupation of the Sudetenland, she mourned as though for a close friend. Czechoslovakia in the distance had become for Tsvetaeva that land of her dreams, that "impossible love" personified by the statue of the young knight on the Prague bridge guarding the river. She asked Teskova to mail her a large photo of that knight, a book about Czechoslovakia, and a long Bohemian crystal necklace. In November, she sent Teskova her first cycle of poems to Czechoslovakia, "September." Her pain, her outrage, had reawakened her creative powers; these poems had come to her like a torrent. Not since her White Army poems had she been so inspired by a cause. People felt sorry for Czechoslovakia, but she wanted more: she wanted active resistance:

> All this is the same faint-heartedness and inertia and *fat* (or craving for it) that has brought about what has happened. I am totally alone in the integrity and clear-sightedness of my outrage. I don't want them [the Czechs] to be pitied at all: one cannot pity a live man in a hole; one has to dig him out and put in his place the one who buried him.[31]

Tsvetaeva suffered during that miserable winter of 1938–39, yet her inner strength would permit no breakdown. No doubt part of her strength was derived from her pride. More than that, she identified with Czechoslovakia, and felt that if she were young, she would have wanted to fight. A small flame of personal faith continued to burn brightly. As she wrote to Teskova at the beginning of that terrible year, 1939: "Well, once more, happy new year! May God give you everything that is good and that is not here, and may God preserve the good that is. And there always is, if only that moral law within us, of which Kant spoke. And that star-studded sky!"[32] But when German troops occupied the rest of Czechoslovakia in March, her tone changed. "March," her second cycle of poems addressed to Czecholovakia, is despairing but defiant:

> Oh tears in my eyes!
> Sobs of anger and of love!
> Oh, Czechoslovakia in tears!
> Spain in blood!
>
> Oh, black mountain
> That has darkened the whole world!
> It's time, it's time, it's time
> To return my ticket to its creator.[33]

The wife of Fedotov recalls this period, when she had occasion to knock at Tsvetaeva's door:

Marina Ivanovna seemed pleased by my visit and began explaining to me that she would have to leave for Russia, that she had to run away because of her neighbors; that she could not keep the boy in school (a French one?) because of his classmates; that finally because of the imminence of war she would simply starve to death and that nobody would publish her, anyway. In the next moment she read to me, to my great joy, her funeral dirge to Czechoslovakia. *Contemporary Notes* actually wanted to publish that poem, but Tsvetaeva had already made up her mind to go to Russia and did not dare to publish in émigré publications.[34]

Mur was in the room, she says, but her presence did not make him switch off the radio or even turn it down.

Tsvetaeva was already on the payroll of the Soviet Embassy, receiving Efron's salary. The hour of the last farewells had come. Salomea Halpern, who had moved to London, came to Paris especially to see her friend off. In early June, Tsvetaeva went with Mur to Slonim to say good-bye. It was an hour of memory, of tenderness, of nostalgia for both of them, although Mur seemed bored. Tsvetaeva read aloud some of her poems. She had no illusions; she might never again be able to publish, she said. Here Mur interrupted: " 'But, Mama, you never want to believe; you'll see, everything will be fine.' " Slonim accompanied them out to the elevator and, speechless from emotion, embraced Tsvetaeva.[35]

In a letter to Teskova dated June 7, Tsvetaeva writes of her imminent departure that "there had been no choice: one must not abandon a person in trouble; I was born with that. And then, too, in a city like Paris Mur would have no life, no chance to grow up. [ . . . ] That's it." But she knew the danger she faced: "Oh, God—what anguish! Right now in the heat of departure, in the heat of my hands—of my head—of the weather, I have not yet fully realized, but I know what awaits me: I know—myself! I will break my neck—looking back at you, at your world, at our world."[36]

On the morning of her last day in Paris, June 12, she wrote her last letter to Ariadna Berg: "I was awakened by the most accurate alarm clock—my heart. We are leaving unaccompanied. As Mur says, 'ni fleurs, ni couronnes,'* like dogs. How sad (and crude), I say. They didn't permit it, but my close friends know and accompany me in their hearts! I know that you, too, will stand invisibly on the pier."[37]

She wrote the last short letter to Teskova when she was on the train to Le Havre. Obviously frightened, she saw out of her window what seemed to be a huge station with green windows, a frightening green garden:

A life of seventeen years comes to an end. How happy I was at times! And the happiest period of my life, don't forget that, was Mokropsy and Vshenory and also my mountain. Strange, yesterday I met its hero [Rodzevich]. I had not seen him for years; he came upon us from behind and without explanation put his arms through Mur's and mine and walked between us as though nothing had happened.

She ended her letter with words of gratitude for everything Teskova had given her: "I am leaving wearing your necklace and the coat with your button, and a belt with your buckle. Everything modest and madly beloved; I'll take it into my grave, or will burn with it. Good-bye! It's not difficult anymore—it is fate."[38]

---

*'No flowers, no wreaths.'

## 25. Return to the Soviet Union

*"There, too, I will be with the persecuted, not with the*
*persecutors, with the victims, not with the executioners."* [1]

**A**t Le Havre, "As soon as I went up on the ship's deck I understood that everything was over," Tsvetaeva told a friend.[2] Actually, in her last years abroad, her world had already collapsed. Now, with the West giving in to Hitler's brutal dictatorship, to Fascism in Italy, and to Stalin's rule, the victory of totalitarianism over the individual seemed assured.

Tsvetaeva arrived in Moscow on June 18, 1939, not as the controversial poet, but as a "White émigrée" and the wife of a Soviet agent. Only Alya greeted her and Mur at the station. Efron was ill; six months after his return in 1937 he had developed a serious cardiac condition, unreported to Tsvetaeva, who learned at the same time that her sister Asya had been arrested in 1937 and was in a prison camp. Alya, who had already distanced herself from her mother in Paris, had now found a man she loved and planned to marry — Samuel Gurevich, called "Mulya."

Efron and Alya lived in Bolshevo, a suburb of Moscow, where NKVD agents and their families were quartered. Tsvetaeva and Mur joined them in the communal dacha they shared with the Klepinin family. Klepinin was also a former White Army officer; he and his wife Nina had worked for the Soviets with Efron in Paris. Her son from a former marriage, Dimitry Sezeman, was Mur's age and became very friendly with him. The accommodations were less than modest, with an outhouse, a communal kitchen, a cellar. Alya spent her days working at the *Revue de Moscou*, a state-sponsored Russian-French publication in Moscow.

Everyday life was difficult. Efron was ill; Mur was disappointed and grumbling, and Tsvetaeva was not easy to get along with. The communal kitchen and lack of privacy heightened her nervous tension. Moreover, her trunk, packed with manuscripts and her personal belongings, had been retained by customs. The family's gloomy mood was further darkened by news of arrests and the disappearance of friends, of trials and executions. In that climate of fear, it is not surprising that Tsvetaeva was unable to record her feelings; not until a year later, in September 1940, did she begin to recount those early days in her notebook.

> June 18th arrival in Russia, on the 19th to Bolshevo. To the dacha. Meeting with Sergey, who is not well. Disquiet. Went to buy some kerosene. Sergey buys apples. Gradually anxiety is gripping me. Difficulties with telephones. Enigmatic Alya, her artificial cheerfulness. I live without documents, don't see anyone. Cats. My dear nonaffectionate adolescent—cat. (All this for my own memory and for no one else.) Mur, even if he reads this, would not understand. But he will not read it since he runs from such things. Cakes, pineapples—that does not make it easier. Walks with Mulya. My loneliness. Dishwater and tears. Undertone and overtone of everything—horror. They promise a partition—and days pass. Promise a school for Murka—days pass. And the unfamiliar wooden landscape, absence of stone: of stability. Sergey's illness. Fear of his heart trouble. Fragments of his life without me—have no time to listen. Hands busy with work, I listen, though ready to spring up. The cellar: a hundred times a day. When is there time to write? . . .

> For the first time the feeling of someone else's kitchen. Terrific heat which I don't notice: streams of sweat and tears into the dishpan. No one to hold on to. I begin to understand that Sergey is powerless, totally powerless in everything. (I, unpacking something: "Didn't you see? Such wonderful shirts!" "I was looking at you!")

> (I unwrap the wound. Raw flesh.) [3]

Tension brought about quarrels in the family. "It's amazing that they weren't all arrested sooner," a neighbor later said. "All they did from morning to night was bicker with each other." [4] Still, Tsvetaeva found time to read her poetry aloud. Dimitry Sezeman, who admired Tsvetaeva for her spiritual will power, has recalled his impressions:

> She sat very straight as only a former pupil of a school for young ladies could. I intentionally stress this rigid erectness of her body because it was characteristic of her entire personality. It outwardly expressed, as

it were, her inner intransigence. . . . When Marina Ivanovna read her poems, one felt that each of them was an irrevocable assertion of something vitally essential, that our agreement or non-agreement was for the poet a question of life or death, that she backed each line with her life.[5]

Despite these pressures, these first two months in Bolshevo were almost a reprieve. The government gave Efron financial support and, in August, Tsvetaeva received her "domestic" Soviet passport. They were together. In her notebook, a year later, Tsvetaeva recalled a visit to an agricultural fair and Alya's happiness: "She was radiant. Wearing a red Czech scarf, my present."[6] This was a happy time for Alya, who was in love and who didn't suspect that Mulya had been assigned by the NKVD to inform on her and her family.[7]

Then, on August 27, disaster struck: Alya was arrested. In those days no reason was given or expected. Tsvetaeva's diary entry for the day of her arrest sounds amazingly understated, even if it was written a year later:

> 27th of August, at night, Alya's arrest. Alya is cheerful, carries herself gallantly. Laughs it off. . . . She leaves without saying good-bye! I: "Well, Alya, how can you go without saying good-bye to anyone?" She, in tears, over her shoulder — waves me away! The commandant (a kind old man) "*That way* is better. Long farewells — too many.tears."[8]

Then, on October 10, they came for Sergey. When they were leading him away, Tsvetaeva made the sign of the cross over him. She never saw him or Alya again. On November 7, they came for the Klepinins.

Recent articles by Irma Kudrova in *Russian Thought* examine the files, long secret, of the case of Sergey Efron.[9] Efron emerges from these interrogations as a man deeply shaken but not broken; courageous in his denial of spying for Western powers and of being in league with the Trotskyists, he remained loyal to his friends. Important facts are revealed for the first time: Efron's heart condition was diagnosed as serious by the prison doctors; he attempted suicide and was placed in a psychiatric ward. He was executed October 16, 1941, as the German army approached Moscow. Contrary to many rumors, he was not shot by Beria himself. Reports differ as to the place of execution. Efron was rehabilitated, thanks to Alya's efforts, in 1956.

Efron's arrest marked the end of Tsvetaeva's relatively "normal" family life in Soviet Russia. She could not stay in Bolshevo; she had no money to buy food and was constantly in fear of being arrested. She had almost no friends; people were afraid of the "White émigrée." Ehrenburg, Zavadsky, Tikhonov, and others who had admired her poetry at a distance avoided her; Valeriya, her stepsister, refused to see her. Her diary entry of September 1940 clearly speaks of this period:

> About myself. Everyone considers me brave. I don't know anyone more timid than myself. I am frightened of everything: of eyes, of darkness, of steps, and more than anything else—of myself, of my head, which has served me so loyally in notebooks while destroying me in life. Nobody sees—nobody knows—that for a year. . . . already, I have been searching with my eyes for a hook, but there is none, because there is electricity everywhere. No chandeliers. For a year I've been trying on death. Everything is ugly and terrifying. To swallow—is disgusting; to jump—is hostile; primordial loathsomeness of water. I do not want to frighten (posthumously), I believe that I am already afraid of myself—posthumously. I do not want to *die*. I want *not to be*. Nonsense. As long as I am *needed* . . . but, oh Lord, how small I am, how incapable I am of doing *anything*. To go on living—go on chewing. Chewing bitter wormwood. How many lines are missed! I don't write anything down. That is finished.[10]

Efron's sister Lilya, who lived in crowded quarters with a close woman friend, offered refuge to Tsvetaeva and Mur. Lilya was a drama teacher; when her students came, Tsvetaeva and Mur had to sit in the communal kitchen or leave the house. The room was so small that Tsvetaeva could not smoke—a deprivation she felt acutely. She tried to find another place to live, a school for Mur, and some income through translations. To her dismay, her trunks had still not been released. She had registered them in Paris under Alya's name, but now Alya was in prison.

Tsvetaeva turned to Pasternak. He could not offer the friendship for which Tsvetaeva had hoped, but when her situation became desperate he offered help, introducing her to a friend of his, Viktor Goltsev, who was in charge of translations for the State Publishing House. Tsvetaeva was commissioned to translate, with the help of literal translations, from Georgian, Polish, and Yiddish poets. Later she translated Baudelaire and Lorca. In fact, this work provided her basic income throughout these difficult years. She earned it the hard way, putting considerable time and effort into every poorly paid word.

She appealed to Aleksandr Fadeyev, a high official of the Union of Soviet Writers, for assistance in finding living quarters and in having her trunks delivered. His suggestion was to apply to the Writers' House in Golitsyno, about one hour from Moscow. His approval arrived in January 1940, a month after Tsvetaeva had moved to Golitsyno.

From Golitsyno, on December 23, 1939, Tsvetaeva addressed a letter to Beria, the head of the NKVD. [11] She gave a summary of her years abroad, stressing her total isolation among the émigrés, and her fervent desire to return to the Soviet Union to see her son grow up there. As for Efron, she pointed out that he was the son of famous revolutionary parents who had suffered for the cause of the People's Will Party. He had made a fateful mistake when he joined the White Army, but he had been very young and had regretted it ever since. Living in Prague and Paris, he published Soviet writers in his journals and became a member of the Eurasian movement. "If I am not mistaken he was called a 'Bolshevik' from 1927 on." When the Eurasians split into a left and a right group, he headed the left group, which joined the Union for Repatriation. "When exactly Sergey Efron began his active Soviet work — I don't know, but it must be known from his earlier records. I think it was around 1930. What I do know with utter certainty is his passionate and constant commitment to the Soviet Union and his passionate service to it." She recalled the unexpected events of 1937 and brought as a witness the French investigator who — during her interrogation — said "But Mr. Efron was tremendously active for the Soviets."

As to the arrest of her daughter — Ariadna — Tsvetaeva called her a loyal patriot. She had returned to the Soviet Union before her father and was very happy here. Then Efron was arrested. Tsvetaeva gives the dates and details of the money accepted for him and Alya in prison. She described her own difficult situation and appealed for justice for her husband, adding that if his arrest was due to a malicious denunciation, the informant should be investigated. "If, however, it was a mistake — I beg you to correct it before it is too late." [12]

Tsvetaeva and Mur lived in Golitsyno for five months. Tsvetaeva had to rent a room outside the Writers' House, but she and Mur were permitted to take their meals there — a minor miracle for them both. Mur was registered in school; their room, although unheated, was adequate, and the meals were prepared for them. The situation offered, if not normalcy, some relief. But twice a month Tsvetaeva took the night train to Moscow to bring money and parcels to the two prisons where Efron and Alya were being held. Not only did she hate to leave Mur alone, but it was bitter cold in the train and eerie in the dark streets. Fear was her constant companion. She stood in line with all the hundreds of other Russian women and hoped, as they did, that her parcels and money would be accepted, indicating that Alya and Efron were still inside and alive.

Anna Akhmatova in the epilogue to her "Requiem" has written of the days when she, too, stood in those lines:

> I've seen how a face can fall like a leaf,
> How, from under the lids, terror peeks,
> I've seen how suffering and grief
> Etches hieroglyphs on cheeks,
> How ash-blonde hair, from roots to tips,
> Turns black and silver overnight.
> How smiles wither on submissive lips,
> And in a half-smile quivers fright.
> Not only for myself do I pray,
> But for those who stood in front and behind me,
> In the bitter cold, on a hot July day
> Under the red wall that stared blindly.[13]

Still, Tsvetaeva survived because Mur, Efron, and Alya needed her. She did not mind her translating work, but she missed the poetry readings and the few friends she had had in the West. She was forced to adjust to a totally different life, a life for which she was as unprepared as she had been to live in Moscow under Communism in 1917. She found out soon enough that friendship in this atmosphere of constant fear was very rare. In the dining room of the Writers' House in Golitsyno, many writers ignored her. She had family members who had been arrested; she had spent time abroad and had not been associated with Soviet organizations—that was more than enough to make her dangerous for others. Another writer, Noye Luriye, who shared meals with her in the Writers' House at Golitsyno, wrote:

> She had the angry manners of a master, a loud and sharp voice. But behind her self-assured tone and judgements one could feel how lost she was and how terribly lonely. Her husband and daughter had been arrested; with her son, I noticed, there was no common language. Writers avoided contact with her because she was a former émigrée. In the eyes of this gray-haired woman with an unusual face, appeared at times such an expression of despair and suffering, that it conveyed stronger than words her condition.[14]

Her night terrors returned, as she wrote to the poet Olga Mochalova:

> Golitsyno, I think January 24, 1940, a new unwelcoming home. Again I don't sleep nights. I am frightened. Too much *glass*—loneliness, night

noises, and fears; now, a car looking for the Devil knows what, now a ghostly cat, then again the rustle of a tree. I jump up, hide myself under a cover, to Mur's bed (do not wake him) and read again, [ . . . ] and again I jump up, and so until daybreak. In daytime—it's the cold, simply freezing; ice-cold hands and feet and brain. [ . . . ] In the house, no butter, no vegetables, only potatoes, and the food ration for writers is not enough—slightly hungry. In the shops nothing except margarine (it disgusts me; cannot overcome it) and once I succeeded in getting some cranberry jam. My head is numb, frozen, and I don't know really which is duller, those word-by-word translations or me? I have no friends and without them it's—the end.[15]

After the torments of the Bolshevo months—the arrests and the abandonment—Tsvetaeva needed to feel life again. Dressed poorly but with an aura of faded elegance, she still managed to make an impression on people. When Yevgeny Tager, a close friend of Pasternak, came to Golitsyno, he approached Tsvetaeva and told her how much he admired her poetry. He was young and handsome and her fire was ignited again. They went for walks together, and Tsvetaeva copied some of her poems for him and addressed a new poem to him. But he soon felt that her behavior was attracting too much attention, and he tried to put some distance between them. Tsvetaeva, however, did not want to understand. As he was leaving on January 22, 1940, she handed him a letter inviting him to come to see her again soon. Though she knew that he was married, she insisted that he come alone "for the whole day—and a very long evening." She gave him the telephone number of Efron's sister so that a meeting could be arranged. He never called, but the day after he left Tsvetaeva wrote two poems. In the first one, about her emptiness when Tager had left, we are reminded of her letters to Bakhrakh, telling him that without "the other" she did not exist.[16]

> He left—I don't eat:
> Emptiness—taste of bread.
> Everything—is chalk.
> Whatever I am reaching for.
>
> He was my bread,
> He was my snow,
> [Now] snow is white no longer
> Bread is no longer good.

The second poem conveys Tsvetaeva's ever-present pain, a pain that she had so desperately tried to quell with passion, with pride, with poetry. Now, she knew that it had been with her since birth and would never leave her.

> It's time! For that fire
> I am too old!
> Love is older than I!
> The mountain
> Of fifty Januaries!
> Love is still older:
> Old as bullrushes, older than the seas . . .
> But the pain in my chest
> Is older than love, older than love.[17]

Tsvetaeva's inspiration had returned, even under the most trying circumstances. Nothing had changed: from the hope for love, followed by disenchantment, bitterness, and pain—a poem was born.

That winter, Mur was frequently ill; Tsvetaeva's trips to Moscow, to publishing houses and to the two prisons, exhausted her. And then at the end of March came another blow: she was told that the Writers' House rules had been changed. Now she would have to pay double for her meals or receive only one portion for the two of them. Tsvetaeva could not afford the double price and had to share her meager food with Mur. This meant not only that she had to look for new housing but that she had to change Mur's school. Because making new arrangements was complicated, Tsvetaeva and Mur spent April and May at Golitsyno, but any sense of permanence was gone.

Tsvetaeva wanted to move to Moscow, where she would be closer to the publishing houses for which she worked and to the prisons where Alya and Efron were locked up. But special permission was required to live there and rents were high. In mid-June, Tsvetaeva was fortunate enough to sublet a room in the Writers' House on Herzen Street, but she knew that at the end of the summer the tenants would return. During June and July, she undertook energetically all the necessary steps with custom officials to have her possessions released. Besides, new friends surrounded her now. Anatoly Tarasenkov, a literary scholar who had been an admirer and collector of Tsvetaeva's works for years, and his young wife, Mariya Belkina, opened their home to her and introduced her to their literary circle.

On July 25 Tsvetaeva finally received her trunks, which contained her manuscripts. She brought a suitcase filled with them to Tarasenkov for safe-keeping, together with a note to the effect that if anything happened to her he would know what to do with them. The fear of arrest was still with her. The rest of her things crowded her small room; she managed to sell some of them and gave others away. She desperately needed a larger room; Mur needed a school; she still had no Moscow residential permit. Her search for a room became desperate. She advertised, wrote appeals to officials, turned again to Pasternak—all without result.

In August, she and Mur moved again to the crowded quarters of Lilya Efron, who was spending the summer months in the country, but there was not enough space for Tsvetaeva's things, and she left some of them, for the time being, in the Herzen Street apartment. She enrolled Mur in school, but she felt desperate and abandoned, unable to write. Memories of her arrival, of Bolshevo, of the arrests surfaced. Yet she blamed her depression largely on the absence of a room in Moscow. On August 31 she wrote angrily to another woman poet, Vera Merkuriyeva:

> Fine, I am not the only one. . . . But my father built the Museum of Fine Arts—the only one in the whole country. He is the founder and the collector, his work of fourteen years. I am not going to talk about myself, and yet I will say in Chénier's words, his last words—"and still something was in there" (and he pointed to his forehead).* I cannot without false humility equate myself with any *kolkhoznik* or someone from Odessa who *also* has not found a place in Moscow. I cannot rid myself of the feeling of being entitled (not even mentioning the fact that there are three of our libraries in the Rumyantsev Museum: my grandfather's, Aleksandr Pavlovich Meyn's, my mother's, Mariya Aleksandrovna Tsvetaeva's, and my father's, Ivan Vladimirovich Tsvetaev's. We have showered Moscow with gifts. But it kicks me out, it ejects me.

This letter shows the extent to which Tsvetaeva had become disoriented: "With the changes of place I gradually lose my sense of reality: there is less and less of me, I'm like that flock that left a tuft of wool on every fence. All that remains is my basic NO." She felt old, defeated:

> If I were ten years younger: no, five years!—part of that load would be lifted—off my pride—by, let's call it for short, 'feminine charm' (I

---

*André Marie de Chénier (1762–1794), a French poet guillotined during the French Revolution.

speak about my men friends). But now, as it is, with my gray head, I don't have the tiniest illusion: everything they do for me, they do for me and not for themselves . . . and that is bitter. I am so used to giving! [ . . . ] This is my misfortune, I have no possessions, all is heart and fate.[18]

Finally, at the end of September, she found a room in a communal apartment in a high-rise building on Pokrovsky Boulevard in Moscow. It was another sublet, but this time the lease was for two years, and Tsvetaeva and Mur were officially registered as Moscow residents. Some sense of stability entered their lives.

In the last days of September, Tsvetaeva was told at Efron's prison that he was no longer on the list of recipients of packages. At the desk an official reassured her that this didn't mean anything. But there was no recourse, no way to find out where Efron was. In this agonizing situation Tsvetaeva kept working on her manuscripts, organizing a new collection of poetry for submission to Goslitizdat, the State Publishing House. "Here I am putting together a book," she wrote in her notebook. "I insert, I check, I spend money to have it copied, again, I revise and am almost sure that they will not take it, it would be a miracle if they would. So, I have done my share, have demonstrated all my good-will (have obeyed)." [19]

In her essay dealing with Tsvetaeva's work on this collection, Viktoria Schweitzer writes: "Apparently one of her friends, possibly Pasternak, who more than anyone took an interest in Tsvetaeva's affairs, persuaded her to try to publish a collection of her poetry in Moscow." [20] Had the book been published, it would have meant not only money but rehabilitation. She knew that both she and Mur were regarded as "family of enemies of the people," which meant they were in constant danger.

Some of the revised versions of these poems, available now, testify to Tsvetaeva's extraordinary courage, a courage that must have revitalized her, for however short a time. The first poem, originally dedicated to Efron in *The Demesne of the Swans*, was in itself a challenge to the regime. People ordinarily tried to hide the fact that a family member was in prison, but Tsvetaeva obviously made no distinction between Efron at the front and Efron in jail. Moreover, this revised version was even more clearly addressed to him, was even more powerful in its love and loyalty. She did not include some of her poems that could be interpreted as showing social consciousness or nostalgia for Russia; instead she chose many of her late, more complex poems which certainly were unacceptable for a critic who adhered to the official dogma of Socialist Realism.

She asked Pasternak's friend Aseyev, who as a Stalin laureate was very influential, to intervene for her. But he recommended submitting a book of translations instead since "they do not take poetry." [21] The state literary publishing house, Goslitizdat, rejected the book because its reviewer found only six or seven of the poems relevant for the Soviet reader. Although Tsvetaeva had expected the rejection, she was hurt by the finality of being reduced to translations alone. There was no place for her in Soviet reality, she felt. Mur reacted to the rejection with total indifference. He understood that Tsvetaeva's poetry was out of place, here even more than abroad; it was not, he felt, about what was needed!

Cheered by her return to poetry, Tsvetaeva congratulated herself in her diary on her forty-eighth birthday: "I am 48 years old today. I congratulate myself, first (knock wood) for surviving; and second, [ . . . ] for forty-eight years of uninterrupted soul." [22] About the same time, she tried to initiate a new relationship with a poet and translator, Arseny Tarkovsky. A draft in her notebook of a letter to him repeats all her usual themes. She invited him to visit her some night soon to listen to her poems. As always, this invitation was to be "their secret," revealing her hope for a closer personal relationship. [23] According to a woman friend, Yelizaveta Yakovleva, who knew Tsvetaeva and Asya from prerevolutionary times and who was now a translator, Tsvetaeva met Tarkovsky at Yakovleva's house, where young poet-translators gathered on Saturdays. It was "love at first sight." [24] Tarkovsky was about fifteen years younger than Tsvetaeva; he admired her early poetry and was drawn to her. He was, however, married and his wife resented Tsvetaeva.

In that fall of 1940 Tsvetaeva seemed to have found a degree of "normalcy." The manuscript for her book would be submitted to a second reading; some of her translations were appearing in Soviet journals; her circle of friends had grown. Her poetry was highly valued in literary circles, and she was flooded with offers of translations. She saw some of her old friends—Yevgeny Lann, Vera Zvyagintseva, Nikolay Aseyev—and new friends—Tager, Goltsev, Tarasenkov, Tarkovsky, Kruchyonykh. As often as she could, she ran to some of these friends' houses to read her poems, escape her black thoughts, and have a good meal.

She always took Mur along as she had taken Alya in revolutionary Moscow. Mur had grown into a very intelligent, handsome, controlled young man who looked older than his fifteen years. Tsvetaeva never let him out of her sight, all the time instructing him like a little boy, which clearly annoyed him. A loner, he rarely laughed and was as alienated in Russia as he had been in France.

Yet, if Tsvetaeva had friends, work, housing, she was as much in need as ever for that kindred soul who would understand her and need her. She thought she had found such a soul in Tanya Kvanina, the young wife of the writer Nikolay Moskvin, whom she had met in Golitsyno. For her part, Kvanina admired Tsvetaeva, but she was young, had grown up in the Soviet world, and never quite understood her. Tsvetaeva must have sensed Kvanina's resistance, and in a letter of November 17, 1940, she declared her love for her and tried to convince her that all that mattered was "to have our heart pound—even if it breaks into smithereens! Mine always broke into smithereens, and all my poems—are those silvery smithereens of my heart."

Tsvetaeva was well aware of how rapidly she scared people off with her stormy feelings:

> Tanya, don't be afraid of me. Don't think that I am intelligent and whatever else, and so on and so forth (substitute all your fears). You can give me so much, so infinitely much; since only the one who makes my heart pound can give me everything. It is my own pounding heart that I need. When I don't love, I am not myself. For such a long time—I have not been myself. With you, I am myself.

In writing to Tanya, Tsvetaeva repeats in much the same words the definition of love she had used with Steiger:

> What I need from a person, Tanya—is love. What I need from the other, Tanya, is need for me, want of me (and if possible dependence on me). Understand me correctly. It means without measure. "I need you like bread." I cannot imagine better words from a person. No, I do: "I need you like air."

She ends the letter with the words: "You know that the one who writes to you is my old self: my young self, the one of twenty years ago, as though those twenty years had never existed! The self that belonged to Sonechka."[25] It is the mention of Sonechka that defines the extent of Tsvetaeva's involvement. Kvanina remained a friend, but she could not respond to Tsvetaeva's passion.

*I think I have loved more than life, a feeling of uyut (securité, safety). It has irretrievably gone out of my life.*[1]

**B**y October 1940 Tsvetaeva's search for emotional safety, her need to be sheltered by the phantasy world of her creativity, had come to an end. Now she was facing the dread of the outside world. A few lines written in February 1941 convey her exhaustion and acceptance of death.

> It's time to take off the amber,
> It's time to change the language,
> It's time to extinguish the lantern
> Above the door.[2]

Yet the year had begun with the "good" news that Alya's case had been decided: she was transferred on January 27, probably to a labor camp. Hoping to hear the same news about Efron, Tsvetaeva had already begun to prepare warm things to send them. But a note asking Tanya Kvanina to find out the price of warm lining ended, "I love you tenderly and hurriedly. I will not live for long, I know."[3]

On April 10, money for Efron was accepted, and on April 11 Alya's first letter arrived with a letter for Mur in the same envelope. Tsvetaeva waited for Mur to come home from school so that they could read their letters together. She answered Alya immediately. After writing briefly about the most important subjects—a parcel for Efron had been accepted, Mur was fine—Tsvetaeva listed the things she was sending to Alya. She would send the carrots she had dried that winter on all the radiators, and she wanted to know which blanket Alya would prefer, her light blue one or her own multi-colored knit one? Perhaps Alya would like her "silver bracelet with a turquoise for the other hand; one can wear it without taking it off." Probably Alya left Bolshevo with one of these bracelets, but offering to send one now shows how little Tsvetaeva understood about Soviet prisons, about beatings and starvation. She reported that she had been accepted as a member of one of the official writers' groups, perhaps hoping that such recognition, however slight, would improve Alya's chances. "In general," she wrote, "I am trying hard."[4] In another letter to Alya, Tsvetaeva mentioned that a big package with warm clothes had been accepted for Efron on May 5. There was still hope!

That spring, Tarkovsky snubbed Tsvetaeva at a book fair. Apparently the friendship was petering out. Her last poem — the very last she ever wrote — was addressed to him and is introduced by a line from one of his poems, "I set the table for six." It echoes her famous poem "Attempt at Jealousy." Contempt and superiority were still her weapons. Pain and rage were again transformed into great poetry.

> I keep changing the first line
> And keep changing one word:
> "I set the table for six . . ."
> You forgot one — the seventh.
>
> .   .   .   .   .   .   .   .   .   .   .   .   .   .   .   .
>
> How could you, how dared you, not understand
> That six (two brothers, the third one
> You yourself — with your wife, father and mother)
> Are seven, since I am in this world!
>
> You set the table for six
> But with six the world is not finished.
> Rather than a scarecrow among the living —
> I want to be a phantom — with your family, (with mine).
>
> Timid, like a thief,
> Oh — not touching a soul!
> I sit down at the absent table setting,
> The uninvited, the seventh one.
>
> There! I knocked over a glass!
> And everything that thirsted to spill out —
> All the salt from my eyes, all the blood from my wounds —
> From the tablecloth onto the floor.

And there is no grave! There is no separation!
The spell is gone from the table, the house is awakened!
Like death to a wedding feast,
I—life, came to supper.

I am no one: not a brother, not a son, not a husband,
Not a friend—and still I reproach you:
You who set the table for six—*souls*,
Not seating me—at the edge.[5]

The poem is a response to exclusion and abandonment not by Tarkovsky alone but by most of her former friends. Tsvetaeva is still able to challenge, to feel superior to all who offend her, but she is tired, resigned. "All the salt from my eyes, all the blood from my wounds" has spilled out. In May, she wrote a short, sad note to Kvanina: "Dear Tanya, you have completely disappeared—as my Sonechka also did. I wish both of you would reappear. Call me [ . . . ] but do not postpone it too long."[6] Did she fantasize about more than friendship? In any case, this infatuation seems also to have ended in rejection. At the same time, the problems of daily life were again increasingly crowding her: she needed money to pay her rent in advance; she hated the communal kitchen and quarreled with the other tenants.

In June, Mur found a girlfriend. Tsvetaeva complained to friends that the girl was not right for him and that he had become "uncontrollable." Mur wrote to Alya that he had two new passions, a girlfriend and soccer. "Mama is angry because she doesn't know anything about my friend, but this is unimportant. In any case I have a fine time with this girl, who is intelligent and graceful—what else do I need?"[7] Mur was growing up and in revolt. Many of Tsvetaeva's contemporaries recall that he was ill-mannered to his mother, that he was often frustrated and angry. Tsvetaeva had again and again expressed her need for full control of her son. Long before, in 1930, she had written to Lomonosova:

How sad [that] you write about your son: "He is quite grown-up. Soon he will marry—will leave." My son is now just five years old. I have been thinking about this since—and perhaps before—his birth. I will, of course, *hate his wife*, because she *is not I* (not the other way around).

I am already sad that he is five, and not four. Mur, surprised: "But, Mama! I am the same! I haven't changed!" "Well, that's just it . . . You'll keep being the same and suddenly—you're twenty. Good-bye Mur!" "Mama! I'll never get married, because a wife is stupidity."[8]

When through Pasternak a meeting with Akhmatova was arranged in the spring of 1941, it must have meant a great deal to Tsvetaeva. The two women had never met, although Tsvetaeva had addressed poems and letters to her famous rival. Akhmatova had come to Moscow from Leningrad to find out more about the fate of her son, imprisoned for the second time. She and Tsvetaeva met at the house of a friend and spent many hours together on two consecutive days. A few months before they met, Akhmatova had written a belated reply to Tsvetaeva's 1916 "Verses to Akhmatova," in which she said:

> Tonight, Marina, you and I
> Are walking through the midnight capital,
> And behind there are millions of such as we,
> And there is no procession more silent,
> All around ring the funeral bells
> And the savage Muscovite moaning
> Of the snowstorm which obliterates our traces.[9]

Now their bond was one of shared suffering, yet as Karlinsky points out, "despite the time the two poets spent together, it seems to have been the same kind of 'non-meeting' as Tsvetaeva's encounter with Pasternak in Paris in 1935."[10] In a second poem, "The Four of Us," written many years later, in 1961, Akhmatova included Tsvetaeva in the circle of poets who were closest to her: Mandelshtam, Pasternak, and Tsvetaeva.


The beginning of the end came on June 22, 1941, when the German armies invaded Russia. Utter panic seized Tsvetaeva at the outbreak of war. No longer able to earn any income from translating, she had, as usual, very little money. But what really overwhelmed her was fear of bombs and fear of her special situation as a relative of "enemies of the people." Rumors circulated that people like her and Mur would be expelled from Moscow. Tsvetaeva told a friend that she was afraid to show her passport. She had probably been told by someone in those long prison lines that passports like hers had a secret, invisible mark that the authorities could recognize.

The first aerial bombardment of Moscow occurred on the night of July 21. Young people volunteered as firefighters, but Tsvetaeva did not want Mur to expose himself to danger on the roof of their building. He refused to listen to her. Petrified at the prospect of losing him, Tsvetaeva did not know what to do, could not decide whether to stay in Moscow or apply to the Writers' Union for evacuation. She asked everyone she met for advice. Mainly she was motivated by her fear for Mur, but he did not want to leave. In Paris, he had insisted that they return to Soviet Russia, but now he was disenchanted, demanding, and angry. Mother and son became increasingly estranged. Tsvetaeva, with all her insight and her awareness of Mur's basically different attitudes, had never succeeded in seeing him as a separate human being. Just as she had with her lovers, she "invented" her son, but unlike them, he had no way out. He was her consolation, her duty, her idol. Now, concerned only for him, she was indifferent even to the safety of her manuscripts, which were still in a suitcase at the Tarasenkovs'. During one aerial alert, she lost control; she shook, her eyes wandered, her hands trembled. Mariya Belkina remembers that when the "all clear" sounded, Tsvetaeva relaxed and smoked, but admitted that she was terrified of bombardments and appalled that Mur was allowed to participate in the civil defense. Later meeting Belkina in the street, Tsvetaeva was almost incoherent in her fear: "He is coming, coming and there's no power that can stop him, he sweeps away everything on his way, destroys everything. One must run away . . . One must." [11]

In August the Writers' Union began evacuating its members to the Tatar Republic. Tsvetaeva leaned toward going with them. When she asked Pasternak's advice, he strongly suggested that she stay in Moscow. Yet he didn't invite her to stay at his dacha in Peredelkino, as she had hoped he would. For Mur's sake she decided to go. On August 8, 1941, they boarded the steamer that would take them on the river Volga to Kazan, and from there on the river Kama to Chistopol and Yelabuga. Pasternak came to see them off. Tsvetaeva seemed distracted and forlorn. Mur was angered by her decision to leave; he kept darting off in all directions and Tsvetaeva was frantic as she waited for him to return. She was leaving Moscow, the city she loved; she was facing the unknown without friends, without money. Did she also know she was saying good-bye to the last fragile link connecting her to Efron?

The trip lasted about two weeks. One of her fellow passengers reported to Alya after the war that Tsvetaeva had been terribly worried about providing for herself and Mur. She had a few hundred rubles and some things she wanted to sell: silver objects and some yarn. She felt unable to work. " 'If I get a job, I will mix everything up because of my fears.' " More than anything she feared filling out questionnaires. She could only wash dishes or scrub floors. She would often approach the ship's rail saying " 'One step that way—and everything is finished.' " [12] Mur, according to the same witness, blamed his mother for everything—their return to Russia, their departure from Moscow. At sixteen, he seemed fully grown-up, with well-defined opinions.

Tsvetaeva said repeatedly: " 'I have to go away so as not to hinder Mur. I stand in his way. He has to live.' " [13]

Most of the evacuees were assigned to stay in Chistopol, a small town in the Tatar Soviet Republic. But Tsvetaeva and Mur were directed, along with a few other families, to Yelabuga, a remote village where Tsvetaeva knew no one. It depressed her from the very first moment. At first, the evacuees were housed in a dormitory. Tsvetaeva finally found a room in a small house in the village. " 'I will stay here,' " she announced. " 'I am not going another step.' " [14] Her landlords have described her as "old and homely; her face tired and worried; her hair, heavily mixed with gray, was combed back. . . . She was poorly dressed: a long, dark dress, an old fall coat, probably brown, and a pea-green knitted beret. . . . Indoors she always wore a big apron with a pocket." [15] Others remembered Tsvetaeva and Mur quarreling behind closed doors: "The son was dissatisfied with their lives; he demanded better clothes for everyday wear and so on." Tsvetaeva had brought bags of sugar, flour, and other provisions, but she was too tired to cook and they went for their meals to a meager wartime kitchen. She tried to sell some of her remaining possessions and look for work as well, all without success.

After only a few days in Yelabuga, Tsvetaeva decided to go to Chistopol to get in touch with Nikolay Aseyev and Aleksandr Fadeyev, leading members of the Evacuation Council of the Writers' Union there, for help in obtaining a residence permit for Chistopol and some work. She had known these writers in Moscow, and may even have hoped to break out of her total isolation. An account published by Kirill Khenkin, who knew Efron during his many years as an NKVD agent, raises the question of terrible complications for Tsvetaeva.

As soon as Marina Tsvetaeva arrived in Yelabuga, the local NKVD representative summoned her and invited her to work for them.

Their provincial agent probably reasoned that since this woman had come from Paris, in Yelabuga she must be unhappy. Since she is unhappy, other dissatisfied elements will seek her out. They will begin to talk, which will allow her to "uncover enemies," that is, to put together a case. And, perhaps, a file of the Efron family had come to Yelabuga with an indication of its involvement with the intelligence agencies. I don't know. . . . In any case, she was offered the opportunity of becoming an informer. . . . She expected that Aseyev and Fadeyev would be as outraged as she was and would protect her against such vile propositions. To protect from what? Be outraged by what?

This was the fall of 1941! Stalin ruled the country! To collaborate with the intelligence agencies, if you want to know, was the highest honor. You, citizeness, to put it straight . . . were offered trust.

And this is why, fearing for themselves, fearing that by referring to them, Marina would ruin them, Aseyev and Fadeyev . . . told her the most innocent thing that people in their position under those circumstances could say. Namely, that everyone had to decide for himself — to collaborate or not with the agencies, that this was a matter of conscience and civic consciousness, an issue of political maturity and patriotism.[16]

If this recollection is true, Tsvetaeva's last days were even more haunted than her friends realized.

On August 24, without Mur, Tsvetaeva boarded a slow riverboat for Chistopol, arriving August 25; two days later she was on her way back. Little was known about her days in Chistopol until 1981, when Lidiya Chukovskaya published her reminiscences, based on the notes she had taken then.[17]


Lidiya Chukovskaya, the daughter of the well-known writer Korney Chukovsky, was a close friend of Akhmatova and a successful author of novels and memoirs in her own right. Widely admired for her uncompromising honesty under the repressive Soviet regime, she has given us a moving account of Tsvetaeva's final days: the ugliness and poverty of the Tatar village, the callousness of Soviet officialdom, and the narrow-mindedness of the average citizen. Against this backdrop stands the tragic figure of the poet — reduced, fearful, and disoriented, an old woman trying to feed her adolescent son by obtaining a dishwasher's job.

Chukovskaya had heard about her, of course, but she met Tsvetaeva for the first time in Chistopol:

The woman in gray looked up at me, slightly bending her head to one side. Her face was the same as the beret: gray. A delicate face but puffy. Sunken cheeks and the eyes yellowish-green staring stubbornly. Her glance heavy, inquisitive. "How glad I am that you are here," she said, stretching out her hand. "My husband's sister, Yelizaveta Yakovlevna Efron, has told me a lot about you. Now I will move to Chistopol and we will be friends." These friendly words were not, however, accompanied by a friendly smile. No smile at all, either on her lips or in her eyes. Neither artificially worldly, nor sincerely happy. She pronounced her friendly greeting in a low, soundless voice, in sentences without intonation.

Chukovskaya was puzzled by Tsvetaeva's quasi-adolescent "Let's be friends" approach, especially since she had met Efron's sister only once, at a shared dinner table.

The next day, a young woman approached Chukovskaya on the street and urged her to come to the building where the Litfond Council, a support organization for members of the Writers' Union, was in session to decide on Tsvetaeva's future. Tsvetaeva, the woman said, was very excited and needed support. She had applied for a residence permit and for a position as a dishwasher in a canteen planned for writers. Chukovskaya raced to the Party office where the meeting was taking place. There, Tsvetaeva grabbed Chukovskaya and begged her to stay with her. " 'My fate is being decided now. . . . If they refuse me a residence permit for Chistopol, I will die. I feel sure they will refuse. I'll throw myself in the river Kama.' " Chukovskaya tried to reassure her, but Tsvetaeva was not listening. Instead, she kept staring fixedly at the door and didn't even turn to Chukovskaya when she talked to her: " 'Here, in Chistopol, there are people, but there [in Yelabuga] is nothing but a village . . . Here there are people . . . In Yelabuga, I am frightened.' "

Finally, one of the Council members emerged and announced that Tsvetaeva's case had been decided in her favor. She was granted a residence permit and had only to find a room. As for her application for the dishwashing job in the writers' canteen, there were many applications and only one position, but her chances were good. Chukovskaya was ready to help in the search for a room in Chistopol, but to her amazement, Tsvetaeva suddenly seemed indifferent. " 'Is it really worth looking for a room?' " she asked. " 'Anyway, I won't find anything. Perhaps it is better to give up at once and to leave for Yelabuga. . . . It's all the same. If I find a room, they won't give me work. I won't have anything to live on.' "

Chukovskaya insisted that many people in Chistopol loved her poems and would help her, and she reminded Tsvetaeva that if she got the dishwashing job she would be able to feed herself and her son. Tsvetaeva was finally convinced. She was ready to start out, but when Chukovskaya told her she wanted to go home to take care of her ten-year-old daughter and her four-year-old nephew, Tsvetaeva cried out: " 'No, no! . . . Alone I cannot. I don't understand directions at all. I cannot find my way anywhere, I don't understand space.' "

So the two of them set off, first to Chukovskaya's home and then on their search for a room. On the way, Tsvetaeva asked Chukovskaya, "'Tell me, please, why do you think that life's still worth living? Don't you understand the future? . . . Don't you understand that everything is finished?'" After Chukovskaya had tended to the children, Tsvetaeva burst out:

> Children, children, to live for the children's sake. . . . If you knew what a son I have, what a gifted, talented youth! But I can't help him with anything. It is only worse for him with me. I am even more helpless than he is. All I have left are my last 200 rubles. If only I could manage to sell that wool . . . If they would take me as a dishwasher, it would be wonderful. I am still capable of washing dishes, but I don't know how to teach children, and I don't know how to work in a *kolkhoz*. I don't know how, I can't do anything. You can't imagine how helpless I am.

As they walked along, Chukovskaya said she was glad Akhmatova was not in Chistopol, where she would have perished. Startled, Tsvetaeva asked why. "'Because she would not have been able to cope with life here,'" Chukovskaya replied. "'You know that she cannot do anything practical at all. Even in city life, even in peacetime.'"

"I saw the gray face at my side twitch."

"'And you think that I—I can?' Marina Ivanovna shouted in a furious voice. 'Akhmatova cannot and I, you think I can?'"

When they came to a street that Chukovskaya considered cleaner and better than the others they had seen, Tsvetaeva exploded: "'What a horrible street. . . . I cannot live here. It's a frightening street.'"

All the more revealing was Tsvetaeva's complete transformation when Chukovskaya brought her to the house of friends, writers who received her with open arms. They loved her poems and were eager to listen to anything she was willing to recite for them. They invited her to stay overnight, promising to help her find a room the next morning.

> Marina Ivanovna was transformed before our eyes. Her gray cheeks gained color. Her eyes turned from yellow to green. Having finished her tea, she changed to a rickety sofa and lit a cigarette. Sitting very straight, she stared with interest at the new faces. I, however, was looking at her, trying to figure out her age. With every minute she was growing younger.

Tsvetaeva told them the story of her life. "What was new to me," Chukovskaya observed, was the precision in her pronunciation of words that corresponded to the precise rigidity of her erect posture, the precise abruptness of her sudden movements, and then also that precision of thought with which she, according to her story, understood how cruelly mistaken her husband and children had been in their eagerness to return to the motherland. She, however, had understood *there*, how it was *here*.

Tsvetaeva ended her story with Efron's and Alya's arrests. Then she began reading her poem "Homesickness," but interrupted herself, saying that she had to leave, though she had been invited to stay the night. She promised, however, to come back that evening to read more poems, to stay overnight and look for a room the next day. But she did not return—not that evening and not ever. Instead, she slept in the dormitory where she had been staying and then returned to Yelabuga.

Three days later Mur called on Aseyev in Chistopol with a letter from Tsvetaeva, "I beg of you, take Mur as your son. [ . . . ] Don't ever abandon him." [18] Tsvetaeva had hanged herself, he explained.

**S** Tsvetaeva had returned to Yelabuga on August 27 or 28, only to commit suicide on August 31. Her landlord had gone fishing, and her landlady and Mur were out. Alone, she found the hook she had been looking for since Bolshevo. She left a note for Mur:

> Murlyga! Forgive me, but to go on would be worse. I am *gravely ill*, this is not me anymore. I love you passionately. Do understand that I could not live anymore. Tell Papa and Alya, if you ever see them, that I loved them to the last moment and explain to them that I *found myself in a trap*. [19]

Mur recorded the events of these desperate weeks in his notebook. Shockingly factual, these dry lines speak either of emotional atrophy or of grief's protective shield, the denial of pain of an injured human being who had never seen himself reflected accurately in his mother's eyes. His was a wound not unlike his mother's:

> On the 8th of August 1941, I was evacuated to Yelabuga with Marina Ivanovna. We arrived on the 17th. On the 26 M. I. went for two days to Chistopol; she returned on the 28th to Yelabuga, where she committed suicide on August 31. She was buried in the Yelabuga cemetery. Her last letter, addressed to me, is in my possession. On September 3, I moved

to Chistopol and from there I left for Moscow on September 28, where I arrived on September 30.[20]

Reports differ, but it seems that Mur did not accompany his mother's casket to the cemetery. Nor did anyone else.

Tsvetaeva's friends blamed themselves for her suicide. Pasternak felt that he would never forgive himself for having failed her. In years to come Alya and many others in the Soviet Union preferred to shift the blame to the hostility to which Tsvetaeva had been exposed in emigration. And still others, among them her sister Asya, accused Mur of having driven his mother to suicide. Writers in the West, on the other hand, believed that Tsvetaeva, unable to publish in the Soviet Union, had no other way out after the arrests of Efron and Alya, especially after she realized that she would be only a burden to Mur.

For many, Tsvetaeva's decision to kill herself was a mystery—certainly it was overdetermined—but she herself offered an answer in her poems. The theme of death and suicide was dominant in her work throughout her life. She had experienced the suicides of the Tsar-Maiden and of Phaedra in her imagination; in her poems, letters, and essays she revealed the anguish and emptiness she felt when she could not find the response she needed, the intensity she sought. Her poetry was her means of reaching out, and life without art had no meaning for her. She sought merger but found it only in short-lived relationships—and in her own creative genius. In Tsvetaeva's letters we see how often she had to choose between passion, however unreal, and depression. Compromise was not for her. Indeed her longing for the absolute continued until she ended her life. By the time she hanged herself, she had come to the end of the road: Efron and Alya had disappeared; Mur did not need her; her passions were not reciprocated. And there was no way for her to reach out with her creativity. "I used to know how to write poems," she said near the end, "but I've forgotten how."[21]

T svetaeva was dead, her remote grave unmarked. Efron was shot in October 1941; Mur, drafted in February 1944, was killed in June the same year. For fifteen years Tsvetaeva's voice would be silenced in the Soviet Union. Abroad, she was considered an esoteric poet, appreciated by only a few.

With Stalin's death and Khrushchev's "thaw," Tsvetaeva's daughter Ariadna was rehabilitated in 1955 after seventeen years in the Gulag and in exile in Siberia. She returned to Moscow and then settled in Tarusa, where her mother had spent so many childhood summers. She devoted the years until her death in 1975 to the rehabilitation of her father, the collecting and publication of her mother's work, and the establishment of an archive to be closed until the year 2000. Anastasiya, a prisoner since 1939, was not released until 1959. Both women wrote about Tsvetaeva's past; each wanted to be regarded as her champion. In the early sixties Anastasiya journeyed to Yelabuga and, unable to find the exact location of her sister's grave, arranged for a cross at an approximate site. A few years later the Union of Writers replaced the cross with a simple monument. Anastasiya died in September 1993, aged ninety-nine.

In 1956, in the Soviet anthology *Literary Moscow* no. 2, Ehrenburg introduced a number of Tsvetaeva's poems with a short essay about her importance. Two more anthologies, in 1956 and 1957, included her poems, but the thaw did not last long and Tsvetaeva found her place in samizdat, the flourishing underground circulation of forbidden works, where, according to Karlinsky, she became the most popular poet of Soviet youth in the sixties and seventies.

In 1961 a slim volume of Tsvetaeva's selected works was published, followed in 1965 by the much more comprehensive volume in the distinguished "Poet's Library" series, edited and annotated by Ariadna Efron and Anna Saakyants. Many separate collections have been published since; the most recent poetry collection appeared in 1990, also in the "Poet's Library" series, introduced and richly annotated by Yelena B. Korkina.

Meanwhile, interest in Tsvetaeva grew abroad. In 1953 the Chekhov Publishing House in Holland (financed in part by American money) published a small volume of her prose. In the same year her friend Yury Ivask included thirteen of her poems in his anthology of Russian émigré poetry. More and more scholarly studies, reminiscences, and previously unpublished letters and poems have appeared. In 1979 Russica, a Russian-language publishing house in New York, came out with a two-volume edition of Tsvetaeva's prose with an introduction by Joseph Brodsky, and in 1980–90 with a five-volume edition of her poems, splendidly edited by Alexander Sumerkin and annotated by Viktoria Schweitzer. Moreover, in Russia, younger poets like Yevgeny Yevtushenko, Bella Akhmadulina, and others have been deeply influenced by Tsvetaeva.

Tsvetaeva said repeatedly that she did not belong to her time. Indeed, she never found a place for herself in life; instead she lived in her fantasy, in a world where she made the rules and had to be in control. In her lifetime, and certainly after her suicide, she was seen as a victim of her time, as of course she was. Still later, some of her admirers in effect took her out of time, attributing her conflicts to the fact that she was born a Poet. In accounting for "a certain *a priori* tragic note" in her work, Joseph Brodsky is not concerned with "first hand tragic experience" or "the purely intrinsic emotional reasons that made her resort to this or that cultural mask."[1]

Brodsky is a poet and critic and the biographer's interests are not his. Yet Viktoria Schweitzer's biography, wonderfully informed by her knowledge of Tsvetaeva's literary milieu, also eschews psychological interpretation in favor of the "born poet" theory. "From this standpoint," one reviewer writes, "Tsvetaeva's reported difficulties with her mother arose simply from her given nature, from her vocation." Yet, for this reviewer, "of the generation intellectually formed by Marx and Freud and all their feminist and structuralist critics, it was impossible . . . not to want to know about Tsvetaeva's relationship with her mother, to her own gender."[2]

It should be said, of course, that Tsvetaeva herself wanted to know about her relationship with her mother and thus explored it directly and indirectly in her own writing. Her letters provide descriptions of her own emotional states of mind that anticipate almost clinically the insights of modern psychologists, sometimes in their language. Tsvetaeva's perception of her own depression is startling.[3]

An excellent recent essay in the New Yorker notes that Tsvetaeva is seen now as "a feminist heroine, fully sexed and unashamed."[4] Many readers will not find this view far-fetched, but it overlooks the complexities of Tsvetaeva's persona by suggesting that she was fulfilled, capable of reciprocity; it blocks out her yearning for self-destruction.

However, there is a new and informed appreciation of Tsvetaeva's insights. Although she was not a feminist—she opposed all movements—her views on women, marriage, motherhood, and creative freedom are of great interest. Her understanding of androgyny expresses itself over a wide range— from the skillful avoidance of gender-specific pronouns to the creation of characters in whom gender distinctions are reversed or combined. Her candor about lesbianism—about sex in general—grips many of today's readers.

On other grounds, too, Tsvetaeva's sense of the modern and what is now called the postmodern world finds receptive readers of many different backgrounds. We know now that her views on technology were rooted in part in the preternatural fear of machinery, the dread of cars and buses reflected in her dreams; she was afraid to cross a city street. But "Poem of the Staircase," written in 1926, transcends her private anxieties and strikes today's readers with its contemporary force:

> We with our crafts, we with our factories
> What have we done with the paradise given us
> A first knife, a first crowbar,
> What have we done with our first day?[5]

Other great artists, of course, shared Tsvetaeva's prescience, but, as she herself predicted, the long eclipse of her work gives her today, a half-century after her death, a special freshness, an extraordinary power.

*Abbreviations*

| | |
|---|---|
| AE | Ariadna Efron, *Stranitsy vospominany* (Pages of recollections) (Paris: LEV, 1979). |
| AT | Anastasiya Tsvetaeva, *Vospominaniya* (Memoirs) (Moscow: Sovetsky pisatel, 1971, 1st ed.). |
| CS | Marina Tsvetaeva, *A Captive Spirit: Selected Prose*, ed. and trans. J. Marin King (Ann Arbor, Mich.: Ardis, 1980). |
| IP | Marina Tsvetaeva, *Izbrannaya proza v dvukh tomakh* (Selected prose in two volumes), ed. Alexander Sumerkin (New York: Russica, 1979). |
| LL | "Letters of Marina Tsvetaeva to R. N. Lomonosova," in *Minuvsheye* (The past) (Paris: Atheneum, 1989). |
| LO | "Marina Tsvetaeva's Letters to Aleksandr Bakhrakh," *Literaturnoye obozreniye* (Literary survey), nos. 8, 9, and 10 (1991). |
| LT | Marina Tsvetaeva, *Pisma k A. Teskovoy* (Letters to A. Teskova) (Prague: Academia, 1969). |
| NP | Marina Tsvetaeva, *Neizdannyye pisma* (Unpublished letters), ed. Gleb and Nikita Struve (Paris: YMCA Press, 1972). |
| PTR | *Pasternak, Tsvetaeva, Rilke: Letters, Summer 1926*, ed. Yevgeny Pasternak, Yelena Pasternak, Konstantin Azadovsky; trans. Margaret Wettlin and Walter Arndt (New York: Harcourt Brace Jovanovich, 1985). |
| SiP | Marina Tsvetaeva, *Stikhotvoreniya i poemy v pyati tomakh* (Lyric and narrative poetry in five volumes), ed. Alexander Sumerkin and Viktoria Schweitzer (New York: Russica, 1980–1990). |
| Sochineniya | Marina Tsvetaeva, *Sochineniya v dvukh tomakh* (Works in two volumes) (Moscow: Khudozhestvennaya literatura, 1980). |
| Vestnik | *Vestnik russkogo kristianskogo dvizheniya* (Messenger of the Russian Christian Movement). |
| WSA | *Wiener slawistischer Almanach* (Vienna Slavic Yearbook). |

## Introduction

1   Marina Tsvetaeva, *A Captive Spirit: Selected Prose*, ed. and trans. J. Marin King (Ann Arbor, Mich.: Ardis, 1980), 338; hereafter cited as CS.

2   Mark Rudman, "Angelic Orders, Spare Moments" (Correspondence of Pasternak, Tsvetaeva, and Rilke), in *Diverse Voices: Essays on Poets and Poetry* (Brownsville, Ore.: Story Line Press, 1993), 225.

3   Simon Karlinsky, *Marina Cvetaeva: Her Life and Art* (Berkeley and Los Angeles: University of California Press, 1966), 7.

4   CS, 153.

5   As quoted by Simon Karlinsky, *Marina Tsvetaeva: The Woman, Her World, and Her Poetry* (Cambridge: Cambridge University Press, 1985), 219, see also 276.

6   Svetlana Elnitskaya, *Poetichesky mir Tsvetaevoy* (Tsvetaeva's poetic world), *Wiener slawistischer Almanach*, special volume 30 (Vienna, 1990).

7   Barbara Shapiro, *The Romantic Mother* (Baltimore: Johns Hopkins University Press, 1983), x.

8   Julia Kristeva, *Black Sun: Depression and Melancholia* (New York: Columbia University Press, 1989), 5.

9   Marina Tsvetaeva, *Stikhotvoreniya i poemy v pyati tomakh* (Lyric and narrative poetry in five volumes), ed. Alexander Sumerkin and Viktoria Schweitzer (New York: Russica, 1980–90), 1:67; hereafter cited as SiP, vols. 1, 2, 3, 4, and 5.

10   CS, 195–96.

11   Ibid., 334.

12   Ibid., 336.

13   Marina Tsvetaeva, *Izbrannaya proza v dvukh tomakh* (Selected prose in two volumes), ed. Alexander Sumerkin (New York: Russica, 1979), 1:398; hereafter cited as IP.

## 1. Family and Background

1   SiP, 1:219.

2   There were actually nine diaries, though only this one has surfaced; the others were in the possession of Marina and Asya Tsvetaeva, but have disappeared. The diary can be found in Tsentralny gosudarstvenny arkhiv literatury i iskusstva (Central state archive of literature and art), fond 237, op. 2, d. 209.

3   CS, 234.

4   SiP, 1:176.

5   CS, 226.

6   Ibid., 227.

7   Ibid., 338.

8   *Nabokov–Wilson Letters*, ed. Simon Karlinsky (New York: Harper and Row, 1979), 33.

9   Ariadna Efron, *Stranitsy vospominany* (Pages of recollections) (Paris: LEV Publishers, 1979), 17; hereafter cited as AE.

10   Anastasiya Tsvetaeva, *Vospominaniya* (Memoirs) (Moscow: Sovetsky pisatel, 1971), 30; hereafter cited as AT. First serialized in *Novy Mir* in the 1960s; published as a book in three editions: 1971, 1974, and 1983.

11   CS, 281.

12   SiP, 1:79.

13   Ibid., 83.

14 Marina Tsvetaeva, *Neizdannyye pisma* (Unpublished letters), ed. Gleb and Nikita Struve (Paris: YMCA Press, 1972), 27. Hereafter cited as NP.

15 Anastasiya's reminiscences are a questionable source. Written under Soviet censorship, their obvious bias has to be taken into account. Though she offers many details about life in the Tsvetaev family, her picture of almost "perfect happiness" is contradicted not only by the evidence in Tsvetaeva's work and letters, but it is also questioned by such Tsvetaeva scholars as Simon Karlinsky, Viktoria Schweitzer, and Irma Kudrova.

16 Véronique Lossky, *Marina Tsvetaeva v zhizne* (Marina Tsvetaeva in life) (New York: Hermitage, 1989), 21.

17 Alice Miller, citing D. W. Winnicott, could be describing Tsvetaeva's plight:

> Every child has a legitimate need to be noticed, taken seriously, and respected by his mother. In the first weeks and months of life he needs to have the mother at his disposal, must be able to use her and to be mirrored by her. This is beautifully illustrated in one of Winnicott's images: the mother gazes at the baby in her arms, and the baby gazes at his mother's face and finds himself therein . . . provided that the mother is really looking at the unique, small, helpless being and not projecting her own introjects onto the child, nor her own expectations, fears and plans for the child. In that case, the child would not find himself in his mother's face but rather the mother's own predicaments. This child would remain without a mirror, and for the rest of his life would be seeking this mirror in vain. Alice Miller, *The Drama of the Gifted Child* (New York: Basic Books, 1981), 32.

18 CS, 271.
19 Ibid., 276.
20 Ibid., 283.
21 Ibid., 280–81.
22 Ibid., 289.
23 Ibid., 320.
24 Ibid., 287.
25 IP, 1:342.
26 Ibid., 2:148.
27 Ibid., 1:343–44.
28 NP, 29.
29 AT, 206.
30 CS, 351.
31 IP, 1:343.
32 SiP, 1:67.
33 CS, 330.
34 Ibid., 329.
35 Ibid., 225.
36 Ibid.
37 Ibid., 230.
38 NP, 402.
39 CS, 252.
40 *Pasternak, Tsvetayeva, Rilke: Letters, Summer 1926*, ed. Yevgeny Pasternak, Yelena Pasternak, Konstantin Azadovsky; trans. Margaret Wettlin and Walter Arndt (New York: Harcourt Brace Jovanovich, 1985), 63; hereafter cited as PTR.

## 2. Growing Up: Reality and Fantasy

1   CS, 308.
2   Ibid., 353.
3   Ibid., 273–74.
4   Ibid., 303.
5   AT, 76.
6   IP, 2:167.
7   Ibid., 168.
8   Ibid., 171.
9   Ibid.
10  Marina Tsvetaeva, *Sochineniya v dvukh tomakh* (Works in two volumes) (Moscow: Khudo-zhestvennaya literatura, 1980), 2:496; hereafter cited as *Sochineniya*.
11  IP, 2:148.
12  Ibid.
13  Ibid., 149.
14  Ibid.
15  Ibid., 150.
16  NP, 271.
17  Ibid., 477. "The Devil" was first published in Paris in 1935 in *Contemporary Annals*, which accepted many of Tsvetaeva's essays. One of the editors, Vadim Rudnev, attracted her particular ire because he often deleted passages he thought would be of no interest to the average reader. Thus ten typewritten pages (two inserts) were left out of the printed text of this essay. This abbreviated text became part of the Russica edition and was translated into English by Janet King as well as into French by Véronique Lossky. Before leaving for the Soviet Union Tsvetaeva instructed a friend to deposit some of her manuscripts, including these inserts, in the library of the University of Basel. These inserts were incorporated in the *Sochineniya*.
18  CS, 301.
19  Ibid., 300. In the text Tsvetaeva says that she read aloud to Valeriya parts of Gogol's *Dead Souls*, but never finished it because she was disappointed in finding neither dead souls nor ghosts.
20  Ibid., 295–96.
21  Ibid., 296.
22  Ibid., 297.
23  Ibid., 298.
24  Ibid., 301.
25  Ibid., 308.
26  Ibid.
27  Sochineniya, 2:143–44.
28  Ibid., 144.
29  Ibid., 146.
30  CS, 306.
31  Ibid., 308.
32  Sochineniya, 2:154.
33  Ibid., 156.
34  Ibid., 155.

35   The fable was I. Krylov's translation from the French of Lafontaine's "Le loup et l'agneau."
36   CS, 333.


3. *Adolescence, Mother's Death*

1    SiP, 1:57.
2    Ellendea Proffer, *Marina Tsvetaeva: A Pictorial Biography* (Ann Arbor, Mich.: Ardis, 1980), 35.
3    AT, 105.
4    CS, 253.
5    In his chapter "On Narcissism: An Introduction" in *Collected Papers* (New York: Basic Books, 1959), 4:46, Freud refers to the fact that narcissistic persons are attracted to "the charm of certain animals which seem not to concern themselves with us, such as cats and the large beasts of prey." Tsvetaeva's Devil had the body of a lioness; she called Kobylyansky "tiger"; she would call her husband "lion" and her son Mur after the cat in E. T. A. Hoffmann's *Kater Murr*.
6    Viktoria Schweitzer, *Byt i bytiye Mariny Tsvetaevoy* (Marina Tsvetaeva's life and being)    is: (Paris: Sintaks, 1988), 47–48.
7    Lossky, *Marina Tsvetaeva v zhizne*, 21.
8    AT, 308.
9    IP, 1:123–24.
10   SiP, 1:17.
11   AT, 189.
12   CS, 183.
13   NP, 402.
14   Pyotr Schmidt was one of the leaders of the sailors' mutiny in the Russian Imperial Navy in October–November 1905. He was court-martialed and executed in March 1906. He later became the hero of Pasternak's long poem "Lieutenant Schmidt," which was discussed at length in his correspondence with Tsvetaeva.
15   PTR, 64.
16   AT, 225.
17   Mariya Aleksandrovna's will left to her daughters only the interest from her capital until they reached forty. Apparently she was afraid that they might give her estate away to revolutionary causes. In fact, it was confiscated by the Bolshevik government.
18   CS, 293.
19   Ibid., 287.
20   Ibid., 293.
21   Ibid.
22   AT, 243–45.
23   CS, 293.
24   Marina Tsvetaeva, *Pisma k A. Teskovoy* (Letters to A. Teskova) (Prague: Academia, 1969), 140; hereafter cited as LT.
25   AT, 338.
26   CS, 199.
27   IP, 1:289.
28   NP, 30.

## 4. Dawning Sexuality

1   SiP, 1:289.
2   N. Valentinov, *Dva goda s simvolistami* (Two years with the Symbolists) (Palo Alto: Stanford University Press, 1969), 151.
3   SiP, 1:8–9.
4   Ibid., 156.
5   Jane A. Taubman, *A Life Through Poetry: Marina Tsvetaeva's Lyric Diary* (Columbus, Ohio: Slavica Press, 1988), 24–25. Taubman introduces an additional reason for Tsvetaeva's fascination with Sarah Bernhardt: the aging actress playing the role of a handsome young man adds to other androgynous elements in the play.
6   "Marina Tsvetaeva's Letters to Aleksandr Bakhrakh," *Literaturnoye obozreniye* (Literary survey) 10 (1991): 106; hereafter cited as I.O. Bakhrakh's letters to Tsvetaeva have not been published, but he published her letters to him in 1960 and 1961 in *Mosty* (Bridges), and in 1991 Professor John Malmstad published a complete, annotated version in *Literary Survey*, nos. 8, 9, and 10.
7   NP, 15–18.
8   IP, 1:344.
9   CS, 294.
10  SiP, 1:36.
11  Ibid., 31.
12  Ibid., 29.
13  Ibid., 110.
14  CS, 113.
15  SiP, 1:28.
16  Ibid., 34.
17  CS, 101.
18  IP, 1:123.
19  CS, 193.
20  IP, 1:186.
21  Karlinsky, *Marina Tsvetaeva: The Woman, Her World, and Her Poetry*, 33.
22  Ibid., 32.
23  NP, 22.
24  As quoted in Karlinsky, *Marina Tsvetaeva: The Woman, Her World, and Her Poetry*, 34.
25  SiP, 1:21.
26  Ibid., 56–57.
27  Ibid., 11.
28  Ibid., 120.
29  Ilya Ehrenburg, *People, Years, and Life* (New York: Knopf, 1962), 124.
30  "Letters of Marina Tsvetaeva to Maksimilian Voloshin," *Novy mir* (New world) 2 (1977): 237–40.
31  Ibid., 237.

## 5. Illusions

1   SiP, 1:134.
2   CS, 69.

3   Ibid., 60.

4   NP, 23.

5   AT, 420.

6   CS, 116.

7   Ibid., 109.

8   Ibid.

9   Ibid., 110.

10  SiP, 1:116.

11  "Letters to Voloshin," Novy mir 2 (1977): 243.

12  "Voloshin's Letter to His Mother, November 1911," Yezhegodnik 8 (1977): 173–74.

13  NP, 25.

14  SiP, 1:[12–13].

15  Nikolay Yelenev, "Kem byla Marina Tsvetaeva?" (Who was Marina Tsvetaeva?), Grani 39 (Frankfurt, 1958): 145.

16  Ibid., 146.

17  SiP, 1:166.

18  Sergey Efron, Detstvo (Childhood) (Moscow: Ole Lukoe, 1912), 106–38.

19  Ibid., 126.

20  LT, 112.

21  Notebook entry, September 1913, "Zapisi o moey docheri" (Notes about my daughter), Vestnik russkogo khristianskogo dvizheniya (Messenger of the Russian Christian movement) 135 (1981): 184; hereafter cited as Vestnik.

22  Ibid., 183.

23  SiP, 1:166.

24  AE, 32.

25  CS, 245.

26  Ibid., 73.

27  SiP, 1:153.

28  Ibid., 138.

29  Ibid., 140.

30  Ibid., 194.

31  Ibid., 182.

## 6. Lesbian Passion

1   SiP, 1:187.

2   CS, 336.

3   Sochineniya, 1:422.

4   SiP, 1:176–87.

5   S. Polyakova, Zakatnye ony dni: Tsvetaeva i Parnok (Those days of yore: Tsvetaeva and Parnok) (Ann Arbor, Mich.: Ardis, 1982), 106.

6   See Diana Lewis Burgin, "Sophia Parnok and the Writing of a Lesbian Poet's Life," Slavic Review 51, no. 2 (Summer 1992):214–31, and her biography of the poet, Sophia Parnok: The Life and Work of a Russian Sappho (New York: New York University Press, 1994).

7   The allusion to Orestes is interesting in the context of the first title given to Tsvetaeva's Letter to an Amazon (1939)—Mon frère féminin, introduction by Ghislaine Limont (Paris: Mercure de France, 1979).

8    Sofiya Parnok, *Sobraniye stikhotvoreny* (Collected poems) (Ann Arbor, Mich.: Ardis, 1979), 141–42.

9    Polyakova, *Zakatnye ony dni*, 87.

10    Ibid., 51.

11    SiP, 1:184.

12    Polyakova, *Zakatnye ony dni*, 54.

13    Ibid., 57.

14    Parnok, *Sobraniye stikhotvoreny*, 131.

15    Ibid., 139.

16    SiP, 1:195.

17    Ibid., 196.

18    Polyakova, *Zakatnye ony dni*, 110–13.

19    Ibid., 113.

20    Ibid., 125.

21    SiP, 1:225.

22    Ibid., 226.

23    *Sochineniya*, 1:65–72.

24    Svetlana Elnitskaya, "Dve 'Bessonnitsy' Mariny Tsvetaevoy" (Marina Tsvetaeva's two 'Insomnias'), paper presented at the Amherst Tsvetaeva conference in 1992.

25    Marina Cvetaeva, *Lettera all'Amazzone*, trans. and ed. Serena Vitale (Milan: Guanda, 1981).

26    Ibid., 102.

27    Ibid., 100.

28    Parnok, *Sobraniye stikhotvoreny*, 234.

29    Ibid., 18.

30    Polyakova, *Zakatnye ony dni*, 70.

## 7. In the Shadow of Revolution

1    SiP, 1:197.

2    IP, 1:364.

3    LO, no. 8, 108.

4    Nadezhda Mandelstam, *Hope Abandoned* (New York: Atheneum, 1974), 462.

5    Ibid., 247.

6    Ibid., 467.

7    SiP, 1:207.

8    LO, no. 10, 101.

9    Osip Mandelstam, *The Complete Critical Prose and Letters* (Ann Arbor, Mich.: Ardis, 1979), 146.

10    Because of publishing problems, *Versts II* would appear a year before *Versts I*.

11    SiP, 1:302. Little is known about this man and her relationship with him.

12    Ibid., 247.

13    Ibid., 2:60.

14    Ibid., 203.

15    Ibid., 205–6.

16    IP, 1:21.

17    Ibid., 21.

18    CS, 90.

## 8. Life under Communism

1    SiP, 2:218.
2    IP, 1:52.
3    Ehrenburg, *People, Years, and Life*, 252.
4    Ibid.
5    IP, 1:83.
6    Ibid., 84.
7    Ibid.
8    "Marina Tsvetaeva's Letters to Yevgeny Lann," in *Wiener slawistischer Almanach*, special vol. 3 (Vienna, 1981): 172; hereafter cited as *WSA*.
9    Marina Tsvetaeva, *Povest o Sonechke* (The tale of Sonechka), in *Neizdannoye: Stikhi, teatr, proza* (Unpublished works: poetry, drama, prose) (Paris: YMCA Press, 1976), 209.
10   In fact, Efron came to collect money for his White Army unit. See Sergey Efron, "Zapiski dobrovoltsa" (Memoirs of a volunteer), *Zvezda* (Star) 10 (1992): 102–6.
11   Schweitzer, *Byt i bytiye*, 317. The identity of that other person is unknown.
12   Viktor Shklovsky, *Sentimental Journey* (Ithaca: Cornell University Press, 1970), 133.
13   SiP, 2:329.
14   Ibid., 68.
15   Ibid.
16   *Psikheya* (Berlin: LEV, 1923; reprint Paris: LEV, 1979).
17   *AE*, 36–37.
18   SiP, 2:327.
19   Ibid., 29.
20   Ibid., 74.
21   IP, 1:84.
22   Ibid., 55.
23   Ibid., 52.
24   Ibid., 60.
25   Ibid., 67.
26   Ibid., 54.
27   Ibid., 69.

## 9. Passion and Despair

1    SiP, 2:252.
2    *Povest o Sonechke*, in *Neizdannoye: Stikhi, teatr, proza*, 213–14.
3    Ibid., 227.
4    Ibid., 219.
5    Ibid., 271.
6    Ibid.
7    Ibid., 312.
8    Ibid.
9    Ibid., 323.
10   Ibid., 337.
11   Ibid., 346–47.

12   Ibid., 348.
13   IP, 1:70.
14   Ibid.
15   Viktoria Schweitzer, "Stranitsy k biografii Mariny Tsvetaevoy" (Pages for a biography of Marina Tsvetaeva), *Russian Literature* 9 (1981): 323–56.
16   IP, 1:88.
17   Schweitzer, "Stranitsy k biografii Mariny Tsvetaevoy," 335–38.
18   Ibid.
19   SiP, 2:275.
20   Schweitzer, "Stranitsy k biografii Mariny Tsvetaevoy," 339.

## 10. Years of Frenzy and Growth

 1   SiP, 2:13.
 2   Ibid., 89.
 3   Letter to Lann, December 1920, *WSA* 3 (1981): 166.
 4   Schweitzer, "Stranitsy k biografii Mariny Tsvetaevoy," 340.
 5   Ibid., 346.
 6   Ibid., 342.
 7   SiP, 2:283–85.
 8   Ibid., 280–81.
 9   G. S. Smith, "Characters and Narrative Modes in Tsvetaeva's 'Tsar'-Devitsa'," *Oxford Slavonic Papers*, n.s., 12 (1979): 119.
10   SiP, 4:80.
11   Ibid., 85.
12   Letter to Lann, December 1920, *WSA* 3 (1981): 167.
13   Ibid., 169.
14   The poem, first published in its full version in *Razluka* (Separation) in 1922 by Helikon in Berlin, was dedicated to Akhmatova. Later, Tsvetaeva rescinded that honor. The second version, without dedication, appeared in print in *Psyche* in 1923, published by Grzhebin, also in Berlin, with other substantial deletions. The *Psyche* version has been the one most frequently reprinted, but because of its deletions I have relied here on the original version.
15   *WSA* 3 (1981): 179.
16   Simon Karlinsky finds that "the poem is an allegory about the terrible and demanding nature of art," which it certainly is, but he avoids a psychological interpretation. Jane Taubman focuses on the importance of Tsvetaeva's overcoming Akhmatova's influence, and Ariadna Efron believed, with no evidence, that the poem was really addressed to Blok.
17   Letter to Lann, January 1921, *WSA* 3 (1981): 180.

## 11. New Poetic Voice and Departure

 1   SiP, 2:135.
 2   Letter to Lann, January 1921, *WSA* 3 (1981): 180.

3   Ibid., 181.
4   Ibid., 185.
5   Ibid., 182.
6   Ibid., 184.
7   Ibid., 185.
8   Schweitzer, "Stranitsy k biografii Mariny Tsvetaevoy," 341.
9   *AE*, 67.
10  Ibid., 42.
11  *IP*, 1:199.
12  Ibid., 201.
13  Ibid., 204.
14  Letter to Voloshin, November 1921, *Yezhegodnik* (Yearbook), 8 (1977): 182.
15  Sergey Volkonsky, Byt i bytiye (Existence and Being) (Paris: YMCA Press, 1924), xi–xii.
16  *Remeslo* (Craft) (Oxford: Willem A. Meeuw, 1981; a reprint of the 1923 Helikon edition),
    x–xi.
17  *WSA* 3 (1981): 187.
18  Karlinsky, *Marina Tsvetaeva: The Woman, Her World, and Her Poetry*, 100–102.
19  *AE*, 87.
20  Ibid., 75.
21  *CS*, 166.

## 12. Russian Berlin

1   *IP*, 2:305.
2   Roman Gul, *Ya unes Rossiyu* (I Took Russia with Me) (New York: "Most" Publishers, 1981),
    58.
3   Ibid., 59.
4   *SiP*, 3:342.
5   *CS*, 126.
6   Ibid., 128.
7   Marina Cvetaeva, *Le notti fiorenti* (Florentine Nights), a bilingual edition in the original
    French and in Italian translation, ed. Serena Vitale (Milan: Mondadori, 1983); hereafter
    cited as *Florentine Nights*.
8   Ibid., 8–10.
9   Ibid., 20.
10  Ibid., 14.
11  Ibid., 22.
12  Ibid., 26–28.
13  Ibid., 56.
14  *AE*, 91.
15  Ibid., 92.
16  *Florentine Nights*, 60.
17  Ibid., 70.
18  Ibid., 82.
19  *SiP*, 3:18.
20  Letter to Pasternak, February 1923, *Vestnik* 128 (1979): 173.

21   *AE*, 96.

22   Boris Pasternak, *I Remember: Sketch for an Autobiography*, trans. David Magarshack (New York: Pantheon, 1958), 107.

23   NP, 273.

24   IP, 1:136.

25   Ibid.

26   LI, 209.

27   LO, no. 8, 107.

13. Prague, Creative Peak

1   SiP, 3:91.

2   Ibid., 130.

3   Ibid., 26.

4   NP, 274.

5   *AE*, 137.

6   LO, no. 8, 107.

7   Letter to Lyudmila Chirikova, April 1923, Novy zhurnal (New journal) 124 (New York, 1976): 148.

8   Olga Kolbasina-Chernova, "O Marine Tsvetaevoy" (About Marina Tsvetaeva), *Mosty*, 15:312.

9   IP, 1:231.

10   SiP, 3:41–43.

11   Letter to Chirikova, April 1923, Novy zhurnal 124 (1976): 148–49.

12   NP, 281.

13   SiP, 4:151.

14   IP, 1:240.

15   "Letters of Marina Tsvetaeva to Roman Gul," Novy zhurnal 58 (1959): 176–77.

16   They have been translated into French by Véronique Lossky.

17   NP, 271.

18   *AE*, 113–14.

19   NP, 278.

20   Letter to Pasternak, February 1923, *Vestnik* 128 (1979): 171.

21   Ibid., 173.

22   NP, 285.

23   Letter to Roman Gul, March 1923, Novy zhurnal 58 (1959): 178.

24   SiP, 3:463.

25   LO, no. 8, 102.

26   Ibid.

27   Ibid., 106.

28   Ibid., 104.

29   Ibid., no. 9, 102.

30   Ibid., 103.

31   Ibid., 104.

32   SiP, 3:89.

33   LO, no. 9, 106.

34   *WSA* 3 (1981): 186–87.

35    LO, no. 10, 103.

36    Ibid., 105.


14. Great Love, Great Pain

1    SiP, 4:168.

2    AE, 152.

3    Schweitzer, Byt i bytiye, 310.

4    SiP, 3:350.

5    Yelenev, "Kem byla Marina Tsvetaeva?" 157.

6    WSA 3 (1981): 227.

7    SiP, 3:351.

8    As quoted by Véronique Lossky in Un itinéraire poétique (Paris: Solin, 1987), 154.

9    LO, no. 10, 108.

10    Ibid., 108.

11    SiP, 3:97–98.

12    Ibid., 103.

13    Ibid., 106.

14    Ibid., 133–34.

15    Ibid., 351.

16    LO, no. 10, 104.

17    Ibid., 110.

18    Schweitzer, Byt i bytiye, 315–18.

19    Ibid., 317.

20    Ibid.

21    SiP, 4:161–67, 168–87.

22    G. S. Smith, "Marina Cvetaeva's Poema Gory: An Analysis," Russian Literature 6, no. 4 (October 1978): 103–23.

23    Sochineniya, 1:536.

24    NP, 92.


15. Resignation and Birth of Son

1    SiP, 3:115.

2    Ibid., 359.

3    Ibid., 351.

4    Ibid.

5    Chernova, "O Marine Tsvetaevoy," Mosty, 15:311.

6    SiP, 3:111–13.

7    NP, 97.

8    Ibid., 74.

9    Ibid., 127.

10    Ibid., 80–81.

11    Ibid., 96.

12    Ibid., 89.

13    Ibid., 94–95.
14    Ibid., 101.
15    Ibid., 114.
16    Dr. Gregory Altshuller, "Marina Tsvetaeva: A Physician's Memoir," *SUN* 4, no. 3 (Winter 1979–80).
17    NP, 132.
18    Ibid., 140.
19    E. T. A. Hoffmann, *Kater Murr*, in *Selected Writings* (Chicago: University of Chicago Press, 1963), 2:11.
20    NP, 174.
21    Ibid., 161.
22    Ibid., 180.
23    Ibid., 188.
24    Ibid., 200–201.
25    Ibid., 292.
26    Ibid.
27    Ibid., 141–42.
28    Ibid., 223.

## 16. Paris, Success and New Problems

1    IP, 1:372.
2    SiP, 4:188–246.
3    PTR, 151.
4    N. V. Reznikova, "Pamyati Mariny Ivanovny Tsvetaevoy" (In memory of Marina Ivanovna Tsvetaeva), *Vestnik* 135 (1981): 159–63.
5    LT, 37.
6    D. Svyatopolk-Mirsky, "O sovremennom sostoyanyy russkoy poezy" (On the contemporary state of Russian poetry), *Novy zhurnal* 131 (1978): 94.
7    LT, 39.

## 17. The Correspondence with Rilke and Pasternak

1    *The Selected Poetry of Rainer Maria Rilke*, intro. by Robert Hass (New York: Random House, 1984), 289.
2    PTR, 53.
3    Ibid., 121.
4    *Selected Poetry of Rainer Maria Rilke*, xxx.
5    PTR, 102.
6    I have been using as my source the English translation (PTR), sometimes drawing on the Russian original.
7    Ibid., 84.
8    Ibid., 81.
9    Ibid., 67.
10    LT, 91.

11  PTR, 103.
12  Ibid., 81–82.
13  Ibid., 84.
14  Ibid., 99.
15  Ibid., 108–9.
16  Ibid., 110, 114.
17  Ibid., 118–19.
18  Ibid., 126.
19  Ibid., 120.
20  Ibid.
21  Ibid., 143.
22  Ibid., 163.
23  Ibid., 160–61.
24  Ibid., 166.
25  Ibid., 181.
26  Ibid., 176.
27  Ibid., 177.
28  Ibid., 189.
29  Ibid., 199.
30  Ibid., 195.
31  Ibid., 196–97.
32  Ibid., 201.
33  Ibid., 197.
34  PTR, 33.
35  Anna A. Tavis, "Marina Tsvetaeva through Rainer Maria Rilke's Eyes," in *Marina Tsvetaeva*, 1892–1992 (Northfield, Vt.: Norwich University Russian School, 1992), 2:219–29.
36  Lossky, *Un itinéraire poétique*, 173.
37  LT, 45.
38  Letter to Daniil Reznikov, March 1926, *Vestnik* 138 (1983): 192.
39  Ibid., 167.
40  PTR, 220. Tsvetaeva would resume her correspondence with Pasternak after Rilke's death in December 1926.
41  Ibid., 204.

## 18. Spiraling Down

1  LT, 62.
2  SiP, 3:363.
3  Ibid., 3:273–77.
4  Svetlana Boym, *Death in Quotation Marks: Cultural Myths of the Modern Poet* (Cambridge, Mass.: Harvard University Press, 1991), 225.
5  Joseph Brodsky, *Less Than One* (New York: Farrar, Straus, and Giroux, 1986), 267.
6  PTR, 216.
7  Ibid., 219.
8  IP, 1:251.
9  Yelena Izvolskaya, "Ten na stenakh" (Shadow on the walls), Opyty (Experiments) 3 (New York, 1954): 157.

10    LI, 49.

11    Ibid., 47.

12    Letter to Pasternak, July 1927, *Novy mir* 4 (1969): 196.

13    Ibid., 200.

14    *AT*, 500.

15    Letter from Pasternak to Gorky, October 1927, *Literaturnoye nasledstvo* (Literary heritage) 70:300.

16    Ibid., 301.

17    LT, 54–55.

18    IP, 2:305.

19    LT, 59.

## 19. Growing Isolation

1    SiP, 4:279.

2    Ibid., 285.

3    LT, 56–57.

4    Ibid., 56.

5    *Sochineniya*, 1:542–49.

6    Ibid., 449.

7    LT, 61.

8    "Letters of Marina Tsvetaeva to R. N. Lomonosova," in *Minuvsheye* (The past) (Paris: Atheneum, 1989), 211; hereafter cited as LL.

9    LT, 65.

10    Ibid., 66.

11    Ibid., 65.

12    *Yevraziya* (Eurasia), November 24, 1928.

13    LT, 71.

14    Ibid., 68.

15    *Vozdushnyye puti* (Aerial ways) 5 (New York, 1967): 9–56.

16    LT, 81.

17    LL, 220.

18    Yelena Korkina, "Poema o tsarskoy semye," *WSA* 32 (1992): 171–200.

19    SiP, 3:380–81.

20    Korkina, "Poema o tsarskoy semye," 181.

## 20. Hitting Bottom

1    SiP, 3:177.

2    Ibid., 373.

3    Marina Tsvetaeva, *Pisma k A. Teskovoy* (Letters to Anna Teskova), ed. I. Kudrova (St. Petersburg: Vneshtorgizdat, 1991), 172.

4    LL, 227.

5    LT, 85.

6    Izvolskaya, "Poet obrechyonnosti" (Poet of doom), *Vozdushnyye puti*, 3 (1963): 158.

7   LT, 87.
8   Ibid., 89.
9   LL, 244.
10  LT, 91.
11  LL, 252.
12  Ibid., 214.
13  Letter to Halpern, September 1931, *Vestnik* 138 (1983): 181.
14  Ibid., 180.
15  Yelenev, "Kem byla Marina Tsvetaeva?" 159.
16  LT, 92.
17  Ibid., 93.
18  SiP, 3:138–39.
19  Ibid., 159–60.

21. *Alienation and Self-Analysis*

1   SiP, 3:164.
2   Karlinsky, *Marina Tsvetaeva: The Woman, Her World, and Her Poetry*, 218–19.
3   Letter to Khodasevich, May 1934, *Novy mir* 4 (1969): 207.
4   LT, 96–97.
5   Ibid., 101.
6   Ibid., 97.
7   SiP, 3:161.
8   LT, 101.
9   IP, 1:367.
10  Ibid., 374.
11  Ibid., 371.
12  Ibid.
13  Ibid., 370.
14  Ibid., 381.
15  Ibid., 387.
16  Ibid., 393.
17  Ibid., 405.
18  Ibid., 406.
19  Letter to Halpern, August 1932, *Vestnik* 138 (1983): 183–86.
20  *Lettera all'Amazzone*, trans. Serena Vitale, 102.
21  Ibid., 96–98.

22. *Indigence and Autobiographical Prose*

1   SiP, 3:169.
2   LI, 212.
3   Ibid., 213.
4   LT, 105.
5   Taubman, *A Life through Poetry*, 252.

6    NP, 411.

7    Ibid., 415.

8    CS, 237.

9    Ibid., 238–39.

10   NP, 430.

11   CS, 235, 237.

12   As quoted by Schweitzer in Byt i bytiye, 420.

13   Letter to Fedotov, May 1933, Novy zhurnal 63 (1961): 170, 172.

14   Ibid., 133 (1978): 199.

15   Letter to Halpern, October 1933, Vestnik 138 (1983): 186.

16   LL, 256.

17   LT, 107.

18   NP, 424.

19   Ibid., 434.

20   SiP, 3:382–83.

21   SiP, 3:174–75.

22   NP, 470.

23   Zinaida Shakhovskaya, "Marina Tsvetaeva," Novy zhurnal 87 (1967): 132.

24   NP, 475.

25   SiP, 3:181–82.

26   NP, 490–91.

27   LT, 112–13.

28   Letter to Halpern, April 1934, Vestnik 138 (1983): 188.

29   LT, 111.

30   NP, 462.

31   Halpern to G. P. Struve, September 1965, Vestnik 138 (1983): 165.

32   SiP, 3:382.

33   Alen Brossa, "Vinovny" (Guilty), Literaturnaya gazeta (Literary gazette) 9 (1992): 22–24.

34   As quoted in Schweitzer, Byt i bytiye, 420. Schweitzer notes that the letter to Bunina was given to her by G. P. Struve, who had withheld it from publication.

35   Ibid., 420.

## 23. Further Withdrawal

1    SiP, 3:196.

2    LT, 124.

3    LT, 134.

4    "Tsvetaeva's Letters to G. F. Fedotov," Novy zhurnal 63 (1961): 164.

5    Pasternak, I Remember, 108.

6    Lazar Fleishman, Boris Pasternak: The Poet and His Politics (Cambridge, Mass.: Harvard University Press, 1990), 192.

7    WSA 3 (1981): 210.

8    Olga Ivinskaya, A Captive of Time (New York: Doubleday, 1978), 71.

9    Paper given by Richard Davis at the International Congress for Soviet and East European Studies, Washington, D.C., 1985.

10   Letter to Pasternak, October 1935, Novy mir 4 (1969): 198.

11  NP, 499.
12  Ibid., 503.
13  Ibid., 504.
14  Pisma Mariny Tsvetaevoy k Ariadne Bergu 1934–1939 (Marina Tsvetaeva's letters to Ariadne Berg 1934–1939) (Paris: YMCA Press, 1990), 43.
15  LT, 130.
16  Ibid., 131.
17  Ibid., 134.
18  Ibid., 135.
19  Elisabeth K. Poretsky, Our Own People (Ann Arbor: University of Michigan Press, 1969).
20  LT, 138–39.
21  Ibid., 140.
22  Shakhovskaya, "Marina Tsvetaeva," Novy zhurnal 87 (1967): 132–33.
23  SiP, 4:336.
24  Kirill Vilchkovsky, "Letter of Marina Tsvetaeva to Anatoly Steiger," Opyty, 5:41.
25  Ibid., 46.
26  Ibid., 50.
27  Ibid., 67.
28  Ibid., 8:9–10.
29  Ibid., 17.
30  LT, 144.
31  SiP, 3:192.
32  LI, 229.
33  Ibid., 230.

## 24. A Fateful Year, 1937

1  CS, 323.
2  SiP, 3:196.
3  Alexander Pushkin, The Poems, Prose, and Plays, selected and ed. Avrahm Yarmolinsky (New York: Random House, 1936), 54.
4  LT, 149.
5  CS, 319.
6  Ibid., 321.
7  Ibid., 324.
8  Ibid., 325.
9  Ibid., 338.
10  Ibid., 336.
11  Ibid., 337.
12  Ibid., 353.
13  As quoted by J. Marin King in CS, 474–75.
14  Ibid., 362.
15  Ibid.
16  For information concerning the mood among NKVD people, see Poretsky, Our Own People.
17  LT, 151–52.
18  CS, 333–34.

19 Ibid., 399.

20 Ibid., 375–76.

21 Ibid.

22 Ibid., 401.

23 Ibid., 381.

24 Ibid., 378.

25 A very different and original interpretation of "Pushkin and Pugachev" is given by Yelena Korkina in a paper presented at the Amherst conference on Tsvetaeva in 1992.

26 LT, 156.

27 Reznikova, "Pamyati Mariny Tsvetaevoy," Vestnik 135 (1981): 163.

28 Berg, Pisma Mariny Tsvetaevoy k Ariadne Bergu, 158–60.

29 SiP, 3:383–84.

30 LT, 158.

31 Ibid., 167.

32 Ibid., 179–80.

33 SiP, 3:208–9. The last line, "it's time to return my ticket to its creator," alludes to the words of Ivan Karamazov in Dostoevsky's Brothers Karamazov.

34 "Tsvetaeva's Letters to G. P. Fedotov," Novy zhurnal 63 (1961): 163.

35 SiP, 3:383–84.

36 LT, 183–84.

37 Berg, Pisma Mariny Tsvetaevoy k Ariadne Bergu, 128–29.

38 LT, 185.

## 25. Return to the Soviet Union

1 Shakhovskaya, "Marina Tsvetaeva," 134.

2 SiP, 1:[34].

3 Ibid., 3:390.

4 Kirill Khenkin, Okhotnik vverkh nogami (Upside down hunter) (Frankfurt: Possev Verlag, n.d.), 47.

5 D. Sezeman, "M. Tsvetaeva v Moskve" (M. Tsvetaeva in Moscow), Vestnik 128 (1979): 178.

6 Mariya Belkina, Skreshcheniye sudeb (Interlocking fates) (Moscow: Kniga, 1980), 68. This book offers a wealth of material about Tsvetaeva's last years after her return to Russia and re-creates the literary milieu of that period.

7 Mulya was suspected of being an informer; after Alya's arrest he went to the prison where she was held, and continued to visit Tsvetaeva. He was arrested in 1950 during Stalin's anti-Jewish "doctors' plot." He was executed in 1952. Lossky, Marina Tsvetaeva v zhizne, 228.

8 SiP, 3:391.

9 Kudrova, "Sergei Efron v zastenkakh Lubyanka" (Sergei Efron in the torture chambers of the Lubyanka), Russkaya mysl 3950 (October 16, 1992), 3951 (October 23, 1992).

10 SiP, 3:391.

11 Letter to Beria, December 23, 1939, Literaturnaya gazeta 3, no. 5413 (1992): 6.

12 Ibid.

13 Anna Akhmatova, Poems, selected and trans. Lyn Coffin (New York: W. W. Norton, 1983), 85.

14  Belkina, *Skreshcheniye sudeb*, 93.

15  NP, 611.

16  Belkina connects these poems with Tager (p. 122). Taubman believes that they were inspired by the pain of Efron's arrest (p. 262).

17  *SiP*, 3:211–12.

18  NP, 611–16.

19  *SiP*, 3:419.

20  Ibid.

21  Belkina, *Skreshcheniye sudeb*, 202.

22  *SiP*, 3:392.

23  Belkina, *Skreshcheniye sudeb*, 170.

24  Ibid., 172.

25  Letter to Kvanina, November 17, 1940, *Vestnik* 128 (1979): 184–87.

## 26. *War, Evacuation, Suicide*

1  *SiP*, 3:392.

2  Ibid., 212.

3  Letter to Kvanina, December 1940, *Vestnik* 128 (1979): 188.

4  NP, 618–21.

5  *SiP*, 3:212–13.

6  Belkina, *Skreshcheniye sudeb*, 218.

7  Ibid., 235.

8  LL, 219.

9  Karlinsky's translation; Karlinsky, *Marina Tsvetaeva: The Woman, Her World, and Her Poetry*, 238.

10  Ibid., 237–38.

11  Belkina, *Skreshcheniye sudeb*, 258.

12  Ibid., 266.

13  Ibid., 267.

14  NP, 642.

15  Ibid., 643.

16  Khenkin, *Okhotnik vverkh nogami*, 49–50.

17  *SiP*, 3:394–416.

18  Belkina, *Skreshcheniye sudeb*, 283.

19  Ibid., 282.

20  *Vstrechi s proshlym* (Meetings with the past) 3 (1980): 304.

21  *SiP*, 3:406.

## *Afterword*

1  Joseph Brodsky, *Less Than One* (New York: Farrar Straus Giroux, 1986), 210.

2  Michèle Roberts, "Silks Thundering," *Poetry Review* 83, no. 3 (1993): 13.

3  Tsvetaeva's knowledge of Freud's work should be researched in the future.

4  Claudia Roth Piermont, "The Rage of Aphrodite," *The New Yorker*, Feb. 7, 1994: 91.

5  *SiP*, 4:265–66.

# Bibliography

## Principal Russian Editions of Marina Tsvetaeva's Works

*Proza* (Prose). Introduced by Valentina S. Coe. New York: Chekhov Publishing House, 1953.

*Izbrannyye proizvedeniya* (Selected works). Compiled and edited by Ariadna Efron and Anna Saakyants. Moscow-Leningrad: Sovetsky pisatel, "Biblioteka poeta," 1965.

*Neizdannoye: Stikhi, teatr, proza* (Unpublished works: Poetry, drama, prose). Paris: YMCA Publishers, 1976. Includes *Juvenilia*, "The Stone Angel," and *Tale of Sonechka*.

*Izbrannaya proza v dvukh tomakh* (Selected prose in two volumes). Edited by Alexander Sumerkin, preface by Joseph Brodsky. New York: Russica, 1979. Includes autobiographical essays, writers' portraits, and theoretical essays.

*Sochineniya v dvukh tomakh* (Works in two volumes). Edited by Anna Saakyants. Moscow: Khudozhestvennaya literatura, 1980.

*Stikhotvoreniya i poemy v pyati tomakh* (Lyric and narrative poetry in five volumes). Edited by Alexander Sumerkin and Viktoria Schweitzer; biographical essay by Viktoria Schweitzer; preface by Joseph Brodsky. New York: Russica, 1980–1990.

*Sochineniya v dvukh tomakh* (Works in two volumes). Edited by Anna Saakyants. Moscow: Khudozhestvennaya literatura, 1988. Includes letters.

*Teatr* (Drama). Edited by Anna Saakyants, preface by Pavel Antokolsky. Moscow: Iskusstvo, 1988.

*Stikhotvoreniya i poemy* (Poetry and narrative poems). Edited by Yelena Korkina. Leningrad: Sovetsky pisatel, "Biblioteka poeta," 1990.

## French/Italian Editions

*Le Notti Fiorentine. Lettera All'Amazzone.* Edited and introduced by Serena Vitale. Milan: Arnoldo Mondadori, 1983. Bilingual: French original and Italian translation.

## English Translations

### PROSE

*A Captive Spirit: Selected Prose.* Edited and translated by J. Marin King. Ann Arbor, Mich.: Ardis, 1980.

*Pasternak, Tsvetayeva, Rilke: Letters, Summer 1926.* Edited by Yevgeny Pasternak, Yelena Pasternak, and Konstantin Azadovsky; translated by Margaret Wettlin and Walter Arndt. New York: Harcourt Brace Jovanovich, 1985.

*Art in the Light of Conscience: Eight Essays on Poetry by Marina Tsvetaeva.* Translated and annotated by Angela Livingston. Cambridge, Mass.: Harvard University Press, 1992.

### POETRY

*The Demesne of the Swans.* Translated, introduced, and annotated by Robin Kemball. Ann Arbor, Mich.: Ardis, 1980.

*Selected Poems of Marina Tsvetayeva.* Translated and introduced by Elaine Feinstein. Oxford: Oxford University Press, revised edition 1981.

*Selected Poems.* Translated by David McDuff. Newcastle-upon-Tyne: Bloodaxe Books, 1987.

*Starry Sky to Starry Sky: Poems by Mary Jane White with Translations of Marina Tsvetaeva.* Stevens Point, Wis.: Holy Cow! Press, 1988.

*In the Inmost Hour of the Soul: Selected Poems of Marina Tsvetaeva.* Translated by Nina Kossman. Clifton, N.J.: Humana Press, 1989.

*After Russia.* Translated by Michael M. Naydan with Slava Yastremski; edited and annotated by Michael Naydan. Ann Arbor, Mich.: Ardis, 1992.

## Biographies and Studies in English

Simon Karlinsky. *Marina Cvetaeva: Her Life and Art.* Berkeley and Los Angeles: University of California Press, 1966.

Olga Carlisle. *Poets on Street Corners: Portraits of Fifteen Russian Poets.* New York: Random House, 1970.

*Tsvetaeva: A Pictorial Biography.* Edited by Ellendea Proffer, introduced by Carl Proffer. Ann Arbor, Mich.: Ardis, 1980.

Ronald Hingley. *Nightingale Fever: Russian Poets in Revolution.* New York: Alfred A. Knopf, 1981.

Simon Karlinsky. *Marina Tsvetaeva: The Woman, Her World, and Her Poetry.* Cambridge: Cambridge University Press, 1985.

Joseph Brodsky. *Less Than One.* New York: Farrar Straus Giroux, 1986. Includes two essays on Tsvetaeva.

Elaine Feinstein. *A Captive Lion: The Life of Marina Tsvetayeva.* London: E. P. Dutton, 1987.

Elizabeth Klosty Beaujour. *Alien Tongues: Bi-lingual Russian Writers of the "First Emigration".* Ithaca and London: Cornell University Press, 1988.

Jane A. Taubman. *A Life Through Poetry: Marina Tsvetaeva's Lyric Diary.* Columbus, Ohio: Slavica, 1989.

Svetlana Boym. *Death in Quotation Marks: Cultural Myths of the Modern Poet.* Cambridge, Mass.: Harvard University Press, 1991.

Viktoria Schweitzer. *Tsvetaeva.* Translated by Robert Chandler and H. T. Willetts; poetry translated by Peter Norman; edited and annotated by Angela Livingstone. London: Harper and Collins, 1992. First published in Russian in Paris by Syntaksis, 1988.

*Sexuality and the Body in Russian Culture.* Edited by Jane T. Costlow, Stephanie Sandler, and Judith Vowles. Stanford, Calif.: Stanford University Press, 1993.

*Articles in English*

Antonina F. Gove. "The Feminine Stereotype and Beyond: Role Conflict and Resolution in the Poetics of Marina Tsvetaeva." *Slavic Review* 36, no. 2 (June 1977): 231–55.

Ieva Vitins. "Escape from Earth: A Study of Tsvetaeva's Elswheres." *Slavic Review* 36, no. 4 (December 1977): 644–57.

Anya M. Kroth. "Androgyny as an Exemplary Feature of Marina Tsvetaeva's Dichotomous Poetic Vision." *Slavic Review* 38, no. 4 (December 1979): 563–82.

Diana Lewis Burgin. "After the Ball Is Over: Sophia Parnok's Creative Relationship with Marina Tsvetaeva." *The Russian Review* 47 (1988): 425–44.

Stephanie Sandler. "Embodied Words: Gender in Cvetaeva's Reading of Pushkin." *Slavic and East European Journal* 34, no. 2 (Summer 1990): 139–57.

Sibelan Forrester. "Bells and Cupolas: The Formative Role of the Female Body in Marina Tsvetaeva's Poetry." *Slavic Review* 51, no. 2 (Summer 1992): 232–46.

Anna A. Tavis. "Russia in Rilke: Rainer Maria Rilke's Correspondence with Marina Tsvetaeva." *Slavic Review* 52, no. 3 (Fall 1993): 494–511.

# Index

Lily Feiler is an independent scholar and translator
living in New York. Her translation of Victor
Shklovsky's *Mayakovsky and His Circle* was nominated
for the 1972 National Book Award for Translation.

Library of Congress Cataloging-in-Publication Data
Feiler, Lily, 1915–
Marina Tsvetaeva : the double beat of Heaven and
Hell / Lily Feiler.
Includes bibliographical references and index.
ISBN 0-8223-1482-7 (alk. paper)
1. Tsvetaeva, Marina, 1892–1941—Biography. 2.
Poets, Russian—20th century—Biography. I. Title.
PG3476.T75Z667 1994
891.71'42—dc20
[B]    94-9243 CIP